George Berkeley, Simon Berington

The Adventures of Sig. Gaudentio di Lucca

Being the substance of his examination before the fathers of the Inquisition at

Bologna, in Italy: giving an account of an unknown country in the midst of the

deserts of Africa. Vol. 1

George Berkeley, Simon Berington

The Adventures of Sig. Gaudentio di Lucca

Being the substance of his examination before the fathers of the Inquisition at Bologna, in Italy: giving an account of an unknown country in the midst of the deserts of Africa. Vol. 1

ISBN/EAN: 9783337309299

Printed in Europe, USA, Canada, Australia, Japan

Cover: Foto ©Andreas Hilbeck / pixelio.de

More available books at www.hansebooks.com

THE ADVENTURES

OF

Sig. GAUDENTIO DI LUCCA.

Being the substance of his examination before the Fathers of the Inquisition at Bologna in Italy:

Giving an account of an UNKNOWN COUNTRY in the midst of the deserts of AFRICA, the origin and antiquity of the people, their religion, customs, and laws.

Copied from the original manuscript in St Mark's library at Venice; with critical notes of the learned Signor RHEDI.

To which is prefixed,

A letter of the secretary of the inquisition, shewing the reasons of Signor GAUDENTIO's being apprehended, and the manner of it.

Translated from the ITALIAN.

EDINBURGH:
Printed by A. DONALDSON and J. REID,
For ALEX. DONALDSON.
MDCCLXI.

THE PUBLISHER TO THE READER.

IT is very natural to think the reader would willingly be apprised of two things relating to these Memoirs: First, how this curious manuscript came to light, considering the dark and deep secrecy with which all things are transacted in the inquisition. Secondly, how it came into the translator's hands. To satisfy such a commendable curiosity, he is to be informed, That the manuscript was sent by the secretary of the inquisition at Bologna to the learned Signor Rhedi, keeper of the library of S Mark at Venice, his intimate friend and correspondent, with the whole account how the author was taken up, and secured in the inquisition, as the letter of the secretary to the same Signor Rhedi will shew: which letter, as it contains a great many curious particulars in the examination of the criminal, (for he was taken up as such, though nothing very material was proved against him; for which reason, he received

received a more favourable treatment than is generally believed to be customary in that dreadful tribunal); so it discovers no indirect practices of the inquisition, but, on the contrary, shews they proceed with a great deal of circumspection within their walls, though all things are involved in impenetrable darkness to those without. Beside, the succession of new popes, and, generally speaking, the change of other officers attending it, might make them be less upon their guard, as the secretary seems to hint in his letter. Neither is there any thing that might do him any harm, in case he were discovered; especially writing to a friend of his own communion, and a priest, as Signor Rhedi was; which is likewise seen by the letter.

As to the second quære, the manuscript came into the publisher's hands, by the means of the same Signor Rhedi, who is an honour to his church, profession, and country, and one of the most learned and polite men in the world. He is not so bigotted to his religion or profession, as to shun the company of the *heretical tramontani*, a title the Italians generally give us; but loves and esteems a learned man, though of a different persuasion. One reason for this may be, that he breathes a freer air at Venice, than they do in the other parts of Italy. The inquisition has
nothing

nothing to do in the Venetian territories. Though they are Roman Catholics, the ſtate admits of no tribunal independent of itſelf. Beſides, as they are a trading people, their commerce obliges them to be civil to perſons of all perſuaſions, eſpecially ſtrangers. But of all others they ſeem to have the greateſt reſpect for the Engliſh; whether it be on account of their power at ſea, or their franknefs in ſpending their money, ſo many of the Engliſh nobility and gentry travelling that way; or from the candour and ſincerity of our nature, ſo oppoſite to the Italians, and therefore the more valued by them: be that as it will, the publiſher, who had ſeveral times made the tour of Italy, was not only intimately acquainted, but had contracted a particular friendſhip with Signor Rhedi, as well on account of their mutual inclinations for learning and antiquity, as for ſeveral reciprocal obligations paſſing between them. The laſt time he was at Venice, which was in company of a perſon of the firſt rank, who liked the place as well as he did, he ſtaid there upwards of fifteen months; during which time he had the opportunity of enjoying the converſation of his learned friend, with as much liberty, as if he had been of the ſame perſuaſion. But the preſent of a gold repeating watch, with ſome other of

our English curiosities, so won his heart, that one day being together in the great library, he unlocks a little grate where he kept his rarities, and turning to me with a smile, Signor Inglese, says he, holding a manuscript in his hand, here is such a curiosity, as I am sure, you never saw, and perhaps never heard of: it is the life of a person who is now in the inquisition at Bologna, taken from his own confession before the inquisitors; with the account of a country in the heart of the vast deserts of Africa, whose inhabitants have lived unknown to all the world upwards of 3000 years, and inaccessible to all the world, but by the way he was carried thither. The inquisitors are so far persuaded of the truth of it, that they have promised him his liberty, if he will undertake to conduct some missionaries the same way, to preach the gospel to a numerous people, who by his account have the greatest knowledge of natural religion and polity of any Heathen nation yet known, even beyond the Chinese. For my own part, I could scarce have believed it, had not the secretary of the same inquisition, who, you may be sure, by his post, is not a man to be imposed upon, assured me of the truth of it: nay, that he himself was present at his seizure and examination, and sent me a copy of his life, which he was
ordered

ordered to give in by the inquisitors; with the whole account of the occasion and manner of his seizure. It seems he had lived some time in Bologna in quality of a physician, under the name of *Signor Gaudentio di Lucca*, which he says is his true name, and confirms it by the place of his birth, the names of his parents, time of his captivity, &c. He had dropped some words of several strange secrets he was master of, with mutterings of an unknown nation, religion, and customs, quite new to the Italian ears; for which reason the inquisition thought fit to seize him, and, by ways and means made use of in that tribunal, obliged him to give an account of his whole life, which is the most surprising I ever read. Here is the secretary's letter, giving a succinct account of the whole affair. I have added, continued he, some critical remarks in proper places, to shew that this account is not so incredible as it may appear at first sight, and that it agrees with some hints left us in the remains of ancient history. Besides, the man stands to the truth of it with a stedfastness that is surprising. He is a person of a very handsome presence, well read, good sense, and, as it appears to the inquisitors, (who are nice judges), of seemingly good morals. He professes himself a zealous Roman Catholic, and that he always was so; for which

which reason, the inquisitors are more civil to him than ordinary. He gives such a rational and circumstantial account of his adventures, that I am of the secretary's opinion, as to the truth of it. But, added he, I wont forestal the satisfaction you will find in the perusal: so delivered the manuscript and the secretary's letter into the publisher's hands, who running his eyes over it for some time, was so struck with the novelty of the thing, that he asked Signor Rhedi, whether he might not take a copy of it. He was answered, he could not permit the manuscript to be taken out of the library; nor could he, with safety to himself, allow a stranger, and of a different religion too, the liberty of staying so long in the library by himself, as the transcribing would take up. The publisher said, he might put what guards upon him he pleased, provided he might but transcribe it. No, says he, that is inconvenient too; but I will order one of my under librarians I can confide in, to write you out an exact copy, with the secretary's letter, and my own remarks, if you think them worth your notice; which he did most faithfully; generously commanding the transcriber, at the same time, not to take any thing of me for his pains. Thus this curious manuscript came to hand, to the infinite satisfaction of the publisher, and he hopes it will prove no less

less to the readers, in the perusal of it. The character of Signor Gaudentio cannot be called in question; nor is the publisher a person so little versed in the nature and ways of the Italians, as to be imposed upon. The translation from the Italian is as exact as possible. This is the previous account the publisher thought proper to give of this affair.

N. B. Great part of the matters treated of in these memoirs, being transacted in a Roman-catholic country, and among Roman Catholics, the reader must not wonder, if they speak of their religion, as if it were the only true one in the world.

It will not be improper to admonish the reader, not to discredit immediately some of the relations contained in these Memoirs; but to suspend his judgment, till he has read Signor Rhedi's remarks; particularly, when he comes to the origin and antiquity of the people the author speaks of. The learned will find in them such a vast knowledge in history, and the most intricate remains of antiquity, as will render them very well worth their notice. The same Signor Rhedi told the publisher, he had inquired into what happened at Venice; particularly what the author mentions of Monsieur Godart, one of the most improbable parts of his adventures, and found the whole to be just as he relates it.

The

The publisher is satisfied the reader will be extremely sorry, as well as himself, for the loss of some sheets belonging to the middle part of this history. How they came to be lost, he cannot tell; but he supposes, by the incivility of the customhouse-officers at Marseilles; for they tumbled over his effects at a very rude rate, and while he had an eye on other matters, they either took some of the loose sheets, or they dropped out in the tumbling; he was very much troubled, when he came to miss them in the course of the translation.

INTRO-

INTRODUCTION.

Giving an account of the causes and manner of the seizure of Signor GAUDENTIO DI LUCCA, and the first part of his examination.

In a letter from the secretary of the INQUISITION to Signor RHEDI.

* S I R,

THE present turn of † affairs which fills the heads of other people with intrigues of state, gives me an opportunity of returning my best thanks, for the rich present you were pleased to send to a person who was yours before by the strictest ties of gratitude. — The cabinet, with the other curiosities, came safe to hand, and shews, that whoever is so happy, as to oblige Signor Rhedi, sows a seed which returns a hundredfold. — The poverty of our ‡ profession hinders me from being capable

---

* The Italian titles of *Illustrissimo, &c.* are left out, as not used in our language.

† He either means the death of some pope, or some extraordinary crisis in the Romish œconomy.

‡ The secretary was a Dominican friar; the Dominicans being masters of the inquisition.

of making a suitable return for your magnificent present; but nothing ought to take from me the desire of expressing my acknowledgments. In testimony of it, and to shew that poverty itself may be grateful, I send you, by the bearer, the account of a man, whose life has filled our inquisitors with wonder and astonishment. He has been in the inquisition at this place about two years: we have employed all our engines to find out the truth of what he is, and can find nothing material against him, unless it be the unheard-of account he gives of himself. Our first inquisitor has obliged him to write his own life, with all the particulars, as succinctly as possible, adding threats withal, that, if we find him in a false story, it shall be worse with him. He tells us strange stories of one of the most beautiful countries in the world, in the very heart of the vast deserts of Africa, inaccessible to all the world but by one way, which seems as extraordinary as the country it leads to. As you are a person of universal knowledge in antiquity, and an admirer of curiosities of this nature, I send you a copy of the manuscript to have your opinion of it; and to give you as clear a notion of the man as I can, you must know, that about three years before he was taken up by the inquisition, he took a neat house at Bologna in quality of a physician, passing through some slight
examination

examination for form's sake, and paying his fees as is customary with strangers. His name, as he says, is *Gaudentio di Lucca*, originally of Lucca *, but born in Ragusa †; he is a tall, handsome, clean-built man, as you shall see in a thousand, of a very polite address, and something so very engaging in his aspect, as bespeaks your favour at first sight. He seems to be near fifty; he is a man of good sense and fine discourse, though his accent is not pure Italian, from his living, as he says, so long in foreign countries. He speaks almost all the oriental languages, and has a very competent share of other parts of learning, as well as that of his profession. We sent to Ragusa and Lucca to inquire about him, but could not get the least information of his being known in those places. The reason of which he has given in his life, as you will see; only at Ragusa, some people remembered there had been a merchant of that name, about five and twenty or thirty years ago, who was either lost, or taken by pirates, and never heard of more.

The inquisition, as you know, Sir, has eyes every where, especially on strangers; we kept an eye upon him from his first settling at Bologna: but as we proceed with

---

* A little republic in Italy.
† A republic in Dalmatia, and tributary to the Turks.

justice as well as caution, we could not discover any sufficient reason to take him up. His life was as regular as that of others of his profession, which he did not follow very closely, but only for form's sake, being chiefly consulted at his own house, on account of some extraordinary secrets he pretended to be master of, without making any visits but to ladies, with whom he grew in prodigious request. They said he had a sweetness and ease in conversation, that was almost bewitching. This unaccountable fondness of the ladies gave us the first suspicion, lest he should instill some ill notions into that sex, so credulous where they are fond, and so incredulous where they dislike. He professed himself a Roman Catholic; seemed to have a competent knowledge, and even veneration, considering he was a physician, for our holy mysteries: so we had nothing against him on that account. We could not find that he wanted for money, though he lived rather genteely than magnificently: we found on several occasions, that money, the idol of other people, was the least of his care; and that he had some secret springs we could not fathom. His house was but decently, though completely, furnished for one of his rank; he kept two servants in livery and a valet de chambre; who, being of this town, knew no more of him than we did. There was an elderly lady dy we thought had been his wife, but it proved she was not; a foreigner, for whom he seemed to have a great respect, and her maid a foreigner also; and an elderly maid-servant of the town. We have them all secured in the inquisition, though he does not know it. The lady has the remains of a wonderful fine face, and an air of quality; she speaks a broken Italian, so that we can get very little out of her, but what agrees with his account. I am confident you will rather be pleased with these particulars than think them tedious. There is something so extraordinary in the man, I ought not to omit the least circumstance. We had several consultations about him in our inquisition, as well as our Leiger intelligences, but could discover nothing of moment. We examined what intercourse he had in other parts, by ordering the postmaster to send us all his letters, which we could easily open, and seal up again with the greatest nicety. But we found he had only two correspondents, one possessed of a moderate income of about four thousand crowns in the bank of Genoa; the other a lady of your city of Venice, whom we discovered to be a celebrated courtezan, who subscribes herself *Favilla*. We find by her last letter, that he had given her very good advice, and persuaded her to become a penitent: you will oblige us if you will inquire what she is. Amorous intrigues not falling under our cognisance, we let him alone for some time, having a person under our examination on suspicion of being a Jew in masquerade, and a spy from the Grand Signor, who kept us employed for some time. Besides, the good advice he gave the courtezan, and he being past his prime, made us less suspicious of the ladies; we supposed they had recourse to him on account of some female infirmities Though the young ladies were most fond of him, his behaviour to them was more an endearing sweetness and courtesy, than love, with very little signs, at least he had the address to conceal them, of more kindness for one than another. In fine, persons of the best rank, of both sexes, began to have a prodigious liking for his company; he stole upon them insensibly. As he increased in this good opinion, he opened himself with greater freedom; he made no shew at all at first, more than a fine presence and a polite address: but, after further acquaintance, they discovered he was master of most sciences, and shewed a superior genius in any thing they could discourse of. We employed proper persons to insinuate themselves into his good liking, and consult him as a friend on several nice points; but he had such a presence of mind, yet appeared so unconstrained in his discourse, that they owned themselves novices in comparison to him.

him. If they talked of politics, he said very judiciously, it was not for men of his rank, to meddle with affairs of state, or examine what persons did in the cabinet. If of religion, he seemed to understand it very well for one of his profession; so that nothing came from him but what was consonant to the Catholic faith; expressing on all occasions a great deference for the authority of the church. But still the more sagacious were persuaded, something more than ordinary lay hid under that specious cover. At length, talking one day with some of our spies about the customs of foreign countries, he said, he had met with a nation in one of the remotest parts of the world, who, though they were Heathens, had more knowledge of the law of nature, and common morality, than the most civilised Christians. This was immediately carried to us, and explained as a reflection on the Christian religion. Another time, as he had a great knowledge in philosophy, he dropt some words as if he had some skill in judiciary astrology; which you know, Sir, is a capital crime with us. We were as good as resolved to seize him, when we were determined to it by the following accident. Two of the most beautiful women in all Bologna had fallen in love with him, either on account of the handsomeness of his person, or, by a whimsicalness peculiar to some women, because he was a stranger, or thinking he might keep their secrets better under the cloak of being a physician; or, in fine, drawn in by some love-potion or other, we cannot tell; but the matter grew to such a height, that on his shewing more distinguishing favour to one of them, as it is natural for our women to be violent in their jealousy, as well as love, the other, to be revenged, said he had bewitched her; which she was sure of, for that, since the very first time she saw him, she thought there was something more in him, than ever she saw in any man in her life. Besides, she said, she had often found him drawing circles and figures on paper, which to her looked like conjuration. Her friends immediately informed our fathers of it; so we resolved to seize him, if it were but to find out his secrets, and see what the man was. There was another reason induced us to it, which the world will hardly believe, though it is matter of fact: that is, we were afraid, the man would be assassinated by some secret means or other, for being so great with our ladies; so, to save his life, and not lose the discoveries we expect from him, it was determined he shou'd be seized immediately. Accordingly, I was deputed, with three under-officers, to do the business, but with all the caution and secrecy usual in such cases. It was done about midnight, when we had watched

watched one of the two ladies he favoured most, into his house. We went in a close coach, and myself and one of the officers stopping at the door, as soon as the servant opened it, stepped in, telling him what we were, and charging him, at his peril, not to make the least noise. The servants being Italians, and knowing the consequence of the least resistance, stood as mute as fishes. We immediately went into the inner parlour, and, contrary to our expectation, found our gentleman, the young lady with her governante, and the elderly lady that belonged to him, sitting very decently at an elegant collation of fruits and sweetmeats, brought, as we supposed, by the fair lady as a present. At our first appearance, he seemed more surprised than terrified; as we make no ceremonies in those cases, we told him our errand, and commanded him to come along with us without the least resistance, or else it should be worse for him. Then we turned to the young lady, whose friends and person we knew, and told her we wondered to find her in such company at such unseasonable hours; but, on account of her friends, would not meddle with her, but bid her for her own sake, as she tendered her life and honour, never to take the least notice of the affair. She trembling, and ready to faint away, after some hesitation, was able to say, that she was come to
consult

consult about her health; that she brought her governante along with her to take off all suspicion, and as she was mistress of herself and fortune, it was not unusual for persons of her rank to be out at that time, considering the heat of the season. She had scarce pronounced these words, when she fell directly into a swoon. Her governante having things proper for such occasions, revived and comforted her as well as she could. But when we were going to take the gentleman along with us, the elderly lady, to whom we suppose he had told his misfortune, instead of falling into fits, flew at us like a tygress, with a fury I never saw in any human creature in my life; tearing at us with her nails and teeth, as if she had been in the most raging madness. We, not accustomed to resistance, considering our character and cloth, and she a woman, were almost motionless, when the servants at the noise came up. We commanded them, in the name of the inquisition, to seize her: the gentleman interposed in our favour, saying some words to her in an unknown language, which he assured us, were to beg her to be pacified, as she tendered his life as well as her own; then the violence of her passion turned another way, and threw her into the strongest convulsions I ever saw. By this time the other two officers were come up, wondering at our delay, and to find resistance fiftance againft the officers of the inquifition. The gentleman, with a becoming fubmiffion, rather than fear, yielded himfelf a prifoner, and begged us to pardon the fudden tranfports of a perfon unacquainted with our cuftoms, whofe life in fome manner depended on his. That fhe was a Perfian lady of quality, brought into this country by great misfortunes, who had once faved his life, as he had been afterwards inftrumental in faving hers. That fhe was difpofed to turn Chriftian, with intention after fome time to end her days in a convent. That for his own part, relying on his innocence, he readily fubmitted to our authority, and offered himfelf to be carried where-ever we pleafed; he uttered all this with an air of conftancy that was furprifing. We immediately took him into the coach, leaving two of the officers with the elderly lady, and commanding them and the gentleman's fervants not to ftir out of the room till further orders. As foon as we arrived at the inquifition, we lodged him in a handfome ftrong room; not fo much like a criminal, as like a perfon for whom we had fome refpect. There we left him to his own thoughts, and returned to his houfe to feize the elderly lady and his papers, having difmiffed the young lady and her governante before. I forgot to tell you, that Signor Gaudentio, by our permiffion, had fpoke to the elderly lady coming

out

out of her fits in Italian, (for we would not let him speak to her in the unknown language, for fear of a combination), and with much pains made her understand, that he begged her, by all that was dear, to submit to whatever we should injoin her; assuring her by that means all would be well for her safety and his own: which last words seemed to give some calm to her tempestuous spirits. You may believe, Sir, we were much surprised at the novelty of the thing, and the account he gave of her quality. But as we often meet with false stories in our employment, that did not hinder us from doing our duty. So I took her by the hand with a great deal of respect, and put her into the coach between myself and my companion; not without apprehensions of some extravagant follies, considering the violence of her temper. But she continued pretty sedate, only seemed to be overwhelmed with grief; we brought her to the inquisition, and lodged her in a very handsome apartment separate from the convent, on account of her sex; with two waiting women to attend her with all respect, till we were better apprised of the truth of her quality. This obliged me to take another journey to Signor Gaudentio's house, to secure his papers, with whatever else might contribute to further our discovery. I found all things in the

same

same order I left them; but being extremely fatigued, I sat down to the elegant collation that was left, and, after a small repast, went to bed in his house, to have the morning before us for securing his effects. I sealed up all the papers I could find, to examine them at more leisure, took an inventory of all the moveables, that they might be restored to him in case he were found innocent; and sent for a proper officer to remain in the house, who was to be responsible for every thing. There were two little cabinets of curious workmanship; one of them, as it appeared, belonged to him, the other to the strange lady; but being full of intricate drawers or tills, we took them both along with us. These and the papers we delivered to the head inquisitors, not being willing to proceed in either of their examinations, till we had got all the light we could, to find out the truth, for that was all our aim; then we could tell what course to take with them. We placed two cunning lay brothers, in the nature of servants, for Signor Gaudentio, who were to insinuate themselves into his favour by their kind offices, compassionating his misfortunes, and advising him to discover the whole truth, in the account of his life, quality, profession, opinions, and, in fine, whatever articles he was to be interrogated on, on, to confess ingenuously what he knew: that that was the only way to find favour at the hands of the inquisitors; that they pardoned almost all faults on a sincere confession, and an assurance of amendment. I visited him myself several times before his examination, and gave him the same advice and assurance; he promised me faithfully he would, and seemed so steady and confirmed in his own innocence, with such an agreeable, yet sincere way in his discourse, as really surprised me, and caused me already to be prejudiced in his favour; adding with a smile, that the history of his life would administer more cause of wonder than indignation.— Not to be too particular, the chief of the inquisition, with myself along with them, set to the scrutiny of his papers. We examined them with all the care imaginable, but could find nothing to ground any material accusation, except some imperfect memoirs of the customs of a country and people unheard of to us, and I believe to all the world beside, with some odd characters, or words, which had no affinity with any language or characters we ever saw. We discovered he had a great knowledge in natural philosophy, with some remarks that were very curious. There was a rough draught of a map of a country, with towns, rivers, lakes, &c. but no climate marked down.

In

In short, all his papers contained nothing but some small sketches of philosophy and physic, with some pieces of poetry of an uncommon taste. Neither could we find any footsteps of judiciary astrology, or calculations of nativities, of which we had the greatest suspicion; only a pair of globes, a set of mathematical instruments, charts of navigation, forms of unknown trees and plants, and such like things, as all gentlemen who delight in travelling are curious to have. There were indeed some lines, circles, segments of circles, which we supposed the informing lady meant; but looked like an attempt to find out the longitude, rather than any magical schemes. —His books were of the same nature; nothing of heresy that we could see, but such as belonged to a man of learning. There were several common books of devotion, such as are approved by our church, and seemed pretty well used; by which we judged him to be really a Catholic, and a person of no bad morals. But as nothing looks so like an honest man as a knave, this did not take away all our suspicion. ——When we came to open the cabinets, in the first of them, which belonged to him, we found in one of the drawers about four hundred and fifty Roman crowns, with other small money, and some foreign coin along with it, as Turkish sequins, and

and some we knew nothing of. The sum not being very extraordinary, we could conclude nothing from thence. In another drawer we found several precious stones, some set, some unset, of a very great value, so far from being counterfeit, that we never saw any so brilliant. Besides, several pieces of native gold, of such fineness, as nothing with us can come up to it. In a third, we found a small heap of medals, most of gold, but of an unknown stamp and antiquity. There were outlandish stones of odd figures enough, which to others might look like talismans, but we took them for some out-of-the-way curiosities. In a private drawer in the centre of the cabinet, there was something wrapt up in a piece of green silk of wonderful fineness, all embroidered with hearts and hands joined together, wrought in gold with prodigious art, and intermixed with different flowers, unknown in our part of the world; in the midst of it was an azure stone, as large as the palm of one's hand, set round with rubies of very great value, on which was most artfully painted in miniature, a woman at length, holding a littl boy in her left hand, the most beautiful creature that ever eyes beheld; clad likewise in green silk spangled with golden suns: their complexion was something darker than that of our Italian ladies; but the

the features, especially the woman's, so uncommonly beautiful as if she had been of another species. Underneath was ingraved with a diamond in a modern hand, *Questo solo.* You may be sure, Sir, this raised our ideas of the man; at first, we thought he had the secret of the philosopher's stone: but in all his inventory we could find no implements of that art. Then we thought he must have been some famous pirate; or one who had robbed the cabinet of some great prince, and was come to live at Bologna in that private manner, under the disguise of a physician. But having been three years in the town, if it had been any European prince, the world would have had an account of it before now: so we concluded that either what he said of that unknown country was true, or that he had robbed some of the eastern princes, and got off clear with his prize. But the picture of the woman made us incline to think, he had married some outlandish queen, and on her death had retired with his effects. The rest of the drawers were full of natural curiosities of foreign plants, roots, bones of animals, birds, insects, &c. from whence very likely he took his physical secrets. The other cabinet, which belonged to the elderly lady, was very rich, but nothing equal to the first; there were a great many small jewels,

jewels, and some very fine pearls, with bracelets, pendants, and other curious ornaments belonging to women ; and a little picture of a very handsome man about thirty, nothing like our gentleman, in a warlike dress, with a Turkish scymitar by his side, who by his mien seemed to be a man of note. But we could find nothing that could give us any knowledge what they were : so that we were at a loss with all our sagacity what to think of the matter, or to find any just cause to keep them in the inquisition : for though we don't discover our motives to other people, we never proceed against any one but on very strong suspicions. On which account we were resolved to make his confinement as easy as possible, till we could see further into the affair. We had thoughts of examining the woman first, to get what we could from her for to interrogate him upon ; but she not understanding Italian enough, we sent to Venice with our accustomed privacy, for some of your people, that trade to the Levant, to be our interpreters. In the mean time we resolved to try what we could get out of him by his own confession ; so we sent for him before us. He came into the room with a modest unconcernedness, that rather argued wonder than fear : we had the cabinet and jewels all before us; shewed them to him all together,

with

with the inventory of his goods, assuring him they should be forthcoming, in case we were apprised of his innocence; but withal advising him, as well as commanding him to confess the truth, and then not a hair of his head should be touched. But if ever we caught him in a false story, all should be confiscated, and he never see sun or moon more. He assured us with great respect, he would own the truth to every thing we should interrogate him about, in an accent that would have persuaded any one of his sincerity, humbly desiring to know what accusations we had against him. We answered, that was not the method of the inquisition; but that he should answer directly to our interrogatories. As the holy office chiefly concerns itself about religion, we asked him first, what religion he was of. The reason of this was, because, though he professed himself a Catholic, we we were to keep up the forms: neither did we know but that he might be some Jew or Turkish spy in masquerade: then his name; place of his birth; where he was educated; how he came by those jewels; what was the occasion of his settling at Bologna; who that elderly lady was; in fine, every thing in general and particular we could think of at first, the better to compare his answers afterwards. He told us, he was a Catholic bred and born; always professed

professed himself such; and in that faith would live and die, let what would happen to him. He explained himself on the chief heads, to shew that he was well instructed in his religion: he appealed to all the inquiries we could make, whether he had not behaved as a Catholic on all occasions; naming a Capuchin in the town, who was his father confessor; to whom, he said, he gave leave to declare all he knew on that head. As to his name, he said, his true name was *Gaudentio di Lucca*, though born at Ragusa. That his father was a merchant trading to the Levant; which employment he designed to follow himself; but in his first voyage was taken by an Algerine pirate, who carried him a slave to Grand Cairo, and sold him to a merchant, of what country nobody knew; which merchant took him along with him, through the vast deserts of Africa, by a way he would describe to us if we required it, till he came to a country, perhaps the most civilized and polite in the whole universe. In that country he lived near five and twenty years, till on the death of his wife, and his only surviving son, whose pictures were in that cabinet, the melancholy disaster made him induce his father-in-law, who was the merchant that had first bought him, to take another journey to Grand Cairo, from whence he might be able to return to his native

native country. This the merchant (for he passed for such, though he was a great ruler in his own country) complied with: but happening to come thither when the plague raged in the city, his father in-law and several of his attendants died of it; leaving him heir to most of his effects, and part of the jewels we saw before us. That being now entirely at liberty, he returned in a French ship trading from Marseilles to the Levant, the master's name *François Xavier Godart*, who by agreement was to land him at Venice; but touching at Candy, they accidentally saved the life of that elderly lady, and brought her off along with them, for which they were pursued by two Turkish vessels, and carried prisoners to Constantinople, but released by the order of the Sultaness mother. That Monsieur Godart was well known at Venice; particularly by Signor Corridani, an eminent merchant there, who could assure us of the truth of what he said. That, in fine, having staid some time at Venice, to see the curiosities and the carnival, an affair relating to the young lady we saw with him, when he was seized, and the love he had for learning, Bologna being a famous university, induced him to settle there, where he presumed we had been very well informed of his behaviour ever since. This, said he, is the most succinct account I can give

give to your Reverences, on the interrogatories you have propofed to me; though my life has been chequered with fuch a variety of incidents, as would take a great deal of time to defcend to pariculars. We looked at one another with fome furprife at this ftrange account, which he delivered with fuch an air of fteadinefs, as fcarce left any room to doubt of the truth of it. However, our fuperior turning to him, faid, Signor Gaudentio, we neither believe nor difbelieve what you tell us; as we condemn no man without a full conviction of his crime, fo we are not to be impofed upon by the accounts people may give of themfelves. What is here before us, fhews there is fomething extraordinary in the cafe. If we find you to be an impoftor, you fhall fuffer as fuch; in the mean time, till we can be better informed, we injoin you to give in your whole life, with all occurrences, except your private fins, if you have any, in writing; which you fhall read to us, and be crofsexamined, as we think proper. It will concern you therefore to be very exact, for nothing will pafs here but innocence, or a fincere repentance.

This, Sir, is the manufcript I fend you, given in by himfelf as ordered; with the inquifitors interrogatories as we examined it, article by article. Which interrogatories

ries I have inserted as they were proposed, with a further account at the end, for the better clearing of the whole. We beg you to inform yourself of the facts, which his memoirs say happened to him at Venice, particularly about Monsieur Godart. Besides, Sir, you that can trace all the branches of ancient history to the fountain-head, are able to form a better judgment of the probability of his relation. He is still in the inquisition, and offers himself to conduct some of our missionaries, to preach the gospel to those unknown people. The length of this only gives me leave to assure you, that I am, with the greatest esteem imaginable,

S I R, &c.

Bologna,   F. ALISIO DE ST IVORIO.
July 29. 1721.

THE ADVENTURES

OF

Sig. Gaudentio di Lucca.

I Should be infensible, Reverend Fathers, if I were not highly concerned to find myself under any accusation before this holy tribunal, which I revere with all the powers of my soul: but especially if your Reverences should harbour any sinister opinion of my religion; for I was born and bred up in the bosom of the most holy catholic church, as well as my parents before me; in the defence of which my ancestors spent part of their blood, against the infidels, and enemies of our faith; and for which faith I am ready to lay down my life. But I am as yet a stranger to your Reverences, and on several accounts may be liable to suspicion. Wherefore I blame not the justice of your proceeding, but rather extol your goodness in allowing me the liberty to clear myself, by a true and sincere declaration of my whole life, wherein, I own, have happened several astonishing

nishing and almost incredible occurrences; all which I shall lay before your Reverences, according to the commands imposed on me, with the utmost candour and sincerity.

My name is *Gaudentio di Lucca:* I was so called, because my ancestors were said to be originally of that place; though they had been settled for some time at Ragusa, where I was born: both which places are not so far off, but they may be very well known to your Reverences. My father's name was *Gasparino di Lucca,* heretofore a merchant of some note in those parts; my mother was a Corsican lady, reported to be descended from those who had been the chief personages in that island. My grandfather was likewise a merchant: but my great-grandfather, Bernandino di Lucca, was a soldier, and captain of the great Venerio's own galley*, who was general for the Venetians in the famous battle of Lepanto against the Turks. We had a tradition in our family, that he was Venerio's son by a Grecian lady of great quality, some say descended from the Paleologi, who had been emperors of Constantinople. But she dying in childbed, and they having been only privately married, Venerio bred him up as the son of a friend of his who was

* This part of the account is certainly true; there was such a captain in the list of the officers in that famous battle.

killed

killed in the wars. That famous battle, in which the Christians and Venerio got so great renown against the Turks, instead of raising my great-grandfather's fortune, was the occasion of his retiring from the wars, and turning merchant. The reason was this: Venerio the Venetian admiral had caused a Spanish captain to be hung up at the yard-arm for mutiny *; which severe

---

* It is likewise true, that there was such a quarrel between Don John of Austria, the generalissimo, and Venerio admiral of the Venetian galleys; which had like to have put the whole Christian fleet at variance together, before the battle, and ruined the hopes of all Christendom. The occasion was as he relates it: Don John, as generalissimo, viewing the whole fleet before the fight, and finding the Venetian galleys too thinly manned, ordered four thousand Spaniards to be put on board the said galleys. But one Mutio Tortona, a Spanish captain, proving mutinous, after a great many injurious words, came to blows with the captain of the Venetian galley where he was; upon which the whole fleet fell to it. Venerio, hearing the uproar, sent his own captain to see what was the matter; but the proud Spaniards treated him no better than they did the rest; so that Venerio himself was forced to come to appease them; but seeing the Spanish captain persist in his mutinous temper, and the affront he had put upon his captain, who was reported to be his son, ordered Tortona and his ensign to be hung at the yard-arm. At this all the Spaniards in the fleet were up in arms, and threatened to cut the Venetians to pieces; but, by the interposition of the other generals, the matter was made up till after the fight; when Venerio, who had behaved with incomparable valour, and, according to Don John's own confession, was the chief occasion of the victory, to appease the haughty Spaniard, had his commission taken from him, and was recalled by the senate.

discipline

discipline so displeased Don John of Austria, generalissimo of the whole fleet, that, after the battle, the Venetians, to appease Don John, and not to be deprived of the succours of the Spaniards against the Turks, were forced to sacrifice Venerio's honour to the resentment of the Spaniards, and put him out of commission *. After this disgrace, Venerio retired; and my great-grandfather, whose fortune depended on his having been bred up to the sea, turned merchant, or rather privateer against the Moors; and, with the knights of Malta, not only did great service against them,

---

* It was Fuscarini, who was made general of the Venetians in Venerio's stead.

Every one who is the least acquainted with history, knows that the battle of Lepanto was the greatest sea-fight that ever was fought between the Christians and Turks; and the victory on the Christians side the most signal. The Spanish galleys were commanded by Don John of Austria, generalissimo: the Pope's galleys, by the famous Colonna: the Genoese by old Dorio, who had gained so much renown against the Turks and French, under Charles V. the Venetians by the great Venerio, one of the bravest soldiers of his time. Haly the Turk, great bassa of the sea, was slain, and almost all the Turkish commanding officers killed or taken. Among the prisoners, were Haly's two sons, nephews to the Grand Signor. Of the common soldiers of the Turks, were slain two and thirty thousand: a hundred and forty-one of the enemy's galleys were taken, forty sunk or burnt; of galliots and other small vessels were taken about sixty. *Vide* the Turkish history, and other accounts of this famous battle, and the whole affair as is there related. The battle was fought on the 7th of October, 1571.

but made a confiderable fortune in the world.

But to return to myfelf: My father, having a plentiful fortune, took particular care of the education of his children: he had only two fons, of whom I was the youngeft, and a daughter, who died young. Finding I had a great inclination to learning, he promoted it, by providing me with the beft mafters, till I was fit to go to the univerfity. The knowledge of languages being of great ufe as well as ornament to young gentlemen, he himfelf, by way of recreation, taught me that mixed language called *Lingua Franca*, fo neceffary in eaftern countries. It is made up of Italian, Turkifh, Perfian, and Arabian, or rather a jargon of all languages together. He fcarce ever fpoke to us but in that language, faying, we might learn Latin from our mafters, and our mother-tongue from our playfellows. The fame reafon induced him to fend me to the famous univerfity of Paris, to learn French at the fame time with my other ftudies. I lived in the college des Quatre Nations, and maintained my thefes of univerfal philofophy under the celebrated Monfieur Du Hamel, who was one of the firft in the univerfity, who decried Ariftotle's philofophy, and leaned towards the opinions of Defcartes.

[*Secretary*,. Here the inquifitors muttered

a little, fearing he was inclined to the Copernican syſtem, which has been condemned at Rome. But, ſince it regarded philoſophical matters only, they paſſed it over.]

I was entering into my nineteenth year, and had ſome thoughts of taking to the church, when my brother wrote me the melancholy account of my father and mother's death, and the unfortunate occaſion of it; which in ſhort was, that having loſt his richeſt ſhip, with all his effects, by pirates, and his chief factor at Smyrna being gone off, his other correſpondents came upon him thick; and not being in a condition to anſwer their calls, it threw him and my mother into a deep melancholy, which ſhortened their days, both dying in three weeks of one another. My brother told me he was not able to maintain me longer at the univerſity, as before; but acquainted me, he had made a ſhift to fit out a ſmall veſſel, wherein he had put his all; and invited me to join the ſmall portion that fell to my ſhare along with him, with which, he ſaid, we could make a pretty good bottom; and ſo retrieve the ſhattered fortune of our family. Not to be too prolix, I followed his advice: he ſold his houſe and gardens to pay his father's creditors, and put what was left, together with my little ſtock, into that unfortunate bottom. We ſet

set sail from Ragusa the 3d of March, *anno Dom.* 1688, very inauspiciously for my dear brother, as will appear by the sequel. We touched at Smyrna, to see if we could hear any thing of my father's factor: and were told, that he was turned Turk, and gone off, very magnificently dressed up in borrowed feathers, to settle at Constantinople; however we picked up something of some honest Christian merchants, with whom he had lodged a part of his effects. This encouraged us to proceed to Cyprus and Alexandria; but, as we were pursuing our voyage one morning, in a prodigious fog, as if the sea was fatal to our family, we spied on a sudden two Algerine rovers bearing down upon us, one on each side. We had scarce time to clear our little vessel, when they fired upon us, and called to us to strike, or we were dead men. My brother and I, considering that our all was at stake, and that we had better die honourably than be made slaves by those unbelieving miscreants, called up our men, who were but twenty-three in all, of whom five were young gentlemen who had engaged to try their fortune along with us. We were armed only with swords, and pistols under our girdles. After a short consultation, it was agreed to fight it out to the last man; and we turned back to back to make head against both sides, my brother in the middle of one rank, and myself

myself in the other. The enemy boarded us in great numbers, looking on us as madmen to pretend to make any resistance; but they were soon made to leap back, at least all that were able; for being close up with them, and they crouded together, we fired our pistols so luckily, that scarce one missed doing execution. Seeing them in this confusion we made a push at them on each side, still keeping our ranks, and drove the remainder headlong off the deck. This we did twice before any of our men dropt. We were grappled so close, they had no use of their cannon or muskets, and scarce thought of firing their pistols at us, expecting we should yield immediately, or to have borne us down with their weight. I am more particular in describing this petty fight, since there are but few examples, where a handful of men made such a long resistance. The arch-pirate, who was a stout, well-built young man, raged like a lion, calling his men a thousand cowards, so loud that his voice was heard above all the cries of the soldiers. The edge of their fury was a little abated after the dropping of so many men; and they began to fire at some distance; which did us more harm than their most furious attacks. My brother, seeing his men begin to drop in their turn, ordered me to face the one ship, while he with his rank leaped in amongst the enemies in the other. He did it with such

such a noble intrepidity, that he made a gap among the thickest of them immediately. But their numbers closing together, their very weight drove him back in spite of all he could do, and he lost several of his men before he could recover his post. The enemy would neither board us, nor leave us; but firing at us continually, still killed some of our men. There were now only eleven of us left; and no hopes of victory, or of quarter after such obstinate resistance. They durst not come to a close engagement with us for all this; when my brother, to die as honourably as he could, once more leaped into the pirate's ship, and seeing their captain in the midst of them, made at him with all his might, calling on the few he had left to second him. He soon cut his way through; but just as he was coming up to him, a cowardly Turk clapt a pistol just below his two shoulder-blades, and, I believe, shot him quite through the heart, for he dropped down dead on the spot. The Turk that shot him was run through the body by one of our men, and he himself with the others that were left, being quite overpowered, were all cut in pieces. I had yet four men left on my side against the lesser ship, and had till then kept off the enemy from boarding; but the pirates giving a great shout at my brother's fall, the captain of the ship I was engaged with, who was the arch-pirate's brother, tier, cried out to his crew, that it was a shame to stand all day firing at five men; and leaping on my deck, made at me like a man of honour, with his pistol steadily poised in his hand: I met him with equal resolution. He came boldly up within sword's length, and fired his pistol directly at my face; he aimed his shot so well, that one of the balls went through my hair, and the other grazed the side of my neck. But before he could second his shot, I gave him such a stroke with my broad sword, between the temple and the left ear, that it cut through part of his scull, his cheek-bone, and going cross his mouth, almost severed the lower part of his face from the upper. I had just the satisfaction to see him fall, when a musket-ball went through the brawny part of my right arm, and, at the same time, a Turk hit me just in the nape of the neck with the butt end of his musket, that I fell down flat on my face, on the body of my slain enemy. My companions, all but one, who died of his wounds soon after, fell honourably by my side. The Turks poured in from both ships like wolves upon their prey. After their barbarous shouts and yelling for the victory, they fell to stripping the dead bodies, and threw them into the sea without any further ceremony. All our crew, beside myself, were slain, or gasping, with threescore and fifteen of the enemy.

The

The reason why we fought so desperately was, that we knew very well, having killed so many at the first attacks, we were to expect no quarter; so we were resolved to sell our lives as dear as we could. When they came to strip me like the rest, I was just come to myself, being only stunned by the stroke of the musket. They found by my cloaths, that I was one of the most considerable persons of the crew. I was got upon my knees, endeavouring to rise, and reaching for my sword to defend myself to the last gasp; I found I could not hold it in my hand, by reason of the wound in my arm, though if I could, it had been needless; for three of them fell down upon me; and pressed me to the deck, while others brought cords and tied my hands, to carry me to the captain. He was dressing a slight wound he had in his leg with a pistol-shot; and four women in Persian habits were standing by; three of whom seemed to be attendants to the fourth, who was a person of the largest size, about five or six and twenty, a most exquisite beauty, except that she had an Amazonian kind of fierceness in her looks. When I was brought thus bound to the captain, they assured him I was the man that had slain his brother, and done the most harm of any. Upon which, starting up in the greatest fury a barbarian was capable of, and calling for a new scymitar he had in his cabin, he said,

" Let

" Let me cleave, if I can, the head of this
" Chriftian dog, as he did my poor brother's;
" and then do you chop him into a thou-
" fand pieces." With that he drew the
fcymitar, and was going to ftrike, when, to
the aftonifhment of the very barbarians,
the ftrange lady cried out, " O fave the
" brave young man!" and immediately
falling down on her knees by me, catched
me in her arms, and clafping me clofe to
her bofom, covered my body with hers,
and cried out, " Strike, cruel man, but
" ftrike through me, for otherwife a hair
" of his head fhall not be hurt." The
barbarians that ftood round us were ftruck
dumb with amazement; and the pirate
himfelf lifting up his eyes towards heaven,
faid, with a groan enough to break his
heart, " How, cruel woman! fhall this
" ftranger in a moment obtain more than
" I can with all my fighs and tears! Is this
" your paramour that robs me of what I
" have fought for with the danger of life?
" No, this Chriftian dog fhall be no longer
" my curfed rival;" and lifting up his
hand, was again going to ftrike, when,
covering me more clofely with her delicate
body, fhe cried out again, " Hold, Hamet!
" this is no rival; I never faw his face be-
" fore, nor ever will again, if you will but
" fpare his life: grant me this, and you
" fhall obtain more from me, than all your
" fervices.

"services could ever do." Here he began to pause a little. For my part, I was as much in amaze as he was. After a little pause, "Cruel woman," said he, "what is the "meaning of this?" Says she, "There is "something in this young man (for I was but "turned of nineteen) that he must not die. "But, if you will engage and swear by the "most holy Alcoran, that you will do him "no harm, I not only promise to be your "wife, but, to take off all umbrage of "jealousy, I give you leave to sell him to "some honourable person for a slave; and "will never see him more." Nor would she part from me, till he had sworn in that solemn manner, never to do me any hurt directly or indirectly; and, for greater security, she ordered one of her own servants to attend me constantly. So I was unbound; and the lady, without so much as looking at me, or staying to receive my thanks, retired with her women into the cabin. The pirate, who had something very noble in his looks for a Turk, confirmed again to me in the hearing of her officer, that I should receive no harm; and then ordered me to be carried under deck to the other end of the ship; commanding his men to steer back for Alexandria, in order, as I supposed, to dispose of me the first opportunity,

that

that he might be rid, as he thought, of so formidable a rival *.

[*Secretary.* Here the superior of the inquisition receiving a message on some other business, we told him we would consider further of the account he had given us, which, we said, might be true, though the adventure was extraordinary; and that we would hear the remaining narrative of his life another time. He assured us with the most natural air, that the whole, let it seem never so extraordinary, was real fact. Whether it were true or false, it did not much concern the holy office, only so far as we might catch him tripping in his story: however, some of the inquisitors asked him the following questions.

1*st Inquisitor.* Why did you not yield at first, considering the prodigious inequality of your strength and numbers, when you might have been ransomed afterwards; and not, like madmen, expose yourselves to be cut in pieces, as they all really were, except yourself?

---

* This is an odd adventure enough; but the circumstances are pretty well connected together. There happen very strange accidents among those lawless eastern people, and the wild Arabs, who observe no rules but what the lions and tigers, could they speak, would make for their own preservation. I fear there are some who profess themselves Christians would do the same.

Gaudentio.

Gaudentio. I told your Reverences, we had put our all in that bottom; which once loſt, we had nothing to ranſom ourſelves with, but in all likelihood muſt have remained in miſerable ſlavery all our life. We were moſt of us raſh young men, of more courage than prudence; we did not doubt but we could keep them off from boarding us, as we did; and thought, by their warm reception, they would have been forced to ſheer off; beſides, fighting againſt Turks and infidels, though for our lives and fortunes, we judged meritorious at the ſame time, and that it might be looked upon as laying down our lives for our holy religion.

2*d Inquiſitor.* You ſaid that the ſtrange lady cried out, "There is ſomething " in that young man, that tells me *he* " *muſt not die:*" I hope you do not pretend to the ſcience of phyſiognomy; which is one of the branches of divination; or that an infidel or Heathen woman could have the ſpirit of prophecy?

Gaudentio. I cannot tell what was her motive for ſaying ſo; I only relate matter of fact. As for phyſiognomy, I do not think there can be any certainty in it. Not but that a perſon of penetration, who has obſerved the humours and paſſions of men, and conſidering the little care the generality of the world take to conceal them; I fay, such a perfon may give a great guefs, *à pofteriori*, how they are inclined; though reafon and virtue may indeed overcome the moft violent. But I entirely fubmit my opinion to your better judgments.

Secretary. I cannot fay, we were diffatisfied with thefe anfwers: we faw he has a very noble prefence; and muft have been extremely handfome in his youth: therefore no wonder a Barbarian woman fhould fall in love with him, and make ufe of that turn to fave his life. However, for the prefent, we remanded him back to his apartment. Some days after he was called again to profecute his ftory.]

While I was under deck in confinement with the pirates, feveral of them were tolerably civil to me; knowing the afcendant the lady had over their captain, and being witneffes, how fhe had faved my life. But yet fhe would not confent to marry him, till fhe was affured I was fafe out of his hands. The arch-pirate never came to fee me himfelf, not being willing to truft his paffion; or elfe to watch all favourable opportunities of waiting on his miftrefs. One day, being indifpofed for want of air, I begged to be carried upon deck to breathe a little;

little; when I came up, I saw the lady, with her women, standing at the other end of the ship on the same account. I made her a very respectful bow at a distance; but as soon as ever she cast her eye on me, she went down into the cabin, I suppose, to keep her promise with the captain, and not to administer any cause of jealousy. I desired to be carried down again, not to hinder my benefactress from taking her diversion. I cannot say I found in myself the least inclination or emotion of love, only a sense of gratitude for so great a benefit; not without some admiration of the oddness of the adventure. When I was below, I asked the most sensible and civilized of the pirates, who their captain was, and who was my fair deliverer. How long, and by what means she came to be among them; because she seemed to be a person of much higher rank. He told me his captain's name was *Hamet*, son to the Dey of Algiers; who had forsaken his father's house on account of his young mother-in law's falling in love with him. For which reason his father had contrived to have him assassinated, believing him to be in the fault. But his younger brother by the same mother, discovered the design. So gathering together a band of stout young men like themselves, they seized two of their father's best ships, and resolved to follow the profession

feffion they were now of, till they heard of their father's death. That as for the lady who had faved his life, fhe was the late wife of a petty prince of the Curdi *, tributary to the king of Perfia, whofe hufband had been lately killed by treachery, or in an ambufcade of the wild Arabs. That, as far as he had been informed, the prince her hufband had been fent by the king his mafter to Alexandria †; who, apprehending an infurection among his fubjects ‡, had ordered him to treat for fome troops of Arabian horfe ‖. That he went there with

a

* The Curdi, or people of Curdiftan, are a warlike nation, paying a fmall tribute to the Perfians, and fometimes to the Turks; their very women are martial, and handle the fword and pike. The country runs from the Aliduli, a mountainous people, made tributary to the Turks by Selim I. father of Soliman the Magnificent, and reaches as far as Armenia.

† Alexandria is a fea-port, at the further end of the Mediterranean, belonging to the Turks, but much frequented by Arabian merchants, both by land and fea. One point of Curdiftan is not far from this port.

‡ This infurrection he fpeaks of, might be the feeds, or the firft plotting of the grand rebellion of Merowits, which began about the date of this account, and caufed fuch a terrible revolution in the Perfian empire; which no one who underftands any thing can be ignorant of.

‖ The Arabian horfes are the beft in the world, though not very large. The horfemen are very dexterous in the eaftern way of fighting. On which account, one cannot wonder, if the king of Perfia, and his rebellious fubjects, made it their intereft to procure as many auxiliaries, as they could. It is very likely the little

parties

a very handsome equipage, and took his beautiful wife along with him. Our captain, continued he, happened to be there at the same time to sell his prizes, and had not only sold several things of great value to the Curdish lord and lady, but had contracted a particular friendship with him, though, as we found since, it was more on account of his fair wife than any thing else. Nothing in the world could be more obsequious than our captain. He attended them, and offered his service on all occasions: you see, he is a very handsome man, and daring by his profession. We could not imagine of a long while, why he made such a stay at that town, contrary to his custom; living at a very high rate, as men of our calling generally do. At length the Curdish lord having executed his commission, was upon the return, when we perceived our captain to grow extremely pensive and melancholy, but could not tell what was the cause of it. He called his brother, who lost his life by your hand, and me to him, and told us in private, he had observed some of the Arabian strangers muttering together, as if they were hatching some plot or other, whether against himself, or the Curd, he could not

parties would always be on watch, to surprise one another when they could find an opportunity. And this petty Curdian prince being zealous for the service of his king, might be taken off by the rebels that way.

tell;

tell; but bid us be sure to attend him well armed where-ever he went. The event proved he had reason for his suspicions; for one evening, as the Curd and his wife were taking the air, with our captain, who was always of the party, passing through a little grove about a league out of town, six Arabian horsemen, exceeding well mounted, came full gallop up to us; and without saying a word, two of them fired their pistols directly at the Curdish lord, who was the foremost, but by good fortune missed us all. The Curd, as all that nation are naturally brave, drew his scymitar, and rushing in among them, cut off the foremost man's head, as clean as if it had been a poppy; but advancing too far unarmed as he was, one of them turned short, and shot him in the flank, that he dropped down dead immediately. Our captain seeing him fall, rushed in like lightning, his brother and myself falling on them at the same time: but the assassins, as if they wanted nothing but the death of the Curd, or saw by our countenance their staying would cost them dear, immediately turned their horses, and fled so swiftly on their jennets, that they were out of sight in an instant. We conducted the poor disconsolate lady and her dead husband back to the town, where those people made no more of it (being accustomed to such things) than if it had been a common accident. When her grief was a little abated, our captain told the lady, that it was not safe for her to return home the same way she came; that, in all probability, those who killed her husband were in confederacy with the disaffected party, and would waylay her, either for his papers, or her goods. That he had two ships well-manned at her service, and would conduct her safe by sea to some part of the Persian empire, from whence she might get into her own country. She consented at last, having seen how gallantly my master had behaved in her defence. So she came aboard with her attendants and effects, in order to be transported into her own country. Our captain, you may be sure, was in no haste to carry her home, being fallen most desperately in love with her: so that instead of carrying her to any of the Persian dominions, he directed his course for Algiers, hearing his father was dead; but meeting with you, it has made him alter his measures for the present. He has tried all ways to gain her love, but she would not give him the least encouragement, till this late accident, by which she saved your life.——When he had ended his relation, I reflected on it a good while, and considering the nature of those pirates, I thought I saw a piece of treachery in the affair, much more black than what he described,

scribed, and could not forbear compassionating the poor lady, both for her disaster, and the company she was fallen into. However, I kept my thoughts to myself. Not long after we arrived at Alexandria, where the pirate sold all our effects, that is, the merchandise he had taken aboard our ship, except some particular things that belonged to my brother and myself, as books, papers, maps and sea-charts, pictures, and the like. He determined to carry me to Grand Cairo*, the first opportunity, to sell me, or even give me away to a strange merchant he had an acquaintance with, where I should never be heard of more.

Nothing remarkable happened during our stay at Alexandria; they told me the captain had been in an extraordinary good humour, ever since the lady's promise to marry him. But she, to be sure he should not deceive her by doing me any injury when I was out of the ship, ordered her officer to attend me where-ever I was carried, till I was put in safe hands, and entirely out of the pirate's power. When we were arrived at Grand Cairo, I was carried to the place where the merchants meet to exchange their commodities; there were persons of almost all the Eastern and Indian

---

* Grand Cairo is the place of residence of the great Bassa of Egypt, higher up the country, on the river Nile.

nations,

nations. The lady's officer, according to his miſtreſs's order, never ſtirred an inch from me to witneſs the performance of the articles. At length, the pirate and a ſtrange merchant ſpied one another almoſt at the inſtant, and advancing the ſame way, ſaluted each other in the Turkiſh language, which I underſtood tolerably well. After ſome mutual compliments, the pirate told him he had met with ſuch a perſon he had promiſed to procure for him two years before, meaning myſelf; only I was not an eunuch, but that it was in his power to make me ſo, if he pleaſed. Your Reverences cannot doubt but I was a little ſtartled at ſuch a ſpeech, and was going to reply, that I would loſe my life a thouſand times, before I would ſuffer ſuch an injury. But the lady's officer turned to the pirate, and ſaid, he had engaged to his lady I ſhould receive no harm; and that he muſt never expect to obtain her for his wife, if ſhe had the leaſt ſuſpicion of ſuch a thing. But the merchant ſoon put us out of doubt, by aſſuring us, that it was againſt their laws to do ſuch an injury to any one of their own ſpecies; but if it were done before, they could not help it. Then turning to me, he ſaid in very good *Lingua Franca*, " Young man, if I buy you, I ſhall ſoon convince you, you need not apprehend any ſuch uſage from me." He eyed me from top to toe, with the moſt penetrating

netrating look I ever saw in my life; yet seemed pleased at the same time. He was very richly clad, attended with two young men in the same kind of dress, though not rich, who seemed rather sons than servants. His age did not appear to me to be above forty, yet he had the most serene and almost venerable look imaginable. His complexion was rather browner than that of the Egyptians, but it seemed to be more the effect of travelling, than natural. In short, he had an air so uncommon, that I was amazed, and began to have as great an opinion of him, as he seemed to have of me. He asked the pirate, what he must give for me; he told him, I had cost him very dear, and with that recounted to him all the circumstances of the fight wherein I was taken; and, to give him his due, represented it nowise to my disadvantage. However, these were not the qualifications the merchant desired; what he wanted was a person who was a scholar, and could give him an account of the arts and sciences, laws, customs, &c. of the Christians. This the pirate assured him I could do; that I was an European Christian, and a scholar, as he guessed by my books and writings; that I understood navigation, geography, astronomy, and several other sciences. I was out of countenance to hear him talk so; for though I had as much knowledge

knowledge of those sciences, as could be expected from one of my years, yet my age would not permit me to be master of them, but only to have the first principles, by which I might improve myself afterwards.

[*Secretary.* The inquisitors demurred a little at this, fearing he might be addicted to judicial astrology; but considering he had gone through a course of philosophy, and was designed for the sea, they knew he was obliged to have some knowledge in those sciences.]

The pirate told him, I had some skill in music and painting, having seen some instruments and books of those arts among my effects, and asked me if it were not so. I told him, all young gentlemen of liberal education in my country learned these arts, and that I had a competent knowledge and genius that way. This determined the merchant to purchase me. When they came to the price, the pirate demanded forty ounces of native gold, and three of those silk carpets he saw there with him, to make a present to the Grand Signior. The merchant agreed with him at the first word; only demanded all the books, globes, mathematical instruments, and, in fine, whatever remained of my effects, into the bargain. The pirate agreed to this, as easily as the other did to the price; so, upon performance of articles on both sides, I was delivered to him.

him. As soon as I was put into his power, he embraced me with a great deal of tenderness, saying, I should not repent my change of life. His attendants came up to me, and embraced me in the same manner, calling me brother, and expressing a great deal of joy for having me of their company. The merchant bid them take me down to the caravansera or inn, that I might refresh myself, and change my habit to the same as they wore. I was very much surprised at such unexpected civilities from strangers. But, before I went, I turned to the pirate, and said to him with an air that made the merchant put on a very thoughtful look, that I thanked him for keeping his promise in saving my life; but added, that though the fortune of war had put it in his power to sell me like a beast in the market, it might be in mine some time or other to render the like kindness. Then turning to the lady's officer, who had been my guardian so faithfully, and embracing him with all imaginable tenderness, I begged him to pay my best respects to my fair deliverer; and assure her, that I should esteem it the greatest happiness to be one day able to make a return for so unparalleled a favour, though it were at the expense of that life she had so generously saved. So we parted, the pirate grumbling a little within himself; and I in an amazing suspense, to know what was likely to become

come of me. As they were conducting me to the caravanfera where they lodged, I was full of the forrowful reflection, that I was ftill a flave, though I had changed my mafter: but my companions, who were fome of the handfomeft young men I ever faw in life, comforted me with the moft endearing words, telling me that I need fear nothing; that I fhould efteem myfelf one of the happieft men in the world, when they were arrived fafe in their own country, which they hoped would be before long; that I fhould then be as free as they were, and follow what employment of life my inclinations led me to, without any reftraint whatfoever. In fine, their difcourfe filled me with frefh amazement, and gave me at the fame time an eager longing to fee the event. I perceived they did not keep any ftrict guard on me; that I verily believed I could eafily have given them the flip; and might have gotten fome Armenian Chriftian to conceal me, till I fhould find an opportunity of returning into my own country. But, having loft all my effects, I thought I could fcarce be in a worfe condition, and was refolved to run all hazards. When I came to the houfe, I was ftruck with wonder at the magnificence of it, efpecially at the richnefs of the furniture. It was one of the beft in all Grand Cairo, though built low according to the cuftom of the

the country. It seems they always staid a year before they returned into their own country, and spared no cost to make their banishment, as they called it, as easy as they could. I was entertained with all the rarities of Egypt; the most delicious fruits, and the richest Greek and Asiatic wines that could be tasted; by which I saw they were not Mahometans. Not knowing what to make of them, I asked them who they were; of what country, what sect and profession, and the like. They smiled at my questions, and told me they were children of the Sun, and were called *Mezoranians*; which was as unintelligible to me as all the rest. But their country, they told me, I should see in a few months, and bid me ask no further questions. Presently my master came in, and embracing me, once more bid me welcome, with such an engaging affability, as removed almost all my fears. But what followed, filled me with the utmost surprise. "Young man," said he, "by the laws of this country you are mine; I have bought you at a very high price, and would give twice as much for you, if it were to be done again: but (continued he, with a more serious air) I know no just laws in the universe, that can make a free-born man become a slave to one of his own species. If you will voluntarily go along with us, you shall enjoy as much freedom as I do myself:

self: you shall be exempt from all the barbarous laws of these inhuman countries, whose brutal customs are a reproach to the dignity of a rational creature, and with whom we have no commerce, but to inquire after arts and sciences, which may contribute to the common benefit of our people. We are blessed with the most opulent country in the world; we leave it to your choice to go along with us, or not; if the latter, I here give you your liberty, and restore to you all that remains of your effects, with what assistance you want to carry you back again into your own country. Only, this I must tell you, if you go with us, it is likely you will never come back again, or perhaps desire it." Here he stopped, and observed my countenance with a great deal of attention. I was struck with such admiration of his generosity, together with the sentiments of joy for my unexpected liberty, and gratitude to my benefactor, coming into my mind all at once, that I had as much difficulty to believe what I heard, as your Reverences may now have at the relation of it, till the sequel informs you of the reasons for such unheard of proceedings. On the one hand, the natural desire of liberty prompted me to accept my freedom; on the other, I considered my shattered fortune; that I was left in a strange country so far from home, among Turks and infidels; the ardour of youth excited me to

push

push my fortune. The account of so glorious, though unknown country, stirred up my curiosity; I saw gold was the least part of the riches of these people, who appeared to me the most civilized I ever saw in my life; but, above all, the sense of what I owed to so noble a benefactor, who I saw desired it, and had me as much in his power now, as he could have afterwards. These considerations almost determined me to go along with him. I had continued longer thus irresolute, and fluctuating between so many different thoughts, if he had not brought me to myself, by saying, What say you, young man, to my proposal? I started out of my reveries, as if I had awaked from a real dream; and making a most profound reverence, My Lord, said I, or rather my father and deliverer, I am yours by all the ties of gratitude a human heart is capable of; I resign myself to your conduct; and will follow you to the end of the world. This I said with such emotion of spirit, that I believe he saw into my very soul; for embracing me once more with a most inexpressible tenderness, I adopt you, said he, for my son; and these are your brothers, pointing to his two young companions; all I require of you is, that you live as such.——Here, Reverend Fathers, I must confess one of the greatest faults I ever did in my life: I never considered whether these men were Christians or Heathens: I engaged myself with a people, where I could never have the exercise of my religion, although I always preserved it in my heart. But what could be expected from a daring young man, just in the heat of his youth, who had lost all his fortune, and had such a glorious prospect offered him for retrieving it?—— Soon after this, he gave orders to his attendants to withdraw, as if he intended to say something to me in private; they obeyed immediately with a filial respect, as if they had indeed been his sons, but they were not; I only mention it to shew the nature of the people I was engaged with: then taking me by the hand he made me sit down by him, and asked me if it were really true, as the pirate informed him, that I was an European Christian? though, added he, be what you will, I do not repent my buying of you. I told him I was, and in that belief would live and die. So you may, said he, (seeming pleased at my answer). But I have not yet met with any of that part of the world, who seemed to have the dispositions of mind I think I see in you, looking at the lineaments of my face with a great deal of earnestness. I have been informed, continued he, that your laws are not like barbarous Turks, whose government is made up of tyranny and brutality, governing all by fear and force, and making slaves of all

who

who fall under their power. Whereas the European Christians, as I am told, are governed by a divine law, that teaches them to do good to all, injury to none; particularly not to kill and destroy their own species; nor to steal, cheat, over-reach, or defraud any one of their just due; but to do in all things just as they would be done by; looking on all men as common brothers of the same stock, and behaving with justice and equity in all their actions public and private, as if they were to give an account to the universal Lord and Father of all. I told him our law did really teach and command us to do so; but that very few lived up to this law; that we were obliged to have recourse to coercive laws and penalties, to enforce what we acknowledged otherwise to be a duty: that if it were not for the fear of such punishments, the greatest part of them would be worse than the very Turks he mentioned. He seemed strangely surprised at this. What, says he, can any one do in private, what his own reason and solemn profession condemns? Then addressing himself to me in a more particular mannner: Do you profess this just and holy law you mentioned? I told him, I did: then, says he, do but live up to your own law, and we require no more of you *. Here he made a little

* If it appear incredible to any one, that Heathens, as these people were, should have such strict ideas of morality and justice, when they see such horrid injustice, frauds,

little noise with his staff, at which two of his attendants came in: he asked them if my

and oppressions among Christians, let them consider, *first*, that the law and light of nature will never be entirely extinguished in any who do not shut their eyes against it; but that they would esteem the injuries they do to others, without any scruple, to be very great hardships if done to themselves: they have therefore the ideas of justice and equity imprinted in their minds, however obscured by their wicked lives. ———— 2*dly*, Let them read the celebrated Bishop of Meaux's universal history, pt. iii. of the morals and equity of the ancient Egyptians under their great king Sesostris, or about that time. ———— 3*dly*, Not only the lives and maxims of the first Heathen philosophers, afford us very just rules of morality, but there are also fragments of ancient history, from the earliest times, of whole Heathen nations, whose lives would make Christians blush at their own immoralities, if they were not hardened in them. The people of Colchos, whom the great Bochart, in his Phaleg. proves to have been a colony of ancient Egyptians, as will be seen in the sequel of these memoirs, or the ancient inhabitants of Pontus, who come from them, were according to Homer the most just of men.

Γαλακτοφάνων δικαιοτάτων ἀνθρώπων.

Milk-eaters the most just of men. *Hom. Il.* K.

Chærilus in Xerxis Diabasi apud Bochart, speaking of the Scythians on the Euxine sea, says, Νομάδων ἦσαν ἄποικοι ἀνθρώπων νομίμων, they were a colony of the Nomades, a just people.

Strabo says, that Anacharsis and Abaris, both Scythians, esteemed by the ancient Greeks, for their peculiar and national affability, probity, and justice: ὅτι ἐθνικόν τινα χαρακτῆρα ἐπέφαινον εὐκολίας, ᾗ τελειότητ⸗, ᾗ δικαιοσύνης.

my effects were come from the pirate. Being anfwered, they were; he ordered them to be brought in, and examined them very nicely. There were among them fome pictures of my own drawing, a repeating watch, two compafs boxes, one of them very curioufly wrought in ivory and gold, which had been my great-grandfather's, given him by Venerio; a fet of mathematical inftruments, draughts of ftatuary and architecture bythe beft mafters; with all which he feemed extremely pleafed. After he had examined them with a great deal of admiration, he ordered one of his attendants to reach him a cabinet full of gold; he opened it to me, and faid, Young man, I not only reftore all your effects here prefent, having no right to any thing that belongs to another man, but once more offer you your liberty, and as much of this gold, as you think fufficient to carry you home, and make you live eafy all your life. I was a little out of countenance, imagining what I faid of the ill morals of the Chriftians, had made him afraid to take me along with him. I told him, I valued nothing now fo much as his company, and begged him not only to let me go along with him, but that he would be

---

συνης. And Nicholaus Damafcenus, of the Galactophagi, εἰσὶ δὲ ϰ) δικαιότατοι, they are the moft juft of men. Vide Bochart, lib. iii. c. 9.

pleafed

pleased to accept whatever he saw of mine there before him: adding, that I esteemed it the greatest happiness, to be able to make some small recompense for the obligations I owed him. I do accept of it, says he, and take you solemnly into my care: go along with these young men, and enjoy your liberty in effect, which I have hitherto only given you in words. Here some of his elder companions coming in, as if they were to consult about business; the young men and myself went to walk the town for our diversion. Your Reverences may be sure, I observed all the actions of these new people, with the greatest attention my age was capable of. They seemed not only to have a horror of the barbarous manners and vices of the Turks, but even a contempt of all the pleasures and diversions of the country. Their whole business was to inform themselves of what they thought might be an improvement in their own country, particularly in arts and trades, and whatever curiosities were brought from foreign parts; setting down their observations of every thing of moment. They had masters of the country at set hours to teach them the Turkish and Persian languages, in which I endeavoured to perfect myself along with them. Though they seemed to be the most moral men in the world, I could observe no signs of religion in them, till a certain occasion that

that happened to us in our voyage, of which I shall speak to your Reverences in its proper place. This was the only point they were shy in; they gave me the reasons for it afterwards; but their behaviour was the most candid and sincere in other matters that can be imagined. We lived thus in the most perfect union all the time we staid at Grand Cairo; and I enjoyed the same liberty that I could have had in Italy. All I remarked in them was an uneasiness they expressed to be so long out of their own country; but they comforted themselves with the thought it would not be long. I cannot omit one observation I made of these young mens conduct while we staid in Egypt. They were all about my own age, strong and vigorous, and the handsomest race of people, perhaps, the world ever produced: we were in the most voluptuous and lewd town in the whole eastern empire; the young women seemed ready to devour us as we went along the streets. Yet I never could perceive in the young men the least propensity to lewdness. I imputed it at first to the apprehension of my being in their company, and a stranger; but I soon found they acted by principle. As young men are apt to encourage, or rather corrupt one another, I own I could not forbear expressing my wonder at it. They seemed surprised at the thought; but the reasons they

they gave were as much out of our common way of thinking, as their behaviour. They told me, for the firſt reaſon, that all the women they ſaw were either married; or particular mens daughters; or common. As to married women, they ſaid, it was ſuch a hainous piece of injuſtice to violate the marriage-bed, that every man living would look upon it as the greateſt injury done to himſelf: how could they therefore in reaſon do it to another? If they were daughters of particular men, bred up with ſo much care and ſolicitude of their parents, what a terrible affliction muſt it be to them, or to ourſelves, to ſee our daughters or ſiſters violated and corrupted, after all our care to the contrary; and this too, perhaps, by thoſe we had cheriſhed in our own boſoms? If common ſtrumpets, what rational man could look on them otherwiſe than brute beaſts, to proſtitute themſelves to every ſtranger for hire? Beſides, their abandoned lewdneſs generally defeats the great deſign of nature to propagate the ſpecies; or, by their impure embraces, ſuch diſorders may be contracted, as to make us hereafter, at beſt, but fathers of a weak and ſickly offspring. And if we ſhould have children by them, what would become of our fathers grandchildren? But what man who had the leaſt ſenſe of the dignity of his own birth, would ſtain his race, and

give

give birth to such a wretched breed, and then leave them exposed to want and infamy? This they said chiefly with reference to the vast ideas they had of their own nation, valuing themselves above all other people; though the consideration holds good with all men. I own, I was mute at these reasons, and could not say but they were very just, though the warmth of my youth had hindered me from reflecting on them before. These reflections appeared so extraordinary in young men, and even Heathens, that I shall never forget them.—Sometime after, I found by their diligence in settling their affairs, and the chearfulness of their countenances, that they expected to leave Egypt very soon; they seemed to wait for nothing but orders from their governor. In the mean time there happened an accident to me, scarce fit indeed for your Reverences to hear; nor should I ever have thought of relating it, had you not laid your commands on me to give an exact account of my whole life. Besides, that it is interwoven with some of the chief occurrences of my life in the latter part of it. Our governor whom they called *Pophar*, which in their language signifies Father of his people, and by which name I shall always call him hereafter, looking at his ephemeris, which he did very frequently, found by computation, that he had still

some

some time left to stay in the country, and resolved to go down once more to Alexandria, to see if he could meet with any more European curiosities, brought by the merchant-ships that are perpetually coming at that season into the port. He took only two of the young men and me along with him, to shew me, as he said, that I was entirely at my liberty, since I might easily find some ship or other to carry me into my own country; and I, on the other hand, to convince him of the sincerity of my intentions, generally kept in his company. The affair I am going to speak of, soon gave him full proof of my sincerity.

While we were walking in the public places to view the several goods and curiosities, that were brought from different parts of the world, it happened that the Bassa of Grand Cairo, with all his family, was come to Alexandria on the same account, as well as to buy some young female slaves. His wife and daughter were then both with him: the wife was one of the Grand Signior's sisters, seemingly about thirty, and a wonderful fine woman. The daughter was about sixteen, of such exquisite beauty, and lovely features, as were sufficient to charm the greatest prince in the world *. When he

* *N. B.* The Bassa of Grand Cairo is one of the greatest officers in the Turkish empire, and the most independent of any subject in Turky; it is customary for the

he perceived them, the Pophar, who naturally abhorred the Turks, kept off, as if he were treating privately with some merchants. But I, being young and inconsiderate, stood gazing, though at a respectful distance, at the Bassa's beautiful daughter, from no other motive but mere curiosity. She had her eyes fixed on my companions and me at the same time, and, as I supposed, on the same account. Her dress was so magnificent, and her person so charming, that I thought her the most beautiful creature I had ever seen in my life. If I could have foreseen the troubles which that short interview was to cost both the Pophar and myself, I should have chosen rather to have looked on the most hideous monster. I observed, that the young lady, with a particular sort of emotion, whispered something to an elderly woman that attended her, and that this last did the same to a page, who immediately went to two natives of the place, whom the Pophar used to hire to carry his things: this was to inquire of them who we were. They, as appeared by the event, told them, that I was a young slave lately bought by the Pophar. After a while, the Bassa with his train went away, and I, for my part, thought no more of

the sultans to give their daughters in marriage to such persons; but they are often disliked by their husbands, on account of their imperious behaviour.

the matter. The next day, as t
and we were walking in one of
gardens; a little elderly man, 1
nuch, with a moſt beautiful y
with him, having dogged us to
part of the walks, came up to 1
dreſſing themſelves to the Pop
him what he would take for
ſlave, pointing at me, becauſe th
ſired to buy him. The Pophar
be more ſurpriſed at this unexp
ſtion, than I ever obſerved him a
before, which confirmed me mor
in the opinion of the kindneſs
me. But ſoon coming to himſelf
a man of great preſence of mind,
ıy calmly, that I was no ſlave;
ſon to be ſold for any price, ſin
free as he was. Taking this fo
to enhance the price, they pro
oriental pearls with other jewels
value; and bid him name wha
have, and it ſhould be paid in
adding, that I was to be the co
the Baſſa's ſon, where I migh
fortune for ever, if I would go
them. The Pophar perſiſted in
ſwer, and ſaid he had no powel
they alledged, I had been bough
but a little before, in the Grar
dominions, and they would hav
I interpoſed, and anſwered b

though I had been taken prisoner by the chance of war, I was no slave, nor would I part with my liberty but at the price of my life. The Baſſa's ſon, for ſo he now declared himſelf to be, inſtead of being angry at my reſolute anſwer, replied with a moſt agreeable ſmile, that I ſhould be as free as he was; making at the ſame time the moſt ſolemn proteſtations by his holy Alcoran, that our lives and deaths ſhould be inſeparable. Though there was ſomething in his words the moſt perſuaſive I ever felt; yet conſidering the obligations I had to the Pophar, I was reſolved not to go; but anſwered with a moſt reſpectful bow, that though I was free by nature, I had indiſpenſable obligations not to go with him, and hoped he would take it for a determinate anſwer. I pronounced this with ſuch a reſolute air, as made him ſee there was no hopes. Whether his deſire was more inflamed by my denial, or whether they took us for perſons of greater note than we appeared to be, I cannot tell; but I obſerved he put on a very languiſhing air, with tears ſtealing down his cheeks, which moved me to a degree I cannot expreſs. I was ſcarce capable of ſpeaking, but caſt down my eyes, and ſtood as immoveable as a ſtatue. This ſeemed to revive his hopes; and recovering himſelf a little, with a trembling voice he replied; Suppoſe it be the Baſſa's daughter, you saw yesterday, that desires to have you for her attendant, what will you say then? I started at this, and casting my eyes on him more attentively, I saw him swimming in tears, with a tenderness enough to pierce the hardest heart. I looked at the Pophar, who I saw was trembling for me; and feared it was the daughter herself that asked me the question. I was soon put out of doubt; for she, finding she had gone too far to go back, discovered herself, and said, I must go along with her, or one of us must die *. — I

* Love-adventures are not the design of these memoirs, as will appear by the rest of his life: otherwise, this account of the Baffa's daughter had like to have made me lay down my pen, without troubling myself to write any further remark. But, when I considered, the man is no fool, let him be what he will, nor could design to embellish his history by this extraordinary adventure, so like the former, and just upon the back of it, I am inclined to believe he wrote the matter of fact just as it happened. More unaccountable accidents than this have happened to some men.

The amorous temper of the Turkish ladies, especially at Grand Cairo, where the women are the most voluptuous in the world, and the surprising beauty of this young man, who, the secretary says, has the noblest presence he ever saw, even at that age, might easily charm a wanton giddy girl at the first sight. Besides, she was informed he was a slave, and might think she could have purchased him for her private gallant; or might be encouraged in it by the lustful elderly woman that attended her. Such things have been done before now; but when she came nearer to the tempting object, and found him to be something more noble than she expected,

— I hope your Reverences will excuse this account I give of myself, which nothing should have drawn from me, though it is literally

pected, her passion might thereby grow to the highest pitch.

Extraordinary beauty, in either sex, is oftentimes a great misfortune; since it frequently leads them into very great follies, and even disasters. What will not heedless youth do, when fired with flattery or charms? It is no new thing for women to fall in love at first sight, as well as men, and on as unequal terms; in spite of all reasons and considerations to the contrary. I believe there may be men in the world, as charming in the eyes of women, as ever the fair Helen appeared to the men. The almost incredible catastrophes caused by her beauty, are so far from being fabulous, that, besides the account Homer gives of her, there is extant an oration of the famous Isocrates *De laudibus Helenæ*, before Alexander the Great's time, which gives a more amazing account of the effects of her beauty, than Homer does. He says, she was ravished for her beauty by the great and wise Theseus, when she was but a girl. She was afterwords courted by all the Grecian princes; and, after her marriage, was carried from Europe into Asia by the beautiful Paris; which kindled the first war that is recorded in history to have been made in those parts of the world. Yet, notwithstanding that false and fatal step, her beauty reconciled her to her husband. The sight of some men may have as violent effects on women.

It is possible the young lady would have been very angry with any one who should have persuaded Signor Gaudentio to do as he did; yet in effect it was the greatest kindness: for this very lady, some time after, became mistress of the whole Ottoman empire. Whereas if she had run away with him, as the violence of her passion suggested, they had both of them been inevitably miserable. Notwithstanding all these reasons, I should

literally true, but your express commands to tell the whole history of my life. — The perplexity I was in cannot be imagined. I considered she was a Turk, and I a Christian; that my death must certainly be the consequence of such a rash affair, were I to engage in it; that whether she concealed me in her father's court, or attempted to go off with me, it was ten thousand to one, we should both be sacrificed: neither could the violence of such a sudden passion ever be concealed from the Bassa's spies. In a word, I was resolved not to go; but how to get off, was the difficulty. I saw the most beautiful creature in the world all in tears before me, after a declaration of love, that exceeded the most romantic tales; youth, love, and beauty, and even an inclination on my side, pleaded her cause. But at length the consideration of the endless miseries I was likely to draw on the young lady, should I comply with what she desired, prevailed above all other. I was resolved to refuse, for her sake more than my own, and was just going to tell her so on my knees, with all the arguments my reason could suggest to appease her; when an attendant came running in haste to the other

not have believed this story, if I had not examined some other facts, which, he said, happened to him at Venice, as incredible as this, and found them to be really true.

person,

perſon, who was alſo a woman, and told her the Baſſa was coming that way. She was rouſed out of her lethargy at this. The other woman immediately ſnatched her away, as the Pophar did me ; and ſhe had only time to call out with a threat, Think better on it, or die. I was no ſooner out of her ſight, but I found a thouſand reaſons for what I did, more than I could think of before, while the inchanting object was before my eyes. I ſaw the madneſs of that paſſion which forced the moſt charming perſon of the Ottoman empire, capable by her beauty to conquer the Grand Signior himſelf, to make a declaration of love, ſo contrary to the nature and modeſty of her ſex, as well as her quality and dignity, and ready to ſacrifice her reputation, the duty ſhe owed her parents, her liberty, perhaps her life, for an unknown perſon, who had been a ſlave but ſome time before. I ſaw on the other hand, that had I complied with the fair charmer's propoſal, I muſt have run the riſk of loſing my religion or life, or rather both, with a dreadful chain of hidden misfortunes, likely to accompany ſuch a raſh adventure. While I was taken up with theſe thoughts, the wiſe Pophar, after reflecting a little upon what had happened, told me, this unfortunate affair wou'd not end ſo, but that it might coſt us both our lives, and ſomething elſe
that

that was more dear to him. He feared so violent a passion would draw on other extremes; especially considering the wickedness of the people, and the brutal tyranny of their government: however, he was resolved not to give me up but with his life, if I would but stand to it myself: adding, that we must make off as fast as we could; and, having so many spies upon us, use policy as well as expedition. Accordingly he went down directly to the port, and hired a ship in the most public manner to go for Cyprus, paid the whole freight on the spot, and told them they must necessarily sail that evening. We should actually have done so, had not our companions and effects obliged us to return to Grand Cairo; but instead of imbarking for Cyprus, he called aside the master of the vessel, who was of his acquaintance, and, for a good round sum, privately agreed with him to sail out of the port, as if we were really on board, while the Pophar hired a boat for us at the other end of the town, in which we went that night directly for Grand Cairo. As soon as we were arrived there, we inquired how long it would be before the Bassa returned to that city. They told us it would be about a fortnight at soonest; this gave the Pophar time to pay off his house, pack up his effects, and get all things ready for his great voyage; but he still had greater apprehensions

sions in his looks than ever I remarked in him. However, he told us, he hoped the affair would end well. In five days time all things were in readiness for our departure. We set out a little before sunset, as is customary in those countries, and marched but a slow pace whilst we were near the town, to avoid any suspicion of flight. After we had travelled thus about a league up by the side of the river Nile, the Pophar leading the van, and the rest following in a pretty long string after him, we met five or six men coming down the river-side on horseback, whose fine turbans and habits shewed they were pages, or attendants of some great person, The Pophar turned off from the river, as if it were to give them way: and they passed on very civilly without seeming to take any further notice of us. I was the hindmost but one of our train, having staid to give our dromedaries some water. Soon after these, came two ladies riding on little Arabian jennets, with prodigious rich furniture, by which I guessed them to be persons of quality, and the others gone before to be their attendants. They were not quite over-against where I was, when the jennet of the younger of the two ladies began to snort and start at our dromedaries, and became so unruly, that I apprehended she could scarce sit him. At that instant, one of the led dromedaries coming pretty near, that and the
rustling

rustling of its loading so frighted the jennet, that he gave a bound all on a sudden, and being on the inside of us towards the river, he ran full speed towards the edge of the bank, where not being able to stop his career, he flew directly off the precipice into the river, with the lady still sitting him; but the violence of the leap threw her off two or three yards into the water. It happened very luckily that there was a little island just by where she fell, and her cloaths keeping her up for some minutes, the stream carried her against some stakes that stood just above the water, which catched hold of her cloaths, and held her there. The shrieks of the other lady brought the nighest attendants up to us; but those fearful wretches durst not venture into the river to her assistance. I jumped off my dromedary with indignation, and throwing off my loose garment and sandals, swam to her, and with much difficulty getting hold of her hand, and loosing her garments from the stakes, I made a shift to draw her across the stream, till I brought her to land. She was quite senseless for some time; I held down her head, which I had not yet looked at, to make her disgorge the water she had swallowed; but I was soon struck with a double surprise, when I looked at her face, to find it was the Bassa's daughter, and to see her in that place, whom I though

I had left at Alexandria. After some time, she came to herself, and looking fixed on me a good while, her senses not being entirely recovered, at last she cried out, " O Mahomet, must I owe my life to this man!" and fainted away. The other lady, who was her confident, with a great deal of pains brought her to herself again; we raised her up, and endeavoured to comfort her as well as we could: No, says she, throw me into the river once more; let me not be obliged to a barbarian for whom I have done too much already. I told her in the most respectful terms I could think of, that providence had ordered it so, that I might make some recompense for the undeserved obligations she had laid on me; that I had too great value for her merit, ever to make her miserable, by loving a slave, such as I was, a stranger, a Christian, and one who had indispensable obligations to act as I did. She startled a little at what I said; but after a short recollection answered, Whether you are a slave, an infidel, or whatever you please, you are one of the most generous men in the world. I suppose your obligations are on account of some more happy woman than myself; but since I owe my life to you, I am resolved not to make you unhappy, any more than you do me. I not only pardon you, but am convinced my pretensions are both unjust, and against my own

own honour. She said this with an air becoming her quality: she was much more at ease, when I assured her I was engaged to no woman in the world; but that her memory should be ever dear to me, and imprinted in my heart till my last breath. Here ten or a dozen armed Turks came upon us full speed from the town, and seeing the Pophar and his companions, they cried out, Stop villains, we arrest you in the name of the Bassa. At this we started up to see what was the matter, when the lady who knew them, bid me not be afraid; that she had ordered these men to pursue me, when she left Alexandria. That hearing we were fled off by sea, she pretended sickness, and asked leave of her father to return to Cairo, there to bemoan her misfortune with her confident; and was in those melancholy sentiments, when the late accident happened to her. That she supposed these men had discovered the trick we had played them in not going by sea, and on better information had pursued us this way. So she dismissed them immediately. I was all this while in one of the greatest agonies that can be expressed, both for fear of my own resolutions and hers: so I begged her to retire, lest her wet cloaths should endanger her health. I should not have been able to pronounce these words, if the Pophar had not cast a look at me, which pierced me through, and

and made me see the danger I was in by my delay. Her resolutions now seemed to be stronger than mine. She pulled off this jewel your Reverences see on my finger, and just said, with tears trickling down her beautiful cheeks, Take this, and adieu! She then pulled her companion away, and never looked at me more. I stood amazed, almost without life or motion in me; and cannot tell how long I might have continued so, if the Pophar had not come and congratulated me for my deliverance. I told him, I did not know what he meant by deliverance, for I did not know whether I was alive or dead, and that I was afraid he would repent his buying of me, if I procured him any more of these adventures. If we meet with no worse than these, says he, we are well enough; no victory can be gained without some loss. So he awakened me out of my lethargy, and commanded us to make the best of our way.

Though the Pophar was uneasy to be out of the reach of the fair lady and her faithless Turks, yet he was not in any great haste in the main, the proper time for his great voyage not being yet come. There appeared a gaiety in his countenance, that seemed to promise us a prosperous journey. For my own part, though I was glad I had escaped my dangerous inchantress, there was a heaviness lay on my spirits, which I could give

give no account of; but the thoughts of such an unknown voyage, and variety of places, dissipated it by degrees. We were eleven in number, five elderly men, and five young ones, myself being a supernumerary person. We were all mounted upon dromedaries, which were very fine for that sort of creature: they are something like camels, but less, and much swifter; they live a great while without water, as the camels do, which was the reason they made use of them, for the barren sands they were to pass over; though they have the finest horses that can be seen in their own country. They had five spare ones to carry provisions, or to change, in case any one of their own should tire by the way. It was upon one of these five that I rode. We went up the Nile, leaving it on our left hand all the way, steering our course directly for the Upper Egypt. I presume your Reverences know, that the river Nile divides Egypt into two parts lengthwise, descending from Abyssinia with such an immense course, that the Ethiopians said it had no head, and running through the hither Ethiopia, pours down upon Egypt, as the Rhine does through the Spanish Netherlands, making it one of the richest countries in the universe. We visited all the towns on that famous river upwards, under pretence of merchandising; but the true reason of our delay was, be-

caufe

cause the Pophar's critical time for his great voyage was not yet come. He looked at his ephemeris and notes almost every hour, the rest of them attending his nod in the most minute circumstances. As we approached the upper parts of Egypt, as nigh as I could guess, overagainst the deserts of Barca, they began to buy provisions proper for their purpose; but particularly rice, dried fruits, and a sort of dried paste that served us for bread. They bought their provisions at different places, to avoid suspicion; and I observed they laid up a considerable quantity, both for their dromedaries and themselves: by which I found we had a long journey to make.—— When we came overagainst the middle coast of the vast desert of Barca, we met with a delicate clear rivulet, breaking out of a rising part of the sands, and making towards the Nile. Here we alighted, drank ourselves, and gave our dromedaries to drink as much as they would; then we filled all our vessels, made on purpose for carriage, and took in a much greater proportion of water than we had done provisions.—— I forgot to tell your Reverence, that, at several places as we passed, they dismounted, and kissed the ground with a very superstitious devotion, and scraped some of the dust, which they put into golden urns, which they had brought with them on purpose, letting me do what I pleased all the while.

while. This fort of devotion I then only guessed, but found to be true afterwards, was the chief occasion of their coming into those parts, though carried on under the pretence of merchandising. They did the same in this place; and when all were ready, the Pophar looking on his papers and needle, cried *Gaulo benim*, which, I was informed, was as much as to say, *Now children for our lives*; and immediately as he had steered south all along before, he turned short on his right hand due west, cross the vast desert of Barca, as fast as his dromedary could well go. We had nothing but sands and sky before us, and in a few hours were almost out of danger of any one's attempting to follow us.

Being thus imbarked, if I may say so, on this vast ocean of sand, a thousand perplexing thoughts came into my mind, which I did not reflect on before. Behold me in the midst of the inhospitable deserts of Africa, where whole armies * had often perished.

* Ancient histories give us several instances of a great number of persons, and even whole armies, who have been lost in the sands of Africa. Herodotus in Thalia, says that Cambyses the son of Cyrus the Great, in his expedition against the Ethiopians, was brought to such straits in those vast deserts, that they were forced to eat every tenth man before they could get back again. The other army, which he sent to destroy the temple of Jupiter Hammon, was entirely overwhelmed and lost
in

rished. The further we advanced, the more our danger increased. I was with men, who were not only strangers to myself, but to all the world beside: ten against one; but this was not all; I was persuaded now they were Heathens and idolaters: for, beside their superstitious kissing the earth in several places, I observed they looked up towards the sun, and seemed to address their oraisons to that planet, glorious indeed, but a planet and a creature nevertheless: then I reflected on what the Pophar said when he bought me, that I was not likely to return. It is possible, thought I, I am destined for a human sacrifice to some Heathen god in the midst of this vast desert. But not seeing any arms they had, either offensive or defensive, except their short goads to prick on their dromedaries, I was a little easy: I had privately provided myself with two pocket-pistols, and was resolved to defend myself till the last gasp. But when I considered that unparallelled justice and humanity I had experienced in their treatment of me, I was a little com-

---

in the sands. *Herodot. Thalia.* The idolaters imputed it as a punishment for his impiety against Jupiter, but it was for want of knowing the danger. ——— I suppose very few are ignorant of the contrivance of Marius the Roman general, to get over the sands to Capsa, to seize Jugurtha's treasure, which he thought secure. *Sallust. de bello Jugarthin.*

forted.

sorted. As for the difficulty of passing the deserts, I reflected that their own lives were as much in danger as mine; that they must have some unknown ways of passing them over, otherwise they would never expose themselves to such evident danger.

I should have told your Reverences, that we set out a little before sun-set to avoid the heats, June the 9th, 1688; the moon was about the first quarter, and carried on the light till nigh dawn of day; the glittering of the sands, or rather pebbly gravel, in which there were abundance of shining stones like jewels or cryftal, increased the light, that we could see to steer our course by the needle very well. We went on at a vast rate, the dromedaries being very swift creatures; their pace is more running than gallopping, much like that of a mule; that I verily believe, from six o' clock in the evening till about ten the next day, we ran almost a hundred and twenty Italian miles: we had neither stop nor let, but steered our course in a direct line, like a ship under sail. The heats were not nigh so insufferable as I expected; for though we saw nothing we could call a mountain in those immense Bares, yet the sands, or at least the way we steered, was very high ground: that as soon as we were out of the breath of the habitable countries, we

had

had a perpetual breeze blowing full in our faces; yet so uniform, that it scarce raised any dust; partly because, where we passed, the sands were not of that small dusty kind, as in some parts of Africa, which fly in clouds with the wind overwhelming all before it, but of a more gravelly kind; and partly from an imperceptible dew, which, though not so thick as a fog, moistened the surface of the ground pretty much. A little after nine next morning we came to some clumps of shrubby trees, with a little moss on the ground instead of grass: here the wind fell, and the heats became very violent. The Pophar ordered us to alight, and pitch our tents, to shelter both ourselves and dromedaries from the heats. Their tents were made of the finest sort of oiled cloth I ever saw, prodigious light and portable, yet capable of keeping out both rain and sun. Here we refreshed ourselves and beasts till a little after six; when we set out again, steering still directly west as nigh as I could guess. We went on thus for three days and nights without any considerable accident; only I observed the ground seemed to rise insensibly higher, and the breezes not only stronger, but the air itself much cooler. About ten, the third day, we saw some more clumps of trees on our right hand, which looked greener and thicker than the former,

mer, as if they were the beginning of some habitable vale, as in effect they were. The Pophar ordered us to turn that way, which was the only turning out of our way we had yet made. By the chearfulnefs of their countenances, I thought this might be the beginning of their country; but I was very much miftaken; we had a far longer and more dangerous way to go, than what we had paffed hitherto. However, this was a very remarkable ftation of our voyage, as your Reverences will find by the fequel. As we advanced, we found it to open and defcend gradually; till at length we faw a moft beautiful vale, full of palms, dates, oranges, and other fruit-trees, entirely unknown in thefe parts, with fuch a refrefhing fmell from the odoriferous fhrubs, as filled the whole air with perfumes *. We rode into the thickeft of it as faft as we could to enjoy the inviting fhade. We eafed our dromedaries, and took the firft care of them; for on them all our fafeties depended. After we had refrefhed ourfelves, the Pophar ordered every one to go to fleep as foon as he could, fince we were like to

---

* The prodigious fertility of Africa, in the vales between the deferts and the fkirts of it, for a great breadth towards the two feas, is recorded by the beft hiftorians; though the ridge of it, over which our author was conducted, and other particular tracts, are all covered with fands.

have

have but little the three following days. I
should have told your Reverences, that as
soon as they alighted, they fell down flat on
their faces, and kissed the earth, with a
great deal of seeming joy and ardour, which
I took to be a congratulation for their happy
arrival at so hospitable a place, but it was on
a quite different account. I was the first who
awoke after our refreshment; my thoughts
and fears, though much calmer than they
had been, would not suffer me to be so sedate as the rest. Finding the hour for departing was not yet come, I got up, and
walked in that delicious grove, which was
so much the more delightful, as the deserts
we had passed were dreadful and horrid.
I passed on, descending towards the centre
of the vale, not doubting but, by the
greenness and fragrancy of the place, I
should find a spring of water. I had not
gone far, before I saw a most delicate rill,
bubbling out from under a rock, forming
a little natural bason, from whence it ran
gliding down the centre of the vale, increasing as it went, till in all appearance
it might form a considerable rivulet, unless
it were swallowed up again in the sands.
At that place the vale ran upon a pretty
deep descent, so that I could see over the
trees and shrubs below me, almost as far as
my eyes could reach; increasing or decreasing in breadth as the hills of sands,

for

for now they appeared to be hills, would give it leave. Here I had the moſt delightful proſpect that the moſt lively imagination can form to itſelf; the ſun-burnt hills of ſand on each ſide, made the greens look ſtill more charming; but the ſinging of innumerable unknown birds, with the different fruits and perfumes exhaling from the aromatic ſhrubs, rendered the place delicious beyond expreſſion. After I had drank my fill, and delighted myſelf with thoſe native rarities, I ſaw a large lion come out of the grove, about two hundred paces below me, going very quietly to the ſpring to lap. When he had drank, he whiſked his tail two or three times, and began to tumble on the green graſs. I took the opportunity to ſlip away back to my companions, very glad I had eſcaped ſo: they were all awake when I came up, and had been in great concern for my abſence. The Pophar ſeemed more diſpleaſed that I had left them, than ever I ſaw him; he mildly chid me for expoſing myſelf to be devoured by wild beaſts: but when I told them of the water and the lion, they were in a greater ſurpriſe, looking at one another with a ſort of fear in their looks, which I interpreted to be for the danger I had eſcaped; but it was on another account. After ſome words in their own language, the Pophar ſpoke aloud in *lingua Franca*,

I

I think, says he, we may let this young man see all our ceremonies, especially since he will soon be out of danger of discovering them, if he should have a mind to do it. At this they pulled out of their stores, some of their choicest fruits, a cruise of rich wine, some bread, a burning-glass, a thurible *, perfumes, and other instruments commonly used in the Heathen sacrifices. I looked aghast at this strange sight; which was such as I had never observed in them before, and began to apprehend that I was now really designed for a human sacrifice † to some infernal god or other; but when I compared the Pophar's late words with what I saw, I scarce doubted of it, and was contriving with myself to sell my life as dear as I could. The Pophar ordered us to bring the dromedaries, and every thing along with us, for fear, as he said, they should be devoured by wild

---

* An instrument to hold incense.

† Our author's fears were not vain, considering the preparatives he saw, and other circumstances. Besides, it is well known, the ancient Africans, particularly the Getulians and Libyans, and even the Carthaginians, made use of human sacrifices to appease their deities. Bochart, in the second part of his *Geographia Sacra*, proves beyond question, that the Carthaginians were part of the people of Canaan driven out by Joshua, who used to sacrifice their children to Moloch, &c. Even in Hannibal's time, when they were grown more polite, they sent privately children to Tyre for a sacrifice to Hercules.

beasts.

beasts. We descended towards the centre of the vale, where I saw the fountain. They went on a great way lower into the vale, till it began to be very steep; but we found a narrow way made by art, and not seeming to have been very long unfrequented, which was more surprising, because I took the place to be uninhabited, and even inaccessible to all but these people. We were forced to descend one by one, leading our dromedaries in our hands: I took particular care to be the hindmost, keeping at a little distance from the rest, for fear of a surprise. They marched down in a mournful kind of procession, observing a most profound silence all the while. At length we came into the finest natural amphitheatre that is possible to describe. There was nothing but odoriferous greens and sky to be seen; except downwards right before us, where we had a most delicious prospect over that glorious vale, winding a little to the right, till it was intercepted by the collateral hills. At the upper part of the amphitheatre, where the break of the hill made that agreeable esplanade, there stood an ancient pyramid, just after the manner of those in Egypt, but nothing near so big as the least of them. In the front of it that faced the vale, the steps were cut out in the form of an altar, on which was erected a statue of a venerable old man, done to the life,

life, of the finest polished marble, or rather some unknown stone of infinite more value. Here, I had not the least doubt, but that I was to be sacrificed to this idol. The Pophar seeing me at a distance called to me, to come and see their ceremonies. Then I thought it was time to speak or never: Father, said I, since you give me leave to call you so, I am willing to perform all your commands, where the honour of the supreme God is not called in question; but I am ready to die a thousand deaths, rather than give his honour to another. I am a Christian, and believe one only God, the supreme being of all beings, and Lord of the universe; for which reason I cannot join with you in your idolatrous worship. If you are resolved to put me to death on that account, I here offer my life freely! if I am to be made a part of your infernal sacrifice, I will defend myself to the last drop of my blood, before I will submit to it. He answered me with a smile, rather than with any indignation, and told me, when I came to be better acquainted with them, I should find they were not so inhuman as to put people to death, because they were of a different opinion from their own. That this was only a religious ceremony they performed to their deceased ancestors *,

and

---

* The earliest accounts of Egypt, from whence these people come, tell us that they had a great veneration

for

and if I had not a mind to assist at it, I might sit down at what distance I pleased.

[*Secretary.* The inquisitors were extremely pleased with the first part of his discourse, wherein he shewed such courage in defence of his religion, and resolution to die rather than join in their idolatrous worship; but all had liked to have been dashed again by the second part, which made one of the inquisitors interrupt his narration, and ask him the following question.

Inquisitor. I hope you do not think it unlawful to persecute, or even to put to death, obstinate heretics, who would destroy the religion of our forefathers, and lead others into the same damnation with themselves. If treason against one's prince may be punished with death, why may not treason against the king of heaven be punished with the like penalty? Have a care you do not cast reflections on the holy inquisition.

Gaudentio. Reverend Fathers! I only relate bare matter of fact, as it was

for their deceased ancestors. See the third part of the Bishop of Meaux's Universal history, quoted above.——— Diodorus Siculus, who lived in the beginning of Augustus's reign, says of the Egyptians, τὸ περὶ τὰς ταφὰς μάλιςα σπυδαζυν, they were particularly diligent about their sepulchres, or in the worship of their dead. The same superstition reigns still among the Chinese, whom I shall shew afterwards to have been a colony of Egyptians, notwithstanding that China and Egypt are so far distant from each other.

spoke

"spoke by the mouth of a Heathen, ignorant of our holy myſteries. I have all the reaſon in the world, to extol the juſtice of the holy inquiſition : nor do I think, but, in ſuch caſes mentioned by your Reverences, it may be lawful to uſe the utmoſt ſeverities to prevent greater evils. But it argued a wonderful moderation in the Pophar, which I found to be his real ſentiments, not unbecoming a Chriſtian in ſuch circumſtances, where it did not tend to the deſtruction of the whole. — But in this, as in all other matters, I ſubmit to your deciſions.

Secretary. I interpoſed in his favour, and put the inquiſitors in mind, that there was nothing but what was juſt in his anſwers : and we ourſelves only uſed thoſe rigours in the laſt extremity, to prevent greater miſchiefs. So they bid him read on.]

When the Pophar had ſaid this, he and the reſt of them fell down on their faces, and kiſſed the earth : then with the burning-glaſs they kindled ſome odoriferous woods ; put the coals in the thurible with the incenſe, and incenſed the idol or ſtatue : that done, they poured the wine on the altar ; ſet bread on the one ſide, and fruits on the other : and having lighted two little pyramids of moſt delicious perfumes at each

each end of the great pyramid, they sat them down round the fountain, which I suppose was conveyed by art under the pyramid *, and issued out in the middle of the amphitheatre. There they refreshed themselves, and gathered the fruits which hung round us in the grove, eating of them very heartily, and inviting me to do the like. I made some difficulty at first, fearing it might be part of the sacrifice; but they assuring me all was but a civil ceremony, I joined them, and did as they did. The Pophar turned to me, and said, My son, we worship one most high God, as you do: what we did just now, was not that we believe any deity in that statue, or adored it as a god; but only respect it as a memorial, and in remembrance of our great ancestor, who heretofore conducted our forefathers to this place, and was buried in this pyramid †. The rest of our forefa-

* The ancient Egyptians had a strange fondness for building pyramids; whether they were for the same end as the tower of Babel, that is, to make themselves a name, or for other ends, we cannot tell. ——— The great pyramid is more ancient than all the rest, insomuch that the best authors do not know when to fix its date, some saying it was built by Mœris their first king, others by Cecrops Lector. But if the account the Pophar gives of their origin, at the next station, be true, it was built before there was any king in Egypt. The river Nile was conveyed by art under the great pyramid.

† One of the ends of building the pyramids, was certainly for burying-places for some great men.

thers,

thers, who died before they were forced to leave this valley, are buried all around us. That is the reason we kissed the ground, not thinking it lawful to stir the bones of the dead. We did the same in Egypt, because we were originally of that land: our particular ancestors lived in that part, which was afterwards called *Thebes* *. The time will not permit me to acquaint you at present, how we were driven out of our native country to this place, and afterwards from this place to the land we are now going to, but you shall know all hereafter. The bread, fruits, and wine we laid on the altar †, as they are the chief support of our being; so we leave them there as a testimony, that the venerable old man, whose statue you see, was, under God, the author and father of our nation. This said, he

---

* Thebes once the most famous city of Egypt, having a hundred gates, &c. was the No-Amon, or Diaspolis of the ancients, *Bochart. Phaleg. lib.* 4. Tacitus says, that, in the time of Germanicus, there was remaining an inscription in the Egyptian language, signifying, *Habitasse quondam (*Thebis) *septingenta millia hominum ætate militari:* That there were once seven hundred thousand inhabitants in Thebes fit to bear arms. *Tacit. Annal. lib.* 2.

† This is certainly rank idolatry, notwithstanding the Pophar calls it but a civil ceremony. Thus the worship the Chinese pay to their dead, and allowed by the Jesuits, was said by them to be but a pious civil ceremony, though it was like this, or rather more superstitious. See the condemnation of it by Pope Clement XI.

told us it was time to make the best of our way; so they all got up, and having kissed the ground once more, the five elderly men scraped a little of the earth, and put it in fine golden vessels, with a great deal of care and respect. After refreshing ourselves again, we made our provision of fruits and water, and leading our dromedaries up the way we came down, mounted, and set out for the remainder of our journey.

We were now past the tropic of Cancer *, as I found by our shadows going southward; and went on thus a little, bending towards the west again, almost parallel to the tropic, the breezes increasing rather stronger than before, so that about midnight it was really cold. We gave our dromedaries water about sun-rising, and refreshed ourselves a little: then set out with new vigour at a prodigious rate: still the breezes fell between nine and ten; however we made shift to go on, because they came again about noon: between three and four was the hottest time of all. Besides, going now parallel to the tropic, we travelled on the hot sands, a very little descending;

---

* When persons are beyond that tropic, at mid-day the shadows of things are towards the south, because the sun is then north of us;

Miranturque umbras transire sinistras.

They might have passed the tropic before, since it runs over part of the desert of Barca, not much southward of Egypt; but it seems they steered westward for some time.

whereas,

whereas, when we pointed southwards towards the line, we found the ground to be insensibly rising upon us * ; but as we went on these almost flats, if it had not been that we were almost on the ridge of Africa, which made it cooler than one can well believe, it had been impossible to bear the heats. When we rested, we not only pitched our tents for ourselves and dromedaries, but the sands were so hot, that we were forced to lay things under our feet to preserve them from burning. Thus we travelled through those dismal deserts for four days, without sight of any living creature but ourselves. Sands and sky were all that presented itself to our view. The fatigue was the greatest I ever underwent in my life. The fourth day about eight in the morning, by good fortune for us, or else by the prudent forecast of the Pophar, who knew all his stations, we saw another vale towards the right hand, with some straggling

---

* His observations are just, since all the new philosophers allow the earth to be spheroidal and gibbous towards the equator. Whoever therefore goes by land, either from the north or south towards the equator, must ascend. This seems to be a very natural reason, why those immense Barcs are not so excessive hot. The highest mountains are considerably nigher the sun than the low lands, yet excessive cold in the hottest climates; in the vales the rays of the sun are cooped in, and doubled and trebled by refraction and reflection, &c. The same air put in a turbulent motion will be hot, and in a direct one cold.

trees here and there, but not seeming nigh so pleasant as the first : we made to it with all our speed, and had much ado to bear the heats till we came to it. We alighted immediately, and led our dromedaries down the gentle descent, till we could find a thicker part of it. The first trees were thin and old, as if they had just moisture enough to keep them alive : the ground was but just covered over with a little sunburnt moss, without any sign of water, but our stock was not yet gone. At length, as we descended, the grove increased every way, the trees were large, with some dates here and there, but not so good as in the other. We rested a little, and then continued to descend for some time, till we came into a very cool and thick shade. Here, the Pophar told us, we must stay two or three days, perhaps longer, till he saw his usual signs for proceeding on his journey ; and bid us be sparing of our water, for fear of accidents. We settled our dromedaries as before: for ourselves, we could scarce take any thing, we were so fatigued, wanting rest more than meat and drink. The Pophar, ordering us some cordial wines they had along with them for that purpose, told us, we might sleep as long as we would ; only bid us be sure to cover ourselves well ; for the nights were long, and even cold about midnight. We were all

soon

soon asleep, and did not wake till four the next morning. The Pophar, solicitous for all our safeties as well as his own, (for this was the critical time of our journey), was awake the first of us. When we were up, and had refreshed ourselves, which we did with a very good appetite, he told us we must go up on the sands again to observe the signs. We took our dromedaries along with us, for fear of wild beasts, though we saw none, walking gently up the sands, till we came to a very high ground. We had but a dreary prospect, as far as our eyes could carry us, of sun-burnt plains, without grass, stick, or shrub, except when we turned our backs to look at the vale where we had lain all night, which we saw spread and extended itself a vast way. He assured us, the notes left for rules by his ancestors, mentioned a spring in that vale below us, which running lower became a rivulet; but that, either by an earthquake, or some flood of sand, it was quite choked up, running under ground, without any one's knowing whether it broke out again, or was entirely swallowed up *. He said also, that, by the most ancient accounts of his forefathers, the sands were not in their times so danger-

* Geographers agree, that rivers, and even great lakes in Africa sink under ground, and are quite lost without any visible outlets. The vast depth of the strata of sand seems more proper to swallow them up there, than in other parts of the world.

ous to pass as they are now, or of such vast extent *, but had fruitful vales much nearer one another than at present. He added, that he wished earnestly to see the signs he wanted for proceeding on our way; since there was no stirring till they appeared: and that, according to his ephemeris and notes, they should appear about this time, unless something very extraordinary happened. This was about eight in the morning, the 9th day after we set out for the deserts. He was every now and then looking southward, or south-west, with great solicitude in his looks, as if he wondered he saw nothing. At length he cried out with great emotions of joy, It is coming! Look yonder, says he, towards the south-west, as far as your eyes can carry you, and see what you can discover. We told him, we saw nothing but some clouds of sand, carried round here and there like whirlwinds. That is the sign I want, continued he; but mark well which way it drives. We said it drove directly eastward, as nigh as we could guess.

---

* There seems to be a natural reason for what he says; for those vast sands, or hills of gravel, were undoubtedly left by the general deluge, as probably all the lesser strata or beds of gravel were. Yet great part of them must have been covered with slime or mud for several years after the deluge, some thinner, some thicker, and consequently more moist and productive accordingly. Nevertheless, the violent rays of the sun still render them more dry and barren, and, in all probability, these deserts will increase more and more, where the country is not cultivated.

It

It does, says he; then turning his face westwards, with a little point of the south, All those vast deserts, says he, are now in such a commotion of storms and whirlwinds, that man and beast will soon be overwhelmed in the rolling waves of sands. He had scarce said this, but we saw, at a vast distance, ten thousand little whirlspouts of sand, rising and falling with a prodigious tumult and velocity * eastward, with vast thick clouds of sand and dust following them. Come, says he, let us return to our resting-place; for there we must stay, till we see further how matters go. As this appeared newer to me than any of the rest, and being possessed with a great idea of the knowledge of the man, I made bold to ask him, what was the cause of this sudden phænomenon: he told me, That, about that full moon, there always fell prodigious

* Though in the vast ocean between the tropics, where promontories do not intervene, the winds are generally easterly, yet there is a perpetual west wind blows into Guinea. —— There are vast rains at the solstices between the tropics, as the accounts of those parts declare; though at that time of the year, more beyond the line than on this side of it. It is not to be questioned, but in such violent changes, particularly before those rains, there must be furious hurricanes of wind and sand, enough to overwhelm whole armies and countries. —— The most incredible part of this narration, is, how they could travel at all under the tropic, in the summer solstice, only, as he says, the ground being very high and open, it must draw air.

rains *, coming from the western part of Africa, on this side the equator, and driving a little south-west for some time at first, but afterwards turning almost south, and crossing the line till they came to the source of the Nile; in which parts they fell for three weeks or a month together; which was the occasion of the overflowing of that river †: but that, on this side the equator, it only rained about fifteen days, preceded by those whirlwinds and clouds of sand, which rendered all that tract impassable, till the rains had laid them again. —— By this time we were come down to our resting-place, and though we did not want sleep or refreshment, yet we took both; to have the cool of the evening to recreate ourselves after so much fatigue, not being likely to move till the next evening at soonest.

At five in the evening, the Pophar called us up to go with him once more to the highest part of the desert, saying he wanted one sign yet, which he hoped to have that evening, or else it would go hard with us

for

---

* Naturalists agree, that beyond the line there are great rains at that season. It is possible, they may begin on this side, being driven by the perpetual west winds into Guinea, and then, by natural causes, turn towards the line and southern tropic.

† The causes of the overflowing of the river Nile, unknown to most of the ancients, are now allowed to be the great rains falling in June and July about the line, and the southern tropic, and the melting of the snow on

the

for want of water, our provision of it being almost spent; and there were no springs in the deserts that we were to pass over, till we came within a long day's journey of the end of our voyage. However, he scarce doubted but we should see the certain sign he wanted this evening: on which account, there did not appear such a solicitude in his countenance as before: for though he was our governor, or captain, and had the respectful deference paid to him; yet he governed us in all respects, as if we were his children, with all the tenderness of a father, as his name imported; though none of the company were his real children. If there were any signs of partiality, it was in my favour, always expressing the most endearing tenderness for me, which the other young men, instead of taking any dislike at, were really pleased with. No brothers in the world could be more loving to one another than we were. The elderly men took delight in seeing our youthful gambols with one another: it is true their nature is,

---

the mountains of the moon lying in that tract. None can wonder there should be snow in those hot climates, who have heard of the Andes or Cordilleras bordering on Peru. Our Italy is very hot, yet the Alps and Apennines are three parts of the year covered with snow.

―――― The Nile overflows in August, which seems to be a proper distance of time for the waters to come down to Egypt, such a vast way off from the cause of it. There is a river in Cochinchina, and elsewhere, that overflows in the same manner.

of the two, a little more inclined to gravity than that of the Italians, who are no light nation; yet their gravity is accompanied with all the serenity and chearfulness imaginable, and I then thought at our first acquaintance, that I had never seen such an air of a free-born people in my life; as if they knew no other subjection but what was merely filial. When we came to the high ground, we could see the hurricanes play still; but, what was more wonderful, very few effects of that aerial tumult came our way, but drove on almost parallel to the equator: the air looked like a brown dirty fog, towards the east and south-east; all the whirlwinds tending towards those parts: it began after some time to look a little more lightsome towards the west; but so, as if it were occasioned by a more strong and settled wind. At length we perceived, at the farthest horizon, the edge of a prodigious black cloud, extending itself to the south-west and western points, rising with a discernible motion, though not very fast. We saw plain enough, by the blackness and thickness of it, that it prognosticated a great deal of rain. —— Here they all fell prostrate on the earth: then raising up their hands and eyes towards the sun, they seemed to pay their adorations to that great luminary. The Pophar, with an audible voice, pronounced some unknown words,

as

as if he were returning thanks to that planet for what he saw. At this I stepped back, and kept myself at a distance; not so much for fear of my life, as before, as not to join with them in their idolatrous worship. For I could not be ignorant now, that they had a wrong notion of God, and if they acknowledged any, it was the sun: which in effect is the least irrational idolatry people can be guilty of *. When they had done their oraisons, the Pophar turned

---

* All idolatry being a worship of creatures instead of the one supreme God, must be irrational. But it is certain, and well attested by ancient history, that the eastern nations worshipped the sun: probably it was the first idolatrous worship that was in the world. The great benefits all nature receives from his influence; the glorious brightness of his rays; the variety, yet constant tenor of his motions, might induce ignorant people to believe him to be of a superior nature to other creatures, though it is evidently certain, he is limited in his perfections, and consequently no God. It is true, the ancient Egyptians, from whom these people sprung, as will be seen afterwards, worshipped the sun in the most early times. There was a priest of the sun in the patriarch Joseph's time. And the Egyptians were some of the first astronomers in the world, contending for antiquity with the Chaldeans. Though both the Chaldeans and Egyptians had their knowledge from the descendents of Sem, or his father Noah, who, by the admirable structure of the ark, appears to have been master of very great sciences. I say, the Egyptians being so much addicted to astronomy, it is probable that glorious luminary was the chief object of their worship. They did not worship idols and beasts till long afterwards. See the learned Bochart's Phaleg. in Misraim.

to me, and said, I see you won't join with us in any of our religious ceremonies; but I must tell you, continued he, that cloud is the saving of all our lives: and as that great sun, pointing to the luminary, is the instrument that draws it up, as indeed he is the preserver of all our beings, we think ourselves obliged to return our thanks to him. Here he stopped, as if he had a mind to hear what I could say for myself. I was not willing to enter into disputes, well knowing that religious quarrels are the most provoking of any: yet I thought myself obliged to make profession of my belief in the supreme God, now I was called upon to the professed worship of a false deity. I answered with the most modest respect I was capable of, that that glorious planet was one of the physical causes of the preservation of our beings, and of the production of all things; but that he was produced himself by the most high God, the first cause and author of all things in heaven and earth; the sun only moving by his order, as an inanimate being, incapable of hearing our prayers, and only operating by his direction. However, I offered to join with him, in returning my best thanks to the most high God, for creating the sun, capable by his heat to raise that cloud for the saving our lives. Thus I adapted my answer as nigh to his discourse as I could, yet not so as to deny my faith. For I could not entirely tell what to make of them as yet; since I observed, they were more mysterious in their religious ceremonies, than in any thing else *; or rather, this was the only thing they were reserved in. He pondered a good while on what I said, but at length he added, You are not much out of the way: you and I will talk this matter over another time; so turned off the discourse; I supposed it to be because of the young men standing by us, who he had not a mind should receive any other notions of religion, but what they had been taught. It was sunset by the time we came down to the grove. We had some small flights of sand, caused by an odd commotion in the air, attended with little whirlwinds, which put us in some apprehensions of a sand-shower; but he bid us take courage, since he could not find in all his accounts, that the hurricanes or rains ever came, in any great quantity, as far as we were, the nature of them being to drive

* This agrees with all ancient accounts of the first people of Egypt; witness their emblems, hieroglyphics, &c. Most of the ancient fables, under which so many mysteries were couched, did not first spring from the Greeks, though improved by them; but from the Egyptians and Chaldeans, who at first held a communication of sciences with one another, but grew to emulosity afterwards. The wonderful things the Egyptian Magi did, in imitation of the miracles wrought by Moses, shew they were great artists.

more parallel to the equator: but he was sure we should have some; and ordered us to pitch our tents as firm as we could, and draw out all our water-vessels, to catch the rain against all accidents. When this was done, and we had eat our suppers, we re-created ourselves in the grove, wandering about here and there, and discoursing of the nature of these phænomena. We did not care to go to rest so soon, having reposed ourselves so well that day, and having all the following night and the next day to stay in that place. The grove grew much pleasanter as we advanced into it; there were a great many dates and other fruits, the natural produce of Africa; but not quite so rich as in the first grove. I made bold to ask the Pophar, how far that grove extended, or whether there were any inhabitants. He told me, he could not tell any thing of either. That it was possible the grove might enlarge itself different ways, among the winding hills: since his accounts told him, there had been a rivulet of water, though now swallowed up; but he believed there were no inhabitants, since there was no mention made of them in his papers. Nor did he believe any other people in the world, beside themselves, knew the way, or would venture so far into those horrid inhospitable deserts. Having a mind to learn whether he had any certain knowledge

of

of the longitude, which creates such difficulties to the Europeans, I asked how he was sure that was the place; or by what rule he could know how far he was come, or where he was to turn to right or left. He stopped a little at my questions; then, without any apparent hesitation, Why, said he, we know by the needle, how far we vary from the north or south point, at least till we come to the tropic *; if not, we can take the meridian and height of the sun, and knowing the time of the year, we can tell how near we approach to, or are off the equator. Yes, said I; but as there are different meridians every step you take, how can you tell how far you go east or west, when you run either way in parallel lines †

---

* Experimental philosophy tells us, that the needle is of little use in navigation, when under the line; but lies fluctuating without turning to any point of itself; because, as some suppose, the current of the magnetic effluvia, flying from pole to pole, has there its longest axis, as the diameter of the equator is longer than the axis of the world. But whether this has the same effect on the needle by land, which is the case, as it has by sea, we must have more certain experiments to know, though it is probable it may.

† Where-ever we stand, we are on the summit of the globe with respect to us. Whoever therefore thinks to go due west, parallel to the equator or east, will not do so, but will cut the line at longrun, because he makes a greater circle. These men therefore, when they thought they went due west, were approaching to the line, more than they were aware of, and supposing the structure of the earth to be spheroidical, went up hill all the way, bating some small inequalities.

to the tropics, or the equator? Here he stopped again, and either could not make any certain difcovery, or had not a mind to let me into the fecret. The firft was moft likely; however, he anfwered readily enough, and faid, You pleafe me with your curious queftions, fince I find you are fenfible of the difficulty. Why, continued he, all the method we have, is, to obferve exactly how far our dromedaries go in an hour, or any other fpace of time: you fee we go much about the fame pace: we have no ftops in our way, but what we know of, to refrefh ourfelves or fo, for which we generally allow fo much time *. When we fet out from Egypt, we went due weft; our beafts gain fo many miles an hour; we know by that, how far we are more weft than we were †. If we decline to the north or the fouth, we know likewife, how many miles we have advanced in fo many hours, and

---

* This muft be underftood according to the foregoing remark.

† At firft fight, it feems to be eafier to find out the longitude by land than by fea, becaufe we may be more certain how far we advance. At fea there are currents, and tides, and fettings in of the fea, which make the fhip to go aflant more or lefs infenfibly. As yet there has been no certain rule found to tell us, how far we advance due eaft or due weft. The elevation of the pole, or the height of the fun, fhews us, how far we decline to the north or fouth; but we have no certain rule for the eaft or weft.

compute

compute how much the declination takes off from our going due weſt. And though we cannot tell to a demonſtrative exactneſs, we can tell pretty nigh. This was all I could get out of him at that time, which did not ſatisfy the difficulty. I afterwards aſked him, how they came to find out this way, or to venture to ſeek out a habitation unknown to all the world beſide. He anſwered, "For liberty, and the preſervation of our laws." I was afraid of aſking any further, ſeeing he gave ſuch general anſwers. By this time it was prodigious dark, though full moon *. We had ſome ſudden guſts of wind that ſtartled us a little; and it lightened at ſuch a rate, as I never ſaw in my life. And although it was towards the horizon, and drove ſidewiſe of us, yet it was really terrible to ſee; the flaſhes were ſo thick, that the ſky was almoſt in a light fire. We made up to our tents as faſt as we could; and though we had only the ſkirts of the clouds over us, it rained ſo very hard, that we had our veſſels ſoon ſupplied with water, and got ſafe into our ſhelter. The thunder was at a vaſt diſtance, but juſt audible, and, for our comfort, drove ſtill to the eaſtward. I do not know in what diſpoſi-

---

* The full moon about the ſummer-ſolſtice generally brings rain, and the overflowing of the Nile is now known to be cauſed by the vaſt rains in the regions near the equator.

tions the elderly men might be, being accustomed to the nature of it; but I am sure I was in some apprehension, fully persuaded, if it had come directly over us, nothing could withstand its impetuosity. I had very little inclination to rest, whatever my companions had; but pondering with myself, both the nature of the thing, and the prodigious skill these men must have in the laws of the universe, I staid with impatience waiting the event.

I was musing with myself on what I had heard and seen, not being able yet to guess with any satisfaction what these people were, when an unexpected accident was the cause of a discovery, which made me see they were not greater strangers to me, than I was to myself. The weather was stifling hot, so that we had thrown off our garments to our shirts, and bared our breasts for coolness sake; when there came a prodigious flash, or rather blaze of lightning, which struck full against the breast of one of the young men opposite to me, and discovered a bright gold medal hanging down from his neck, with the figure of the sun engraved on it, surrounded with unknown characters; the very same in all appearance I had seen my deceased mother always wear about her neck, and since her death I carried with me for her sake. I asked the meaning of that medal, since I had one
about

about me, as it appeared, of the very fame make. If the Pophar had been ftruck with lightning, he could not have been in a greater furprife than he was at thefe words: You one of thefe medals! faid he; how, in the name of wonder, did you come by it? I told him my mother wore it about her neck, from a little child; and with that pulled it out of my pocket. He fnatched it out of my hands with a prodigious eagernefs, and held it againft the lightning perpetually flafhing in upon us. As foon as he faw it was the fame with the other, he cried out, Great fun, what can this mean? Then afked me again, where I had it? how my mother came by it? who my mother was? what age fhe was of when fhe died? As foon as the violence of his ecftafy would give me leave, I told him my mother had it ever fince fhe was a little child: that fhe was the adopted daughter of a noble merchant in Corfica, who had given her all his effects when my father married her: that fhe was married at thirteen; and I being nineteen, and the fecond fon, I gueffed fhe was towards forty when fhe died. It muft be Ifiphena, cried he, with the utmoft ecftafy, it muft be fhe. Then he caught me in his arms, and faid, You are now really one of us, being the fon of my father's daughter, my dear fifter Ifiphena. The remembrance of whom made the tears run down

down the old man's cheeks very plentifully.— She was loft at Grand Cairo about the time you mention, together with a twin-fifter who I fear is never to be heard of. Then I reflected I had heard my mother fay, fhe had been informed, the gentleman who adopted her for his daughter, had bought her when fhe was a little girl of a Turkifh woman of that place; that being charmed with the early figns of beauty in her, and having no children, he adopted her for his own. Yes, faid the Pophar, it muft be fhe; but what is become of the other fifter? For, faid he, my dear fifter brought two at one unfortunate birth, which coft her her life. I told him I never heard any thing of the other. Then he acquainted me that his fifter's hufband was the perfon who conducted the reft to vifit the tombs of their anceftors, as he did now: that the laft voyage, he took his wife with him, who out of her great fondnefs had teafed him and importuned him fo much to go along with him, that, though it was contrary to their laws, he contrived to carry her difguifed in man's cloaths, like one of the young men he chofe to accompany him in the expedition: that ftaying at Grand Cairo till the next feafon for his return, fhe proved with child of twins; and, to his unfpeakable grief, died in childbed. That when they carried her up to Thebes to be

interred

interred with her ancestors, of which I should have a more exact information by and by, they were obliged to leave the children with a nurse of the country, with some Egyptian servants to take care of the house and effects; but before they came back, the nurse with her accomplices ran away with the children, and, as was supposed, murdered them, rifled the house of all the jewels and other valuable things, and were never heard of afterwards. But it seems they thought it more for their advantage to sell the children, as we find they did, by your mother; but what part of the world the other sister is in, or whether she be at all, is known only to the great author of our being. However, continued he, we rejoice in finding these hopeful remains of your dear mother, whose resemblance you carry along with you. It was that gave me such a kindness for your person the first time I saw you, methought, perceiving something I had never observed in any other race of people. But, said he, I deprive my companions and children here of the happiness of embracing their own flesh and blood, since we all sprung from one common father, the author of our nation, with whom you are going to be incorporated once more. Here we embraced one another with a joy that is inexpressible. Now all my former fears were entirely vanished: though I had lost the country where I was born, I had found another, of which

I could nowife be afhamed, where the people were the moft humane and civilized I ever faw, and the foil the fineft, as I had reafon to hope, in the world. The only check to my happinefs was, that they were infidels. However, I was refolved not to let any confideration blot out of my mind that I was a Chriftian. On which account, when the Pophar would have tied the medal about my neck, as a badge of my race, I had fome difficulty in that point, for fear it fhould be an emblem of idolatry, feeing them to be extremely fuperftitious. So I afked him, what was the meaning of the figure of the fun, with thofe unknown characters round about it? He told me the characters were to be pronounced *Omabim*, i. e. *The fun is the author of our being*, or more literally, *The fun is our father*. *Om* or *On* fignifies the fun [This will be explained in another place]. *Ab* fignifies *Father*, *Im* or *Mim*, *Us*. This made me remember, they had told me in Egypt that they were children of the fun; and gave me fome uneafinefs at their idolatrous notions. I therefore told him, I would keep it as a cognifance of my country; but could not acknowledge any but God to be the fupreme author of my being. As to the fupreme author, faid he, your opinion is little different from ours*.

* Thefe people are fomething like the Chinefe, who worfhip the material heaven, or fky, which fome miffionaries could think compatible with Chriftianity.

But let us leave thefe religious matters till another time: we'll clofe this happy day with thankfgiving to the fupreme being for this difcovery: to-morrow morning, fince you are now really one of us, I will acquaint you with your origin, and how we came to hide ourfelves in thefe inhofpitable deferts.——

[*The reader is defired not to cenfure or difbelieve the following account of the origin and tranfmigration of thefe people, till he has perufed the learned remarks of Signor Rhedi.*]

The next morning the Pophar calling me to him, Son, faid he, to fulfil my promife which I made you laft night, and that you may not be like the reft of the ignorant world, who know not who their forefathers and anceftors were *; whether they

sprung

---

* It would certainly be a great fatisfaction to moft nations to know from what race of people, country, or family, they fprung originally. This ignorance is owing chiefly to the Barbari Tramontani †, and other northern nations, who have from time to time over-run the face of Europe, leaving a mixture of their fpawn in all parts of it; fo that no one knows, whether he came originally from Scythia or Afia, from a civilized nation, or

† Signor Rhedi being an Italian, one cannot wonder he fpeaks fo contemptibly of the northern people; the Italians call them all Barbari.

sprung from brutes or barbarians, is all alike to them, provided they can but grovel on the earth, as they do: you must know therefore, as I suppose you remember what I told you at our first station, that we came originally from Egypt. When you asked me, how we came to venture through these inhospitable deserts, I told you, it was for liberty, and the preservation of our laws; but as you are now found to be one of us, I design to give you a more particular account of your origin. Our ancestors did originally come from Egypt, once the happiest place in the world; though the name of *Egypt*, and *Egyptians*, has been given to that country, long since we came out of it: the original name of it was *Mezzoraim* *, from the first man that peopled it, the

from the greatest brutes; and though wars and invasions have destroyed, or interchanged the inhabitants of most countries; yet this man's observation is a just censure of the neglect of most people, with respect to their genealogy and knowledge of their ancestors, where they have been settled in a country for several ages. But there are matters of greater moment in this man's relation, true or false, which lead us into some curious remains of ancient history.

* The original name of Egypt was *Misraim*; from Misraim, Mesoraim, or Metsoraim, as the learned Bochart explains it, lib. 4. of *Geograph. Sacra in Misraim*, M. Du Pin's history of the Old Test. c. 6. and others. All ancient authors agree, that it was once the richest and happiest country in the world; flourishing
with

the father of our nation; and we call ourselves *Mezzoranians* from him. We have
a tradition delivered down to us from our
first ancestors, that when the earth first rose
out of the water *, six persons, three men
and three women, rose along with it: either sent by the supreme deity to inhabit it,
or produced by the sun †. That Mezzoraim

with plenty, and even learning, before the patriarch Abraham's time. There is a very remarkable fragment of
Eupolemus an ancient Heathen writer, taken from the
Babylonian monuments, preserved by Eusebius, lib. 9.
Præparat. Evan. The words are, Βαβυλωνιης λίγε.
πρῶτον γενέσθαι Βῆλον, ὃν ειναι Κρόνον ἀδελφὸν τȣ Μεσραιμ
πατρὸς Αἰγυπτίων. The whole fragment, in our mother
tongue, signifies, that, according to the Babylonians, the
first was Belus, the same with Kronos or Saturn; from
him came Ham or Cham, the father of Canaan, brother
to Mesraim, father of the Egyptians.

* This is an obscure notion of Noah's flood, known
to all nations, at least the eastern, as appears by the
oldest remains; of which see Bochart on that article,
lib. 1. "The earth rose out of the water," or the waters sunk from the earth. These people might mistake
something of that undoubted and ancient tradition. But
Misraim could not be ignorant of the flood, his father
Ham having been in the ark, whether ignorance or other
motives made his posterity vary in the account; but it is
evident the ancients had a notion of the general deluge,
as may easily be proved by the remains of Heathen authors bearing testimony to the scripture-account of it.

† The ancient Egyptians thought men, as well as insects, were produced out of the slime of the Nile, by
the heat of the sun, and called themselves *Aborigines*,
as several other nations did. Though this wise man is
inclined

raim our first founder was one of those six; who increasing in number, made choice of the country now called *Egypt* *, for the place of his habitation, where he settled with sixty of his children and grandchildren, all of whom he brought along with him, governing them as a real father, and instructing them to live with one another, as brothers of one and the same family †. He was a peaceable man, abhorring the shedding of blood ‡, which he said would be

inclined to think they were created by God; as it is evident and certain they were; for since we see one single insect cannot be produced without a cause, it is nonsense, as well as impossible, to imagine an infinite series of men and animals could be produced without a separate cause: on which account Atheism is one of the most foolish and absurd notions in the world.

* Herodotus tells us, the Egyptians pretended to be the first inhabitants of the earth; though the Ethiopians contended with them for antiquity. I must quote the words in Latin, out of Laurenzo Valla's translation, because I have him not in Greek, *Omnium hominum priores se extitisse arbitrabantur.* They esteemed themselves, says he, to have been the first of all men. *Herodot. lib.* 2. *Euterpe.*

† It is certain from Bochart, and other learned authors, that the Egyptian government, as well as that of most nations, was at first patriarchal: till Nimrod founded the first kingdom or empire in the world; whose example others followed, according to their power. However, the patriarchal government was soon broke in upon in Egypt, since they had kings in Abraham and Isaac's time, as we learn from the Old Testament. See Bochart's *Geographia Sacra.*

‡ The celebrated Bishop of Meaux, in part 3. of his Univ.

be punished by the supreme ruler of the world; extremely given to the search of sciences, and contemplation of the heavens *. It was he who was the first inventor

Univ. Hist. gives us a wonderful description of the justice and piety of the first Egyptians, who had such a horror of shedding man's blood, that they punished their criminals after they were dead; which was as much *in terrorem*, considering their superstitious reverence for their deceased friends and parents, as if they had been punished when alive. The reason why the ancient moral Heathens abhorred the shedding of blood, might be, that Noah's sons having lived before the deluge, knew that the wickedness of the world was the cause of that dreadful judgment; and shedding of blood being the first crime punished by God, they might take warning by such terrible examples, though the impiety of some nations soon obscured this innate light of nature, particularly the descendents of Ham; all but this Misraim; who with his family, by all accounts, first peopled Egypt; and they were noted for justice and knowledge. It will be made evident in the subsequent remarks, that these Hicksoes were the descendents of wicked Canaan, or Cush, who destroyed the peaceable state of the first Egyptians, and introduced idolatry among them; which made great numbers of them fly into other parts of the world to save themselves.

* The same learned Bishop of Meaux, and other historians, assure us, as it is a thing well known to all the learned, that arts and sciences were brought to very great perfection in the earliest times in Egypt. Moses was instructed in the sciences of the Egyptians. Triptolemus, the founder of agriculture, came out of Egypt. Bacchus, the inventor of wine, according to the ancients, came out of Egypt, or Libya, which borders upon it; though it was first learned from Noah. Pythagoras,

tor of all our arts, and whatever is useful for the government of life, sprung from him. Though his grandson Thaoth * rather excelled him, particularly in the more sublime sciences. Thus our ancestors lived four hundred years, increasing and spreading over all the land of Egypt, and abounding with the blessings of peace and knowledge; without guile or deceit, neither doing or fearing harm from any; till the wicked descendents of the other men, called *Hicksoes* †, envying their happiness, and the

thagoras, and other learned men, went into Egypt to be instructed by the priests, &c. Herodotus says the same of himself.

* This Tha-oth, the famous philosopher of the Egyptians, was before Mercury or Trismegistus; though some take him to be the same. All allow him to be extremely ancient, but cannot fix the time when he lived. Historians murder his name at a strange rate. Bochart calls him *Ta-utus*, lib. 2. cap. 12. Clemens Alex. lib. 6. Strom. says, he wrote forty-two books of astrology, geography, physic, policy, theology, religion, and government. Joseph Ben-Gorion, *de divisione Gentium*, calls him *Tutis*; some call him *Theut*, others, *Teut*, *Taut*, *Thoth*, &c. But, according to this man, his name was *Tha-oth*. It is certain, however, that he was the great master of the Egyptians; but derived his learning from Noah, who might have the knowledge of arts and sciences from the antediluvian world, or from the columns of Seth, which, Josephus says, contain the principles of astrology, and were erected before the flood by the nephews of Seth: one of which columns, as he says, remained in Syria in his time. *Joseph. Ant. lib.* 2. *c.* 2.

† The same Josephus, lib. 2. *contra Appion*, says, that

the richnefs of their country, broke in upon them like a torrent, deftroying all before them, and taking poffeffion of that,

that *Hyckfoes* or *Hyckloes*, an old Egyptian word, fignifies Βασιλεῖς ποιμένες, *king fhepherds*, or kings of beafts, given them by the native Egyptians, as a name of difgrace and contempt. It is out of all controverfy that there was a great revolution in Egypt, about four hundred years after the flood, or a little before Abraham's time. Monfieur Du Pin makes the time from the flood to 'Abraham's birth three hundred and fifty years; and about four hundred to his being called by God. It is certain alfo, there were kings in Egypt in Abraham's time. It is probable thefe kings were the Hyckfoes, or king-fhepherds, who altered the government of the ancient Egyptians, and continued about five kings reigns. For when the patriarch Jofeph called his father and brethren into Egypt, he bid them afk the land of Gofhen to inhabit, becaufe, faid he, all fhepherds are an abomination to the Egyptians. By which it appears the fhepherds were lately driven out. In all likelihood thefe were the kings who introduced idolatry and the adoration of brute-beafts among the Egyptians, for which reafon they called them in derifion king-fhepherds, or king-beafts.——— The great Bochart, in his Phaleg. looks upon this revolution in Egypt to have been before Abraham's time, and fo far from being a fiction, that he fays in exprefs words, *Caflucos et Caphthoræos* (whom he proves to be the people of Colchos, for all it is fo far from Egypt) *ex Ægypto migraffe certum eft ante Abrahami tempora.* "It is certain," fays he, "that the Cafluci and the Caphthoræi went out of Egypt before Abraham's time." *Bochart Phaleg. lib.* 4. *c.* 31. Herodotus in Euterpe fays, that the people of Colchos were originally Egyptians; though fome fay they went back fome ages after, and fettled in Paleftine, and were called after that Philiftines.

ha py

happy place our anceſtors had rendered ſo flouriſhing. The poor innocent Mezzoranians abhorring, as I ſaid, the ſhedding of blood, and ignorant of all violence, were ſlaughtered like ſheep all over the country; and their wives and daughters violated before their eyes. Thoſe whom their mercileſs enemy ſpared, were made ſlaves to work and till the earth for their new lords.

Secretary. Here the inquiſitors interrupted him, and aſked him, whether he thought it unlawful in all caſes to reſiſt force by force, or whether the law of nature did not allow the Mezzoranians to reſiſt thoſe cruel invaders even to the ſhedding of blood; as alſo to puniſh public malefactors with death for the preſervation of the whole. Their intent was, as they are cautious of any new opinions, to know whether he might not be a dogmatizer, and advance ſome erroneous notions, either by holding that to be lawful, which was not ſo; or denying things to be lawful, which really may be allowable by the light of nature.

Gaudentio. Doubtleſs they might lawfully have reſiſted even to the ſhedding of blood in that caſe, as public criminals may be put to death. I only acquaint your Reverences with the notions peculiar to theſe people; as for the puniſhment of their criminals, your Reverences will ſee, when I come to their laws and

and cuſtoms, that they have other ways and means of puniſhing crimes as effectual as putting to death; though living entirely within themſelves, free from all mixture and commerce with other people, they have preſerved their primitive innocence in that reſpect to a very great degree. *Inquiſitor.* Go on.

The Pophar continuing his relation, added: But what was moſt intolerable was, that theſe impious Hickſoes forced them to adore men and beaſts, and even inſects, for gods; nay, and ſome to ſee their children offered in ſacrifice to thoſe inhuman deities *. This dreadful inundation fell at firſt only on the lower parts of Egypt, which was then the moſt flouriſhing. As many of the diſtreſſed inhabitants as could eſcape their cruel hands, fled to the upper parts of the country, in hopes to find there ſome little reſpite from their misfortunes. But alas! what could they do? they knew no uſe of arms: neither would their laws ſuffer them to deſtroy their own ſpecies; ſo that they expected every hour to be devoured by their cruel enemies. The heads of the families in ſuch diſtreſs were divided in

---

* Theſe Hickſoes being in all appearance the deſcendents of wicked Canaan or Cuſh, were ſo abominably impious, as to ſacrifice human victims and children to their falſe gods; and even were the firſt authors of all impiety and idolatry.

their

their counsels, or rather they had no counsel to follow: some of them fled into the neighbouring deserts, which you have seen are very dismal, on both sides the upper part of that kingdom; they were dispersed like a flock of sheep scattered by the ravenous wolves. The consternation was so great, they were resolved to fly to the fartheſt parts of the earth, rather than fall into the hands of those inhuman monsters. The greatest part of them agreed to build ships, and try their fortune by sea. Our great father Mezzoraim had taught them the art of making boats *, to cross the branches of the great river [Nile]; which some, said he, had learned by being preserved in such a thing from a terrible flood that overflowed all the land †. Which instrument of their preservation they so improved afterwards, that they could cross the lesser

---

* It is highly probable the Egyptians had the knowledge of shipping long before the Greeks, whose finest ship was Argo, built by Jason to fetch the golden fleece from Colchos. The first notion of shipping was undoubtedly taken from the ark; the Egyptians were necessitated to make use of boats, by reason of the annual overflowing of the river Nile, and to pass the different branches into which that famous river divides itself in the Lower Egypt. The Sidonians, whom Bochart proves to be the descendents of Canaan, had the use of shipping, as he also proves, before the children of Israel departed out of Egypt.

† In all appearance this must have been Noah's flood, which it is much Signor Rhedi passes over in his remarks.

sea

sea * without any difficulty. This being resolved on, they could not agree where to go: some being resolved to go by one sea, some by the other. However they set all hands to work; so that in a year's time they had built a vast number of vessels; trying them backwards and forwards along the coasts, mending what was deficient, and improving what they imagined might be for their greater security. They thought now, or at least their eagerness to avoid their enemies made them think, they could go with safety all over the main sea. As our ancestors had chiefly given themselves to the study of arts and sciences, and the knowledge of nature, they were the most capable of such enterprises of any people in the world. But the apprehension of all that was miserable being just fresh before their eyes, quickned their industry to such a degree, as none but men in the like circumstances can have a just idea of. Most of these men were those who had fled in crouds from Lower Egypt. The natural inhabitants of the upper parts, though they were in very great consternation, and built ships as fast as they could, yet their fears were not so immediate, especially seeing the Hicksocs remained

---

* Egypt is bounded on the one side by the end of the Mediterranean; on the other side by the Red sea, dividing it from Arabia: this he calls the lesser sea, as being much narrower than the Mediterranean.

yet quiet in their new poſſeſſions. But news being brought them, that the Hickſoes began to ſtir again, more ſwarms of their cruel brood ſtill flocking into that rich country, they reſolved now to delay the time no longer, but to commit themſelves, wives, and children, with all that was moſt dear and precious, to the mercy of that inconſtant element, rather than truſt to the barbarity of their own ſpecies. They who came out of the Lower Egypt, were reſolved to croſs the great ſea *, and with immenſe labour

---

* This great ſea, as diſtinguiſhed from the leſs, muſt be the Mediterranean. Thoſe who fled by that ſea, muſt be thoſe who went to Colchos: they could not go by land over the iſthmus, becauſe the Hickſoes poured in upon them that way: we muſt not ſuppoſe they went all the way by ſea to Colchos, quite round by the ſtreights of the Helleſpont. They muſt croſs the end of the Mediterranean, and go by land the ſhorteſt way they could till they came to the borders of the Euxine ſea. It is almoſt incredible men ſhould go ſo far to ſeek an habitation. But Bochart ſays, it is certain the people of Colchos came out of Egypt; they muſt therefore have been driven out by ſome terrible enemies. You will ſay, Why may not this firſt revolution in Egypt, which Bochart ſpeaks of, have been made by the great Semiramis, wife to Ninus, the ſon of Nimrod? It is anſwered in the firſt place, becauſe Joſephus calls the firſt invaders of Egypt, βασιλεῖς ποιμένες, king-ſhepherds, which cannot agree with the great heroine Semiramis. 2dly. Becauſe it is not credible, notwithſtanding the contrary opinion of moſt hiſtorians, that Ninus, the huſband of Semiramis, could be ſo early as they make him to be, i. e. the ſon of Nimrod, but ſome other Ninus

bour were forced to carry their materials partly by land, till they came to the outermoſt branch of the Nile, ſince their enemies coming over the iſthmus, though they hindered them from going out of their country by land, unleſs by the deſerts, yet had not taken poſſeſſion of that part of the country. It is needleſs to recount their cries and lamentations at their leaving their dear country. I ſhall only tell you, that they ventured into the great ſea, which they croſſed, and never ſtopped till they came to another ſea *, on the ſides of which they fixed their habitation, that they might go off again in caſe they were purſued. This we learned from the account of our anceſtors who met with ſome of them that came to viſit the tombs of their deceaſed parents, as we do; but it is an immenſe time ſince, and we never heard any more of them. — The other part, who were much the great-

---

long after him: for though Semiramis conquered Egypt, and afterwards loſt her army againſt the Ethiopians, this could not be ſo ſoon after the flood; becauſe hiſtorians deſcribe that army to conſiſt of three hundred thouſand men inſtructed in diſcipline after a military manner, armed with warlike chariots, &c. as were the Ethiopians againſt her, and even ſuperior to her. I ſay, it is not credible ſuch great armies could be raiſed ſo ſoon after the flood, if ſhe was daughter-in-law to Nimrod the great hunter, who was the ſon of Cuſh, and great-grandſon to Noah.

* *i. e.* the Euxine ſea.

er number, went down the lesser sea *, having built their ships on that sea; they never stopped or touched on either side, till they came to a narrow part of it †, which led them into the vast ocean; there they turned off to the left into the eastern sea ‡. But whether they were swallowed up in the merciless abyss, or carried into some unknown regions, we cannot tell, for they were never heard of more. Only of late years, we have heard talk at Grand Cairo, of a very numerous and civilized nation in the

---

* *i. e.* the Red sea. There were several other revolutions in Egypt, as by the Ethiopians, after Semiramis was conquered; who were expelled again, either by the great Sesostris, of whom Herodotus relates such famous exploits; or a little before by his predecessor. The Canaanites also, who were driven out of Palestine by Joshua, conquered part of it, as we shall see afterwards. Long after that, it was subdued by Nabuchodonosor, who destroyed the renowned city of Thebes, with her hundred gates. Bochart in Nineve. Then the Persians under Cambyses the son of Cyrus the Great. In fine, the Romans made a province of it in Augustus's time. Strabo says of that famous city of Thebes, νυνὶ δὲ κωμηδὸν συνοικεῖται. At present, says he, it is but a poor village.

Atque vetus Thebe centum jacet obruta portis.
                                                    Juven. sat. 1.

† This must be the streights of Babelmandel, which let them into the vast eastern ocean.

‡ It is likely that colony was carried to China; for, let what will come of this man's relations, there are very strong reasons to believe, that the Chinese, notwithstanding the vast distance from Egypt, came originally from

the eastern parts of the world, whose laws

from that country, about the time of the invasion of the king-shepherds, which was before Jacob and his sons went into the land of Egypt. For whoever compares the account given by the learned Bishop of Meaux, in the third part of his Universal History, of the lives and manners of the first Egyptians, with those of the Chinese, will find them to agree in a great many points. As, 1*st*, their boasted antiquity; 2*dly*, their so early knowledge of arts and sciences: 3*dly*, their veneration for learned men, who have the preference before others: 4*thly*, their policy: 5*thly*, their unaccountable superstition for their deceased parents: 6*thly*, their annual visiting the family of their ancestors: 7*thly*, their peaceable dispositions: 8*thly*, their religious worship. As for this last, it is well known the first Egyptians worshipped the sun, long before the gods Apis, and Isis, and Anubis, were introduced among them by their idolatrous invaders. And the Chinese to this day worship the material heaven, as is seen in the condemnation of the Jesuits by Clem. XI. Lastly, the use of pyramids in Egypt, which were like ancient idols among the Chinese. See the account of them in Moreri. The only difficulty is to know how they got from Egypt to China, which is not so insupportable as people may imagine. It is certain, the Egyptians, as has been remarked, had a very early knowledge of navigation. It is certain also, that, in those barbarous invasions, the invaders of kingdoms almost destroyed all before them. Since we find therefore in the most ancient histories, that there was a most terrible revolution in Egypt about that time made by the people, whose customs the Egyptians had in abomination, the Chinese might seek their fortune by sea, and might be carried beyond the Persian gulf, till they came to Cochin China, from whence they might get into the main continent, and so people that vast empire; preserving their ancient laws and customs inviolable. So that, whatever becomes of this man's relation, it is extremely probable, the Chinese came first from Egypt.

and customs have some resemblance to ours; but who, and what they are, we cannot tell, since we have never met with any of them.

The father of our nation, since we separated ourselves from the rest of the world, who was priest of the sun at No-om *, (called afterwards by those miscreants No-Ammon †, because of the temple of Hammon), was

---

* *No-om*, or *No-on*, signifies, in the old Mezzoranian, or old Egyptian language, the house of the sun. Their words are made up of monosyllables put together like the Chinese, which is another reason why the Chinese ought to be looked upon as a colony of the Egyptians. *Vid:* the remarks of the foregoing part of this relation. The patriarch Joseph married the daughter of the priest of On; which, several learned men say, is the same with Heliopolis, or city of the sun. From No comes the Egyptian nomes, or divisions of the country, which the great Bochart in his Phaleg says is an Egyptian, not a Greek word, though dynasty is Greek. Bochart, lib. 4. c. 24. Hence very likely came the Nomades, and Numidæ, from their wandering and frequently changing their habitation, or names; the first and most ancient of all nations lived thus.

* That is, the house or temple of Ham, or Hammon; or Charnoon, or Chum, as Bochart varies it. This Ham was the Tyrian Jupiter, and in this place was afterwards situated the great city of Thebes, as has been observed before, called by the Greeks *Diospolis*, or the city of Jupiter. Cadmus, who was of Thebes in Palestine, being driven out from thence by Joshua, built it; but was driven out from it, and forced to retire to Tyre, from whence he conducted a colony of Tyrians, or banished Canaanites, into Bœotia, where he built Thebes also, or rather the citadel of Thebes, called Cadmeia. *Vide Bochart,*

in

was not asleep in this general consternation; but did not as yet think they would come up so high into the land. However, he thought proper to look out for a place to secure himself and family in case of need. He was the descendent, in a direct line, from the great Tha-oth; and was perfectly versed in all the learned sciences of his ancestors. He guessed there must certainly be some habitable country, beyond those dreadful sands that surrounded him, if he could but find a way to it, where he might secure himself and family; at least, till those troubles were over: for he did not at that time think of leaving his native country for good and all. But, like a true father of his people, which the name of *Pophar* implies, he was resolved to venture his own life, rather than expose his whole family to be lost in those dismal deserts. He had five sons, and five daughters married to as many sons and daughters of his deceased brother*. His two

in Cadmus and Hermione. Which last the same author says, came originally from mount Hermon in Palestine; and as that word in the Canaanean languages signifies a serpent, from hence arose the fable of the serpent's teeth turning into men. The temple of Jupiter Ammon, or Hammon, in Africa, was built by the Chinani, who spread themselves from Egypt into Libya.

* It is certain that the ancients, particularly the eastern nations, married their nigh relations, as well as the Jews, to keep up their names or tribes; but we do not find

two eldeſt ſons had even grandchildren, but his two youngeſt ſons as then had no children. He left the government and care of all to his eldeſt ſon, in caſe he himſelf ſhould miſcarry; and took his two youngeſt ſons, who might beſt be ſpared along with him. Having provided themſelves with water for ten days, with bread and dried fruits, juſt enough to ſubſiſt on, he was reſolved to try five days journey endwiſe through theſe ſands; and if he ſaw no hopes of making a diſcovery that time, to return again before his proviſions were ſpent, and then try the ſame method towards another quarter. In ſhort, he ſet out with all ſecrecy, and pointing his courſe directly weſtward, the better to guide himſelf, he came to the firſt grove that we arrived at, in a little more time than we took up in coming thither. Having now time enough before him, and ſeeing there was water and fruits in abundance, he examined the extent of that delicious vale: he found it was large enough to ſubſiſt a great many thouſands, in caſe they ſhould increaſe, and be forced to ſtay there ſome

---

find in hiſtory that they married their own ſiſters, till the Perſian kings, who were condemned for it by the Greeks. The Egyptians under the Ptolemies followed that barbarous cuſtom, though they begun with Ptolemy Lagus, one of the captains of Alexander; the Incas in America did the ſame, not to profane their blood, as they ſaid, with other mixtures.

generations,

generations, as in effect they did. After this they laid in provisions as before, with dates and fruits of the natural produce of the earth, finer than ever were seen in Egypt, to encourage them in their transmigration, and so set out again for his native country. The time prefixed for his return was elapsed by his stay in viewing the country; so that his people had entirely given him up for lost. But the joy for his unexpected return, with the promising hopes of such a safe and happy retreat, made them unanimously resolve to follow him. Wherefore, on the first news of the Hicksoes being in motion again, they packed up all their effects and provisions as privately as they could; but particularly all the monuments of arts and sciences left by their ancestors, with notes and observations of every part of their dear country, which they were going to leave, but hoped to see again when the storm was over. They arrived without any considerable disaster, and resolved only to live in tents till they could return to their native homes. As they increased in number, they descended further into the vale, which there began to spread itself different ways, and supplied them with all the necessaries and conveniencies of life; so that they lived in the happiest banishment they could wish; never stirring out of the vale for several years, for fear of being discovered. The
Pophar

Pophar finding himself grow old, (having attained almost two hundred years of age *), though he was hale and strong for his years, resolved to visit his native country once more before he died, and get what intelligence he could for the common interest. Accordingly, he and two more disguised themselves, and repassed the deserts again. They just ventured at first into the borders of the country: but, alas! when he came there, he found it all over-run by the barbarous Hickfoes. All the poor remains of the Mezzoranians were made slaves; and those barbarians had begun to build habitations, and establish themselves, as if they designed never more to depart the country. They had made No-om one of their chief towns *,

* The regular lives of the first Egyptians, and of these people descended from them, together with the climate, their diet of fruits and liquors, their exemption from violent passions, without being corrupted by the spurious spawn of other nations, and the like, might contribute very much to the length of their lives, and strength proportionably. The Macrobii, or long-livers, a people of Ethiopia, and a colony of the ancient Egyptians, lived to a vast age, and were called *Macrobii* from their long lives. See Herodotus of the Ethiopians; and what he says of their strength in the bow, which they sent to Cambyses, when he had denounced war against them; saying, that when he could bend that bow, he might make war against them; which bow only Smerdis, Cambyses's brother, could bend, and for that reason was afterwards put to death by his brother out of envy.

* It seems Thebes, though afterwards such a prodigious city, was then but the head of the name of that man's family.

where

where they erected a temple to their ram-god *, calling it *No-Hammon* †, with such inhuman laws and cruelties, as drew a flood of tears from his aged eyes ‡. However, being a man of great prudence and foresight, he easily imagined, by their tyrannical way of living, they could not continue long in that state without some new revolution. After making what observations he could, and visiting the tombs of his forefathers, he returned to the vale, and died in that place where you saw the pyramid built to his memory. Not many generations after, according as he had foreseen, the natives, made desperate by the tyrannical oppressions of the Hicksoes, were forced to break in upon their primitive laws, which forbade them to shed blood; made a general insurrection, and, calling in their neighbours around them, fell upon the Hicksoes when they least expected it, and drove them out of the country. They were headed by a brave man of a mixed race, his mother being a beautiful Mezzoranian, and his father

* Jupiter Hammon, whom Bochart proves to have been Ham or Cham, the son of Noah, was represented with a ram's head, which was held in such abomination by the first Egyptians, from whence they called those first invaders Hicksoes.

† No-Hammon, the house of the ram-god.

‡ It is likely he means *Busiridis aras*, so infamous in antiquity; or the cruel Busiris, who sacrificed his guests.

Though

father a Sabæan *. After this young conqueror had driven out the Hickfoes, he eftablifhed a new form of government, making himfelf king over his brethren, (but not after the tyrannical manner of the Hickfoes), and grew very powerful. Our anceftors fent perfons from time to time to inform themfelves how matters went. They found the kingdom in a flourifhing condition, indeed, under the conquering Sofs †, for fo he

Though hiftorians do not agree about the time when Bufiris lived, which fhews he was very ancient; yet all agree, he was a monfter of cruelty, and became a proverb on that account. This was a very natural reafon for the Egyptians to difperfe themfelves into fo many colonies as they did, to avoid fuch cruelties.

* Thefe Sabæans were the defcendents of fome of the fons of Chufh, or Chufs, a very tall race of men, great negotiators, and more polite than the other Arabians. *Bochart. in Seba filio Chus*, where he quotes a paffage out of Agatharcides of the handfomenefs of the Sabæans,

Τὰ σώματά ἐςι τῶν κατοικȣ́ντων ἀξιολογώτερα.

The bodies of the inhabitants [the Sabæans] are more majeftic than other men.

† This muft be the great Sefoftris or Sefofis, of whom the learned Bifhop of Meaux, as alfo Herodotus, fays fuch glorious things. Though authors do not fay precifely when he lived, all acknowledge him to have flourifhed in the earlieft times. He extended his conquefts over the greateft part of the eaft, and almoft over the known world, as fome fay, Where his enemies were cowards, and made no refiftance, he fet up ftatues of them refembling women. *Herodot. lib. 2. Euterpe. Monf. de Meaux, par. 3. Hift. Univ.* This great conqueror's name is very much varied by authors.

was

was called. He and his fucceffors made it one of the moft powerful kingdoms of the earth; but the laws were different from what they had been in the time of our anceftors, or even from thofe the great Sofs had eftablifhed. Some of his fucceffors began to be very tyrannical; they made flaves of their brothers, and invented a new religion; fome adoring the fun, fome the gods of the Hickfoes; fo that our anceftors, as they could not think of altering their laws, though they might have returned again, chofe rather to continue ftill unknown in that vale, under their patriarchal government. Neverthelefs, in procefs of time, they increafed fo much, that the country was not capable of maintaining them; fo that they had been obliged to return, had not another revolution in Egypt forced them to feek out a new habitation. This change was made by a race of people called *Cnanim* *, as wicked and barbarous in effect, but

---

* Thefe in all appearance were the wicked Canaaneans, who being to be deftroyed, and being driven out of Canaan by Jofhua, difperfed themfelves, and invaded the greateft part of the countries round about them. *Bochart in Canaan* proves almoft demonftrably, that they difperfed themfelves over all the iflands and fea-ports of Europe, Afia, and Africa. In his preface he quotes a moft curious paffage out of *Procopius de bello Vandelico*, of a pillar that was found in Africa, with a Phœnician or Canaanean infcription, which fignifies in Greek,

N   ΗΜΕΙΣ

but more politic, than the Hickſoes; though ſome ſaid they were originally the ſame people, who being driven out of their own country by others more powerful than themſelves, came pouring in, not only over all the land of Mezoraim, but all along the coaſts of both ſeas, deſtroying all before them, with greater abominations than the Hickſoes had ever been guilty of: in ſhort, a faithleſs and moſt perfidious race of men, that corrupted the innocent manners * of the whole earth. Our forefathers were in the moſt dreadful conſternation ima-

ΗΜΕΙΣ ΕΣΜΕΝ ΟΙ ΦΕΥΓΟΝΤΕΣ ΑΠΟ ΠΡΩΣ-
ΟΠΟΥ ΙΗΣΟΥ ΤΟΥ ΛΗΣΤΟΥ ΥΙΟΥ ΝΑΥΗ.

We are thoſe who fled from the face of Jeſus, or Joſhua the robber, the ſon of Nave. Euſebius, in *Chronico,* has much the ſame; and St Auſtin, in his *City of God,* ſays, that the ancient country-people about Hippo in Africa, who were the remains of the ancient Carthaginians, if you aſked them who they were, would anſwer, We are originally Canaani, or Canaaneans.

* The celebrated Bochart, ſo often quoted, proves that the Phœnicians or Carthaginians, whom he alſo proves to have been Canaaneans, were the perſons who ſpread idolatry, with all the tribe of the Heathen gods, and their abominable rites, over the whole world. *Bochart in Canaan.* The ſame author ſays, the Phœnicians or Canaani, invaded Egypt about that very time. This he proves directly: and that they had their caſtra about Memphis; as alſo that Cadmus and Phœnix, whom he makes contemporaries with Joſhua, having fled before him, came out of Egypt afterwards, and built Thebes in Bœotia. See alſo *Herodotus in Euterpe.*

ginable.

ginable. There was now no prospect of ever returning into their ancient country. They were surrounded with deserts on all sides. The place they were in began to be too narrow for so many thousands as they were increased to: nay, they did not know but the wicked Cnanim, who were at the same time the boldest and most enterprising nation under the sun *, might find them out some time or other. Being in this distress, they resolved to seek out a new habitation; and, to that end, compared all the notes and observations on the heavens, the course of the sun, the seasons, and nature of the climate, and whatever else might direct them what course to steer. They did not doubt but that there might be some habitable countries in the midst of those vast deserts, perhaps as delicious as the vale they lived in, if they could but come at them. Several persons were sent out to make discoveries, but without success. The sands were too vast to tra-

* Herodotus says, that they sailed (even in those early days) from the Red sea, round Africa, and came back to Egypt through the streights, and up the Mediterranean. *Herodot. Melpomene*, and *Bochart*. That Hanno the elder, by order of the senate of Carthage, sailed round the greatest part of the world, and after his return delivered to them an account of his voyage, which is called the Periplus of Hanno. He affected to be honoured as a god for it, and lived before Solomon's time. *Bochart in Canaan, lib.* 1. *c.* 37.

vel over without water, and they could find no springs nor rivers. At length the moſt ſagacious of them began to reflect, that the annual overflowing of the great river Nile, whoſe head could never be found out, muſt proceed from ſome prodigious rains which fell ſomewhere ſouthward of them about that time of the year; which rains, if they could but luckily time and meet with, might not only ſupply them with water, but alſo render the country fertile where they fell. Accordingly the chief Pophar, aſſiſted by ſome of the wiſeſt men, generouſly reſolved to run all riſks to ſave his people. They computed the preciſe time when the Nile overflowed, and allowed for the time the waters muſt take in deſcending ſo far as Egypt. They thought therefore, if they could but carry water enough to ſupply them till they met with theſe rains, they would help them to go on further. At length, five of them ſet out, with ten dromedaries, carrying as much water and proviſions as might ſerve them for fifteen days, to bring them back again in caſe there was no hopes. They ſteered their courſe as we did, though not quite ſo exact the firſt time, till they came to the place, where we are now. Finding here, as their notes tell us *, a lit-

---

* Thoſe wiſe ancients kept records of every thing that was memorable and uſeful for their people. If this had been the practice of the Europeans, we ſhould not have loſt ſo many ſecrets of nature as we have.

tle

tle rivulet, which is since swallowed up by the sands, they filled their vessels, and went up to take an observation; as we did: but seeing the signs of the great hurricanes, which was our greatest encouragement, it had like to have driven them into despair; for the Pophar knowing the danger of being overwhelmed in the sands, thought of nothing but flying back as fast as he could, fearing to be swallowed up in those stifling whirlpools. This apprehension made him lay aside all thoughts of succeeding towards that climate; and now his chief care was how to get back again with safety for himself and his people. But finding all continue tolerably serene where they were, they made a halt in order to make some farther observations. In the mean time, they reflected that those hurricanes must be fore-runners of tempests and rain. Then they recollected, that no rain, or what was very inconsiderable, ever fell in Egypt*, or for a

---

* This is well known by all the descriptions of that country, the inundation of the Nile supplying the want of it, and making it one of the most fertile kingdoms in the world; every one knows it was once the granary of the Roman empire. However, some small rain falls sometimes: nor is there any more higher up in the country. The overflowing of the Nile is known to be caused by vast rains falling under the line, or about that climate; and since those don't take Egypt and the adjoining part of Africa in their way, they must by consequence run parallel with the line; which was a very natural and philosophical observation of these wise men.

great way south of it, till they came within the tropics; and thence concluded, that the rains must run parallel with the equator, both under it, and for some breadth on both sides, till they met the rise of the river Nile, and there caused those vast inundations so hard to be accounted for by other people. That, in fine, those rains must last a considerable while, and probably, though beginning with tempests, might continue in settled rain, capable of being passed through. Then he at first resolved to venture back again to the first vale: but being a man of great prudence, he presently considered, that as he could not proceed on his way without rains, so he could not come back again but by the same help, which coming only at one season, must take up a whole year before he could return. However, he was resolved to venture on, not doubting but if he could find a habitable country, he should also find fruits enough to subsist on, till the next season. Therefore he ordered two of his companions to return the same way they came, to tell his people not to expect him till the next year, if Providence should bring him back at all; but if he did not return by the time of the overflowing of the Nile, or thereabouts, they might give him over for lost, and must never attempt that way any more. They took their leaves of one another as if it were the last adieu, and

and set out at the same time; two of them, for their homes in the first vale, and the other three for those unknown regions; being destitute of all other helps but those of a courageous mind. The three came back to this place, where it thundered and lightened as it does now; but the Pophar observed it still tended sidewise, and guessed, when the first violence was over, the rains might be more settled. The next day it fell out as he foresaw; whereupon, recommending himself to the great author of our being, he lanched boldly out into that vast ocean of sands and rain, steering his course southwest, rather inclining towards the south. They went as far as the heavy sands and rains would let them, till their dromedaries could hardly go any further. Then they pitched their tents and refreshed themselves just enough to undergo new labour, well knowing all their lives depended on their expedition. They observed the sands to be of a different kind from what they had seen hitherto, so fine, that any gust of wind must overwhelm man and beast, only the rains had clogged and laid them.

Not to prolong your expectation too much: they went on thus for ten days, till the rains began to abate; then they saw their lives or deaths would soon be determined. The 11th day the ground began to grow
harder

harder in patches, with here and there a little mofs on the furface, and now and then a fmall withered fhrub. This revived their hopes, that they fhould find good land in a fhort time, and in effect, the foil changed for the better every ftep they took; and now they began to fee little hills covered with grafs, and the valleys fink down as if there might be brooks and rivers. The twelfth and thirteenth day cleared all their doubts, and brought them into a country, which, though not very fertile, had both water and fruits, with a hopeful profpect further on of hills and dales, all habitable and flourifhing. Here they fell proftrate on the earth, adoring the creator of all things, who had conducted them fafe through fo many dangers, and kifling the ground, which was to be the common nurfe for them, and, as they hoped, for all their pofterity: when they had repofed themfelves for fome days, they proceeded further into the country, which they found to mend upon them the more they advanced into it. Not intending to return till next year, they fought the propereft place for their habitation; and fetting up marks at every moderate diftance not to lofe their way back again, they made for the higheft hills they could fee, from whence they perceived an immenfe and delicious country every way; but, to their greater fatisfaction, no inhabitants. They wandered thus

thus at pleasure through those natural gardens, where there was a perpetual spring in some kinds of the produce of the earth, and the ripeness of autumn with the most exquisite fruits in others. They kept the most exact observations possible. Whichever way they went, there were not only springs and fountains in abundance, but, as they guessed, (for they kept the higher ground), the heads of great rivers and lakes, some of which they could perceive; so that they were satisfied there was room enough for whole nations, without any danger, as they could find, of being disturbed. By their observation of the sun, they were nigher the equator than they had imagined *, so that they there passed the middle space between the tropic and the line. Being come back to their first station, they there waited the proper season for their return. The rains came something sooner than the year before, because they were further west-

---

* Though we may imagine a lesser circle parallel to the tropics and the equator, which is called *maximus parallelorum*; yet whoever travels either by land or sea, parallel, as he thinks, to the equator, does not so, but will approach to it; nay and cross it at last, (unless he goes spirally), and make indentures as he goes along: the reason is, because where-ever we are, we are on the summit of the globe with respect to us, and our feet make a perpendicular to the centre; so that if we go round the globe, we shall make a great circle, and by consequence cut the equator.

ward,

ward. The hurricanes were nothing like what they were in the vaſt ſands. As ſoon as they began to fix in ſettled rains, they ſet out again as before, and in twenty days time from their laſt ſetting out, happily arrived at the place where they left their dear friends and relations, whoſe joy for their ſafe and happy arrival was greater than I can pretend to deſcribe. Thus this immortal hero accompliſhed his great undertaking, ſo much more glorious than all the victories of the greateſt conquerors, as it was projected, formed, and executed by his own wiſdom and courage; not by expoſing and ſacrificing the lives of thouſands of his ſubjects, perhaps greater men than himſelf, but by expoſing his own life for the ſafety of thoſe that depended on him.

It were too tedious to recount to you all the difficulties and troubles they had, both in reſolving to undertake ſuch a hazardous tranſmigration, as well as thoſe of tranſporting ſuch a multitude, with their wives and children, and all their moſt precious effects, over thoſe mercileſs ſands, which they could only paſs at one ſeaſon of the year. But the voyage being at length reſolved on, and the good Pophar wiſely conſidering the difficulties, and neceſſity, the mother of invention, urging him, at the ſame time, to gain as much time as he could, ſince the vale where they were at preſent

present was sufficient to maintain them till the rains came; got all his people hither in the mean time, to be ready for the season. The new-born children were left with their mothers, and people to take care of them, till they were able to bear the fatigue. Thus, in seven years time, going backwards and forwards every season, they all arrived safe, where we ourselves hope to be in ten or twelve days time. This great hero we deservedly honour, as another Mesraim, the second founder of our nation, from whose loins you yourself sprung by the surer side, and are going to be incorporated again with the offspring of your first ancestors.

Here he ended his relation, and your Reverences may easily believe, I was in the greatest admiration at this unheard-of account. As it raised the ideas I had of the people, so I could not be sorry to find myself, young and forlorn as I was before, incorporated with, and allied to such a flourishing and civilized nation. My expectation was not disproportionable to my ideas: I was persuaded I was going into a very fine country; but the thoughts of their being Pagans left some little damp on my spirits, and was a drawback to my expected happiness. However, I was resolved to preserve my religion, at the expense of all that was dear to me, and even of life itself.

By

By this time, the Pophar ordered us to refresh ourselves, and prepare all things for our departure, though the storm of thunder and lightning did not cease till towards morning. At length, all things being ready for our moving, we marched on slowly till we came into the course of the rains. It was the most settled and downright rain (as the saying is) that ever I saw; every thing seemed to be as calm, as the tempest was violent before. Being accustomed to it, they had provided open vessels on each side of the dromedaries, to catch enough for their use as it fell, and they covered themselves and their beasts with that fine oiled cloth I mentioned before. All the sands were laid, and even beaten hard by the rains, though heavy and cloggy at the same time. We made as much way as possible, for five days, just resting and refreshing ourselves when absolutely necessary. I must own, nothing could be more dismal than those dreary solitary deserts, where we could neither see sun nor moon, but had only a gloomy, malignant light, just sufficient to look at the needle, and take our observations. On the sixth day we thought we saw something move sidewise of us, on our right hand, but seemingly passing by us; when one of the young men cried, *There they are*, and immediately crossed down to them. Then we perceived

perceived them to be perſons travelling like ourſelves, croſſing in the ſame manner up towards us. I was extremely ſurpriſed to find, that thoſe deſerts were known to any but ourſelves. But the Pophar ſoon put me out of pain, by telling me, they were ſome of their own people, taking the ſame ſeaſon to go for Egypt, and on the ſame account. By this time we were come up to one another. The leader of the other caravan, with all his company, immediately got off their dromedaries, and fell proſtrate on the earth before our Pophar; at which he ſtept back; and cried, *Alas! is our father dead?* They told him, Yes; and that he being the firſt of the ſecond line, was to be regent of the kingdom, till the young Pophar, who was born when his father was an old man, ſhould come to the age of fifty. Then our people got off, and proſtrated themſelves before him *, all but myſelf. They took no notice of my neglect, ſeeing me a ſupernumerary perſon, and by conſequence a ſtranger; but as ſoon as the ceremonies were over, came and embraced me, and welcomed me into their brotherhood with the moſt ſincere cordiality, as if I had been one of their nation. The Pophar ſoon told them what I was, which made them repeat their careſſes with

---

* The eaſtern manner of ſhewing reſpect.

new ecftafies of joy peculiar to thefe people. After reiterated inquiries concerning their friends, and affurances that all was well, except what they had juft told him, the Pophar afked them, how they came to direct their courfe fo much on the left hand, expecting to have met them the day before; and they feeming to point as if they were going out of their way. They told us, they were now fenfible of it, and were making up for the true road as faft as they could: but that the day before, they had like to have loft themfelves by the darknefs of the weather, and their too great fecurity; for, bearing too much on the left hand, one of their dromedaries floundered, as if he were got into a quickfand *. The rider thinking it had been nothing but fome loofer part of

* Perfons may wonder to hear of quickfands in the midft of the fun-burnt deferts of Africa, But the thing will not feem fo improbable, when we come to examine the reafons of it. Without doubt, our author does not mean fuch quickfands as are caufed by the coming in of the tide under the fands; a man of fenfe would be incapable of fuch a blunder. But that there fhould be fome ftagnating waters in the low fwamps of the fands, is fo far from being incredible, that it can be hardly thought to be otherwife. It is very well known, there are vaft lakes in fome parts of Africa, which have no vifible outlets. There are rivers alfo that lofe themfelves in the fands, where finking under for fome time, they may form fandy marfhes, or quickfands, as the author calls them.

the

the sand, thought to go on, but fell deeper the further he went, till the commander ordered him to get off immediately, which he did with so much haste, that not minding his dromedary, the poor beast going on further into the quicksands, was lost. Then the Pophar told them, there was such a place marked down in their ancient charts, which, being so well acquainted with the roads, they had never minded of late years: that he supposed those quicksands to be either the rains, which had sunk through the sands, and meeting with some strata of clay, stagnated, and were forming a lake; or more probably, it was the course of some distant river, rising perhaps out of a habitable country, at an unknown distance, but had lost itself in those immense sands. However, he congratulated them on their escape, and, like a tender father, gently chid them for their too great security in that boundless ocean. Our time not permitting us to stay long, each caravan set out again for their destined course, having but five or six days journey to make, that is, as far as we could travel in so many days and so many nights; for we never stopped but to refresh ourselves. The rains had so tempered the air, that it was rather cold than hot, especially the nights, which grew longer, as we approached the line. Here we steered our course more to the west again,

again, but not so as to leave the ridge of the world. I observed, the more we kept to the west, the more moderate the rains were, as indeed they slackened in proportion as we came nigher our journey's end; because coming from the west, or at least with a little point of the south, they began sooner than where we set out. The tenth day of our journey, I mean from the last grove or resting-place, one of our dromedaries failed. We had changed them several times before, to make their labour more equal. They would not let it die, for the good it had done; but two of the company having water enough, and knowing where they were, staid behind, to bring it along with them. We now found the nature of the sands and soil to begin to change, as the Pophar had informed me: the ground began to be covered with a little moss, tending towards a green sward, more like barren downs than sands; and I unexpectedly perceived in some places, instead of those barren gravelly sands, large spaces of tolerable good soil *. At length, to our inexpressible

* It was observed in some of the former remarks, that not only the deserts of Africa, but all the strata, or great beds of gravel, which are found in all parts of the world, probably were caused by the universal deluge. Nor can they be well accounted for otherwise. The deeper the beds of gravel are, the more they shew, by the heterogeneous stuff lodged with them, that they were

expressible joy and comfort, at least for myself, who could not but be in some suspense in such an unknown world, we came to patches of trees, and grass, with slanting falls and heads of vales, which seemed to enlarge

were brought thither, not produced there *ab origine*. The vast falls and gullets which are seen on the skirts of all the mountains in the world, evidently shew they were caused by some violent agitation, which carried the loofer earth and small stones along with it : for which nothing can be more natural, than the supposition of a flood, or agitated fluid, which, by its violence and shakings, carried all that was moveable before it for some time. This gravel was incorporated with the loose earth before the flood, and was carried to and fro, while the waters were in their greatest agitation, washing and melting the loose earth from the gravel and stones. But when the waters came to their highest pitch, and began to subside, the stones and gravel would sink sooner than lighter things, and so be left almost in a body in those strata they appear in. This might be illustrated much further, if there were occasion. The vast numbers of petrified shells and scallops, which are found in all parts of the world, on the higher grounds, could never be a mere *lusus naturæ*, as some too curious philosophers imagine, but must be accounted for by such a flood ; and these appearing in all parts of the universe, the flood must have been universal. The sudden change of soils in every region, with the exceeding richness of some more than others, and that too sometimes all at once, is to be accounted for from the same cause : for the same violence of waters washing the earth from the stones, must naturally make an unequal accumulation of both. As for Africa, all the ancients speak of the incredible fertility of it in some places, and the extreme barrenness of the deserts in others.

themselves beyond our view *. The rains were come to their period; only it looked a little foggy at a great diftance before us, which was partly from the exhalations of the country after the rains †; partly from the trees and hills ftopping the clouds, by which we found that the weather did not clear up in the habitable countries fo foon as in the barren deferts. The Pophar told me, that, if it were not for the hazinefs of the air, he would fhew me the moft beautiful profpect that ever my eyes beheld. I was fenfibly convinced of it by the perfumes of the fpicy fhrubs and flowers, which ftruck our fenfes with fuch a reviving fragrancy, as made us almoft forget our paft fatigue, efpecially me, who had not felt the like even in the firft vale: neither do I believe all the odours of the Happy Arabia could ever come up to it. I was juft as if I had rifen out of the moft delicious repofe. Here the Pophar ordered us to ftop for refrefhment, and added, that we muft ftay there till next day. We pitched our tents on the laft defcent of thofe immenfe

---

* The prodigious height of the fands in Africa, in thofe parts which lie between the tropics, may not only be the caufe of the fands or gravel finking in greater quantities at the decreafe of the flood; but the moft extenfive vales may have their rife from very fmall gullets at firft.

† It is very natural to think, that thofe barren funburnt deferts fend up but few exhalations.

Bares,

Bares, by the side of a little rill that issued out of the small break of the downs, expecting further orders.

The cause of our stay here, where we were out of danger, was not only for our companions we had left behind us, but on a ceremonious account, as your Reverences will see by and by : they were also to change their habits, that they might appear in the colours of their respective tribe or name, which were five, according to the number of the sons of the first Pophar, who brought them out of Egypt, whose statue we saw at the pyramid. By their laws all the tribes are to be distinguished by their colours; that where-ever they go, they may be known what name they belong to; with particular marks of their posts and dignities; as I shall describe to your Reverences afterwards. The grand Pophar's colour, who was descended from the eldest son of the ancient Pophar, was a flame colour, or approaching nigh the rays of the sun, because he was chief priest of the sun. Our new regent's colour was green, spangled with suns of gold, as your Reverences saw in the picture ; the green representing the spring, which is the chief season with them. The third colour is a fiery red, for the summer. The fourth is yellow, for autumn ; and the fifth purple, representing the gloominess of winter;

ter; for these people, acknowledging the sun for the immediate governor of the universe, mimic the nature of his influence as nigh as they can. The women observe the colours of their respective tribes, but have moons of silver intermixed with the suns, to shew that they are influenced in a great measure by that variable planet. The young virgins have the new moon; in the strength of their age the full moon; as they grow old, the moon is in the decrease proportionably. The widows have the moon expressed just as it is in the change; the descendents of the daughters of the first Pophar were incorporated with the rest. Those of the eldest daughter took the eldest son's colour, with a mark of distinction, to shew they were never to succeed to the popharship, or regency, till there should be no male issue of the others at age to govern. This right of eldership, as these people understand it, is a little intricate; but I shall explain it to your Reverences more at large, when I come to speak more particularly of their government. When they are sent out into foreign countries, they take what habit or colour they please, and generally go all alike, to be known to each other; but they must not appear in their own country but in their proper colours, it being criminal to do otherwise. They carry marks also of their families, that

in

in cafe any mifdemeanor fhould be committed, they may know where to trace it out; for which reafon, now they drew near their own country, they were to appear in the colours of their refpective nomes; all but myfelf, who had the fame garment I wore at Grand Cairo, to fhew I was a ftranger, though I wore the Pophar's colour afterwards, as being his relation, and incorporated in his family. When they were all arrayed in their filken colours, fpangled with funs of gold, with white fillets round their temples, ftudded with precious ftones, they made a very delightful fhew, being the handfomeft race of people this day in the univerfe, and all refembling each other, as having no mixture of other nations in their blood.

The fun had now broke through the clouds, and difcovered to us the profpect of the country, but fuch a one as I am not able to defcribe; it looked rather like an immenfe garden than a country: at that diftance I could fee nothing but trees and groves; whether I looked towards the hills or vales, all feemed to be one continued wood, though with fome feemingly regular intervals of fquares and plains, with the glittering of golden globes or funs through the tops of the trees, that it looked like a green mantle fpangled with gold. I afked the Pophar, if they lived all in woods, or

whether

whether the country was only one continued immense forest. He smiled and said, When we come thither, you shall see something else besides woods; and then bid me look back, and compare the dreary sands we had lately passed with that glorious prospect we saw before us: I did so, and found the dismal barrenness of the one enhanced the beautiful delight of the other. The reason, says he, why it looks like a wood, is, that, besides innumerable kinds of fruits, all our towns, squares, and streets, as well as fields and gardens, are planted with trees, both for delight and conveniency, though you will find spare ground enough for the produce of all things sufficient to make the life of man easy and happy. The glittering of gold through the tops of the trees, are golden suns on the tops of the temples and buildings: we build our houses flat and low on account of hurricanes, with gardens of perfumed ever-greens on the top of them; which is the reason you see nothing but groves.

We descended gradually from off the desert through the scattered shrubs, and were saluted every now and then with a gale of perfumes quite different from what are brought to the Europeans from foreign parts. The fresh air of the morning, together with their being exhaled from the living stocks, gave them such a fragrancy as cannot

cannot be expreffed. At length we came to a fpacious plain a little fhelving, and covered with a greenifh coat, between mofs and grafs, which was the utmoft border of the defert ; and beyond it a fmall river, collected from the hills, as it were weeping out of the fands in different places ; which river was the boundary of the kingdom that way. Halting here, we difcovered a fmall company of ten perfons, the fame number, excluding me, with ours, advancing gravely towards us : they were in the proper colours of the Nomes, with fpangled funs of gold, as my companions wore, only the tops of their heads were fprinkled with duft, in token of mourning. As foon as they came at a due diftance, they fell flat on their faces before the Pophar, without faying a word, and received the golden urns with the earth which we brought along with us. Then they turned, and marched directly before us, holding the urns in their hands as high as they could, but all in a deep and mournful filence. Thefe were deputies of the five Nomes fent to meet the urns. We advanced in this filent manner without faying one word, till we came to the river, over which was a ftately bridge with a triumphal arch on the top of it, beautified with funs of gold, moft magnificent to behold. Beyond the bridge, we immediately paffed through a kind of
circular

circular grove, which led us into a moſt delightful plain, like an amphitheatre, with five avenues or ſtreets leading to it: at the entrance of each avenue ſtood an innumerable multitude of people repreſenting the five Nomes, or governments of thoſe immenſe kingdoms, all in their different colours, ſpangled with ſuns of gold, which made the moſt glorious ſhow in the world. As ſoon as we entered the amphitheatre, our ſilence was broke with ſhouts of joy that rended the very ſkies; then the whole multitude falling flat on their faces, adoring the urns, and thrice repeating their ſhouts and adorations, there advanced ten triumphant chariots, according to the colours of the Nomes with ſuns as before; nine of the chariots were drawn with ſix horſes each, and the tenth with eight for the Pophar regent. The five deputies, who were the chief of each Nome, with the urns and companions, mounted five of the chariots, the other five were for us, two in a chariot; only being a ſupernumerary, I was placed backwards in the Pophar's chariot, which he told me was the only mark of humiliation and inequality I would receive. We were conducted with five ſquadrons of horſe, of fifty men each, in their proper colours, with ſtreamers of the ſame, having the ſun in the centre, through the oppoſite avenue, till we came into another amphitheatre

of

of a vast extent, where we saw an infinite number of tents of silk of the colour of the Nomes, all of them spangled with golden suns: here we were to rest and refresh ourselves. The Pophar's tent was in the centre of his own colour, which was green, the second Nome in dignity, in whose dominions and government we now were.

I have been longer in this description, because it was more a religious ceremony than any thing else, these people being extremely mysterious in all they do *. I shall explain the meaning to your Reverences as briefly as I can. The stopping before we came to the bridge on the borders of those inhospitable deserts, and walking in that mournful silent manner, not only expressed their mourning for their deceased

---

* The ancient Egyptians were so mysterious, particularly in their religious ceremonies, and *arcana* of government, that, in all probability, the ancient fables, which very few yet understand rightly, had their rise from them; though the learned Bochart, in his Phaleg. derives them chiefly from the Canaanites, who dispersing themselves all over the world, when they fled from Joshua, imposed upon the credulous Greeks by the different significations of the same words in their language. It is observable by the by, that the most ancient languages, as the Hebrew, with its different dialects, of which the Canaanean or Phœnician language was one, the Chinese language, &c. had a great many significations for the same word, either from the plain simplicity or poverty of the ancient languages, or more probably from an affected mysteriousness in all they did.

ancestors, but also signified the various calamities and labours incident to man in this life, where he is not only looked upon to be, but really is, in a state of banishment and mourning; wandering in sunburnt deserts, and tossed with storms of innumerable lawless desires, still sighing after a better country. The passage over the bridge, they would have to betoken man's entrance into rest by death. Their shouts of joy, when the sacred urns arrived in that glorious country, not only signified the happiness of the next life, (for these people universally believe the immortality of the soul, and think none but brutes can be ignorant of it), but also that their ancestors, whose burial-dust they brought along with them, were now in a place of everlasting rest.

[*Inquisitor.* I hope you don't believe so of Heathens, let them be ever so moral men, since we have no assurance of happiness in the next life mentioned in the holy scripture, without faith in Christ.

Gaudentio. No, Reverend Fathers; I only mention the sense in which these men understand the mysteries of their religion. As I believe in Christ, I know there is no other name under heaven by which men can be saved.

Inquisitor. Go on.]

Every ceremony of these people has some mystery

mystery or other included in it; but there appeared no harm in any of them, except their falling prostrate before the dust, which looked like rank idolatry: but they said still, they meant no more than what was merely civil, to signify their respect for their deceased parents*.

I shall not as yet detain your Reverences with the description of the beauties of the country through which we passed, having so much to say of the more substantial part; that is, of their form of government, laws, and customs, both religious and civil; nor describe their prodigious magnificence, though joined with a great deal of natural simplicity, in their towns, temples, schools, colleges, &c. Because, being built mostly alike, except for particular uses, manufactures, and the like; I shall describe them all in one, when I come to the great city of Phor, otherwise called, in their sacred language, *No-om* †: for if I should stay to

---

* See the remarks before on that head, and the accounts of the worship of the Chinese, who were originally Egyptians, in the disputes between the Dominicans and Jesuits, where the latter maintained the idolatrous ceremonies and offerings made to their deceased ancestors, to imply nothing but a natural and civil respect. The Dominicans, on the contrary, very justly held them to be idolatry, as they were judged to be, and condemned as such by Clement XI.

† Josephus against Appion distinguishes two languages of the ancient Egyptians, the one sacred, the other common. Their sacred language was full of mysteries, perhaps like the Cabala of the Jews.

describe

describe the immense riches, fertility, and beauties of the country, this relation, which is designed as a real account of a place wherein I lived so many years, would rather look like a romance than a true relation. I shall only tell your Reverences at present, that after having taken a most magnificent repast, consisting of all the heart of man can conceive delicious, both of fruits and wines, while we staid in those refreshing tabernacles, we passed on by an easy evening's journey to one of their towns, always conducted and lodged in the same triumphant manner, till we came to the head of that Nome, which I told your Reverences was the green Nome, belonging to the Pophar regent, second in dignity of the whole empire. Here the urn of dust belonging to that Nome was reposited in a kind of golden tabernacle set with precious stones of immense value, in the centre of a spacious temple, which I shall describe afterwards. After a week's feasting and rejoicing, both for the reception of the dust, and the safe return of the Pophar and his companions, together with his exaltation to the regency, we set out in the same manner for the other Nomes, to reposit all the urns in their respective temples. These are five, as I informed your Reverences before. The country is something mountainous, particularly under the line, and not very

very uniform, though every thing else is; containing valleys, or rather whole regions running out between the deserts; besides vast ridges of mountains in the heart of the country, which inclose immense riches in their bowels. The chief town is situated as nigh as possible in the middle of the Nomes, and about the centre of the country, bating those irregularities I mentioned. The four inferior Nomes were like the four corners, with the flame-coloured Nome, where the grand Pophar, or regent *pro tempore* resided, in the centre of the square. Their method was to go to the four inferior Nomes first, and reposit the urns, and then to complete all at the chief town of the first Nome. These Nomes were each about eight days very easy journey over. Thus we went the round of all, which I think, as I then remarked, was a kind of political visitation at the same time. At length we came to the great city of Phor, or No-om, there to reposit the last urn, and for all the people to pay their respects to the grand Pophar, if in being, or else to the regent. By that time, what with those who accompanied the procession of the urns, and the inhabitants of that immense town, more people were gathered together, than one would have almost thought had been in the whole world; but in such order and decency, distinguished in their ranks,

ranks, tribes, and colours, as is not eafy to be comprehended. The glittering tents fpread themfelves over the face of the earth.

I fhall here give your Reverences a defcription of the town, becaufe all other great towns or heads of the Nomes are built after that model, as indeed the leffer towns come as nigh it as they can, except, as I faid, places for arts or trades, which are generally built on rivers or brooks, for conveniency; fuch is the nature of the people, that they affect an exact uniformity and equality in all they do, as being brothers of the fame ftock.

The town of Phor, that is, the Glory or No-om, which fignifies the houfe of the fun, is built circular, in imitation of the fun and its rays. It is fituated in the largeft plain of all the kingdom, and upon the largeft river, which is about as big as our Po, rifing from a ridge of mountains under the line, and running towards the north, where it forms a great lake, almoft like a fea, whofe waters are exhaled by the heat of the fun, having no outlet, or fink under ground in the fands of the vaft deferts encompaffing it. This river is cut into a moft magnificent canal, running directly through the middle of the town. Before it enters the town, to prevent inundations, and for other conveniencies, there are prodigious

digious basons, and locks, and sluices, with collateral canals, to divert and let out the water, if need be. The middle stream forms the grand canal, which runs through the town, till it comes to the grand place; then there is another lock and sluice which dividing it into two semicircles or wings, and carrying it round the grand place, forms an island with the temple of the sun in the centre, and meeting again opposite to where it divided, so goes on in a canal again. There are twelve bridges with one great arch over each, ten over the circular canals, and two where they divide and meet again. There are also bridges over the strait canals, at proper distances. Before the river enters the town, it is divided by the first great lock into two prodigious semicircles encompassing the whole town. All the canals are planted with double rows of cedars, and walks the most delightful that can be imagined. The grand place is in the centre of the town, a prodigious round, or immense theatre, encompassed with the branches of the canal, and, in the centre of that, the temple of the sun. This temple consists of three hundred and sixty-five double marble pillars, according to the number of the days of the year*, repeated with three stories one above

* Our author seems to be a little out in this place; for it is certain, the ancient Egyptians did not make their year

above another, and on the top a cupola open to the sky for the sun to be seen through. The pillars are all of the Corinthian order *, of a marble as white as snow, and fluted. The edges of the flutes, with the capitals cornished, are all gilt. The inner roofs of the vast galleries on these pillars, are painted with the sun, moon, and stars, expressing their different motions; with hieroglyphics known only to some few of the chief elders or rulers. The outsides of all are doubly gilt, as is the dome or grand concave on the top, open in the middle to the sky. In the middle of this concave is a golden sun, hanging in the void, and supported by golden lines or rods from the edges of the dome. The

year to consist of so many days, unless you will say, that these people, being very great astronomers, were more exact in their observations.

* It is generally supposed, that the different orders of pillars, as the Doric, the Ionic, Corinthian, &c. came first from the Greeks, as their appellations, being Greek, would make us believe; but the famous and ancient palace of Persepolis, notwithstanding its Greek name, where there were hieroglyphics and inscriptions in characters none could understand, besides other reasons, shew that the invention came from Egypt, or from the ancient Chaldeans, or rather from Seth, Noah, and the ancient Hebrews. It is likewise very observable, that the invention of arts and sciences came from the east, and can be traced no higher than Noah's flood; unless you will allow the fables of Seth, alledged by the learned Josephus in his antiquities, quoted above. All which is a very natural confirmation of the account given by Moses, against our modern sceptics.

artificial

artificial sun looks down, as if it were shining on a globe of earth, erected on a pedestal altar-wise, opposite to the sun, according to the situation of their climate to that glorious planet; in which globe or earth are inclosed the urns of their deceased ancestors. On the inside of the pillars, are the seats of the grandees or elders, to hold their councils, which are all public. Opposite to the twelve great streets, are so many entrances into the temple, with as many magnificent stair-cases between the entrances, to go into the galleries or places where they keep the registers of their laws, &c. with gilt balustrades looking down into the temple. On the pedestals of all the pillars were ingraven hieroglyphics and characters known to none but the five chief Pophars, and communicated under the greatest secrecy to the successor of any one of them, in case of death, loss of senses, and the like. I presume, the grand secrets, and *arcana* of state, and, it may be, of their religion, arts, and sciences, are contained therein. The most improper decorations of the temple, in my opinion, are the flutings of the pillars, which rather look too finicial for the august and majestic simplicity affected by these people in other respects.

The fronts of the houses round the grand place are all concave, or segments of circles, except where the great streets meet, which

are

are twelve in number, according to the twelve signs of the zodiac, pointing to the temple in strait lines like rays to the centre. This vast round is set with double rows and circles of stately cedars before the houses, at an exact distance; as are all the streets on each side, like so many beautiful avenues, which produce a most delightful effect to the eye, as well as conveniency of shade. The cross streets are so many parallel circles round the grand place and temple, as the centre, making greater circles as the town enlarges itself. They build always circular-wise till the circle is complete; then another, and so on. All the streets, as I said, both straight and circular, are planted with double rows of cedars. The middle of the areas between the cuttings of the streets are left for gardens and other conveniencies, enlarging themselves as they proceed from the centre or grand place. At every cutting of the streets, is a lesser circular space set round with trees, adorned with fountains, or statues of famous men; that, in effect, the whole town is like a prodigious garden, distinguished with temples, pavilions, avenues, and circles of greens; so that it is difficult to give your Reverences a just idea of the beauty of it. I forgot to tell your Reverences, that the twelve great streets open themselves as they lengthen, like the *radii* of a wheel, so that at the first
coming

coming into the town, you have the profpect of the temple and grand place directly before you ; and from the temple a direct view of one of the fineft avenues and countries in the world. Their principal towns are all built after this form. After they have taken a plan of the place, they firft build a temple ; then leave the great area, or circular market-place, round which they build a circle of houfes, and add others as they increafe, according to the foregoing defcription ; ridiculing and contemning other countries, whofe towns are generally built in a confufed number of houfes and ftreets, without any regular figure. In all the fpaces or cuttings of the ftreets, there are either public fountains brought by pipes from a mountain at a confiderable diftance from the town; or, as I faid before, ftatues of great men holding fomething in their hands to declare their merit ; which, having no wars, is taken, either from the invention of arts and fciences, or fome memorable action done by them for the improvement and good of their country. Thefe they look upon as more laudable motives, and greater fpurs to glory, than all the trophies erected by other nations, to the deftroyers of their own fpecies. Their houfes are built all alike, and low, as I obferved before, on account of ftorms and hurricanes, to which the

country

country is subject; they are all exactly of a height, flat-roofed, with artificial gardens on the top of each *, full of flowers and aromatic shrubs; so that when you look from any eminence down into the streets, you see all the circles and avenues like another world under you; and if on the level, along the tops of the houses, you are charmed with the prospect of ten thousand different gardens meeting your sight where-ever you turn; insomuch, that I believe the whole world besides cannot afford such a prospect. There are a great many other beauties and conveniencies according to the genius of the people; which, were I to mention, would make up a whole volume. I only say, that the riches of the country are immense, which in some measure are all in common, as I shall shew when I come to the nature of their government; the people are the most ingenious and industrious in the world; the governors aiming at nothing but the grandeur and good of the public, having all the affluence the heart of man can desire, in a

---

* The ancient Babylonians had artificial gardens, or *horti pensiles*, on the tops of their houses, as early as the great Semiramis; though Herodotus derives their invention from a later Babylonian queen, who being a Mede by nation, and loving woods, and not being permitted to go out of the palace, had those artificial gardens made to divert her.

place

place where there has been no war for near three thousand years; there being indeed no enemies but the inhospitable lands around them, and they all consider themselves as brothers of the same stock, living under one common father; so that it is not so much to be wondered at, if they are arrived to such grandeur and magnificence, as persons in our world can scarce believe or conceive.

When the ceremonies for the reception of the urns were over, religious ceremonies with these people always taking place of the civil*, they proceeded to the inauguration of the Pophar regent; which was performed with no other ceremony, for reasons I shall tell your Reverences afterwards, but placing him in a chair of state with his face towards the east, on the top of the highest hill in the Nome, to shew that he was to

---

* The most polite nations of antiquity, even among the Heathens, gave the preference to religion before all other considerations. As for the Christian religion, though of late persons of some wit, little judgment, and no morals, call it in question, it is well known, men become more men as they become Christians. The light of faith brought in learning, politeness, humanity, justice, and equity, instead of that ignorance, and a brutal barbarity, that overspread the face of the earth; and the want of it will lead us in time into the same enormities which religion has taught us to forsake; on which account it is the part of all wise governments to countenance and preserve religion.

inspect, or overlook all, looking towards the temple of the sun, which stood directly eastward of him, to put him in mind that he was to take care of the religion of his ancestors in the first place. When he was thus placed, three hundred sixty-five of the chief of the Nome, as representatives of all the rest, came up to him, and making a respectful bow, said, *Eli Pophar*, which is as much as to say, *Hail father* of our nation; and he embracing them as a father does his children, answered them with *Cali Benim*, that is, *My dear children*. As many of the women did the same. This was all the homage they paid him, which was esteemed so sacred as never to be violated. All the distinction of his habit was one great sun on his breast, much bigger than that of any of the rest. The precious stones also, which were set in the white fillet binding his forehead, were larger than ordinary, as were those of the cross circles over his head, terminated on the summit with a large tuft of gold, and a thin plate of gold in the shape of the sun, fastened to the top of it horizontally; all of them, both men and women, wore those fillet-crowns with a tuft of gold, but no sun on the top, except the Pophar.

As soon as the ceremonies and rejoicings were over, which were performed in tents at the public expense, he was conducted, with

with the chearful acclamations of the people, and the sound of musical instruments, to a magnificent tent in the front of the whole camp, facing the east, which is looked upon as the most honourable, as first seeing the rising sun; and so on, by easy journeys, till he came to the chief town of that Nome. The reason why these ceremonies were performed in the different Nomes, was to shew that they all depended on him, and because the empire was so very populous, it was impossible they could meet at one place. I cannot express the caresses I received from them, especially when they found I was descended from the same race by the mother's side, and so nearly related to the Pophar. When I came first into their company, they all embraced me, men and women, with the most endearing tenderness; the young beautiful women did the same, calling me brother, and catching me in their arms with such an innocent assurance, as if I had been their real brother lost and found again. I cannot say but some of them expressed a fondness for me that seemed to be of another sort, and which afterwards gave me a great deal of trouble; but I imputed it to the nature of the sex, who are unaccountably more fond of strangers, whom they know nothing of, than of persons of much greater merit, who converse with them every day. Whether it proceeds from the want of a sufficient solidity in their judgment, or from a levity and fickleness in their nature, or from the spirit of contradiction, which makes them fond of what they mostly should avoid; or thinking that strangers are not acquainted with their defects, or, in fine, are more likely to keep their counsel; be that as it will, their mutual jealousies gave me much uneasiness afterwards. But to say a word or two more of the nature of the people, before I proceed in my relation; as I told your Reverences, they are the handsomest race of people I believe nature ever produced, with this only difference, which some may think a defect, that they are all too much like one another: but if it be a defect, it proceeds from a very laudable cause; that is, from their springing from one family, without any mixture of different nations in their blood *; they have neither wars, nor traffic

---

* Tacitus says much the same of the Germans, *Ipse eorum opinionibus accedo, qui Germaniæ populos nullis aliarum nationum connubiis infectos, propriam et sinceram et tanquam sui similem gentem exstitisse arbitrantur* †. I agree, says he, with their opinion, who think the people of Germany so peculiarly like one another, because they have not been corrupted by marriages with other nations. They were noted in Augustus's time to have blue eyes, as most of the native Germans have to this day. I remember I saw a review of a German regiment in the city of Milan, where almost every one of

† *Tacitus de moribus Germanorum.*

fic with other people, to adulterate their race, for which reason they know nothing of the vices such a commerce often brings along with it. Their eyes are something too small, but not so little as those of the Chinese; their hair is generally black, and inclined to be a little cropped or frizzled *, and their complexion brown, but their features are the most exact and regular imaginable; and in the mountainous parts towards the line, where the air is cooler, they are rather fairer than our Italians †; the men are universally well shaped, tall and slender, except through some accidental deformity, which is very rare; but the women, who keep themselves much within doors, are the most beautiful creatures, and the finest shaped in the world, except, as I said, being too much alike. There is such an innocent sweetness in their beauty, and such a native modesty in their countenance, as cannot be described. A bold forwardness in a woman is what they dislike;

the common soldiers had blue eyes. No wonder therefore, if these Africans, our author speaks of, should be so like one another.

* The ancient Egyptians, according to Herodotus and Bochart, were so.

† Though our Italians are something more swarthy than the northern Tramontani; yet our ladies keeping much in the house from their childhood, have very fine skins, and excel all others for delicacy of features *.

* I fancy Signor Rhedi never saw our English beauties.

and to give them their due, even the women are the moſt chaſte I ever knew, which is partly owing to the early and provident care of their governors. But as I deſign to make a ſeparate article of the education of their young people, I ſhall ſay no more at preſent on that head.

The viſitations which we made to carry the urns, gave me an opportunity of ſeeing the greateſt part of their country as ſoon as I came there; though the Pophar, with a leſs retinue, and with whom I always was, viſited them more particularly afterwards. The country is generally more hilly than plain, and in ſome parts even mountainous; there are, as I ſa:d, vaſt ridges of mountains, which run ſeveral hundred miles, either under, or parallel to the equator. Theſe are very cold, and contribute very much to render the climate more temperate than might otherwiſe be expected, both by refrigerating the air with cooling breezes, which are wafted from thence over the reſt of the country, and by ſupplying the plains with innumerable rivers running both north and ſouth, but chiefly towards the north *. Theſe hills, and the great woods

* It is remarkable that moſt ſprings riſe from the north ſide of the hills, and more rivers run northward than ſouthward, at leaſt on this ſide of the line, though the obſervation does not always hold; the reaſon may be,. for that there are more miſts and dews hanging on the north ſide, becauſe the ſun dries up the moiſture on the

woods they are generally covered with, are the occasion of the country's being subject to rains *; there are vast forests and places, which they cut down and destroy as they want room, leaving lesser groves for beauty and variety, as well as use and conveniency. The rains and hilliness of the country make travelling a little incommodious, but then they afford numberless springs and rivulets, with such delicious vales, that, adding this to the honesty and innocence of the inhabitants, one would think it a perpetual paradise. The soil is so prodigious fertile, not only in different sorts of grain and rice, with a sort of wheat much larger and richer in flower than any Indian wheat I ever saw; but particularly in an inexhaustible variety of fruits, legumes, and eatable herbs of such nourishing juice, and delicious taste, that to provide fruit for such numbers of people is the least of their care. One would think the curse of Adam had scarce reached that part of the world; or that Providence had proportioned the fertility of the country to the innocence of the inhabitants; not but the industry and ingenuity of the people,

---

the south side of the mountains, more than on the north; though perhaps all springs don't rise from rain and mists, &c. yet most do.

* It is well known to the naturalists, that great woods and hills collect clouds and vapours, and consequently cause it to rain more there than in other places.

joined

joined with their perpetual peace and rest from external and almost internal broils, contribute very much to their riches and fertility. Their villages being most of them built on the rivulets for manufactures and trades, are not to be numbered. Their hills are full of metallic mines of all sorts, with materials sufficient to work them; silver is the scarcest, and none more plentiful than gold; it comes out oftentimes in great lumps from the mineral rocks, as if it wept out from between the joints, and was thrown off by the natural heat of the earth, or other unknown causes: this gold is more ductile, easier to work, and better for all uses, than that which is drawn from the ore. Their inventions not only for common conveniencies, but even the magnificence of life, are astonishing. When I spoke of their fruits, I should have mentioned a small sort of grape that grows there naturally, of which they make a wine, sharp at first, but which will keep a great many years, mellowing and improving as it is kept; but the choicest grapes, which are chiefly for drying, are cultivated among them, and a very little pains does it. Their wines are more cordial than inebriating; but a smaller sort, diluted with water, makes their constant drink. I don't remember I ever saw any horned beasts in the country, except goats of a very large size, which

which serve them for milk, though it is rather too rich : deer there are innumerable, of more different kinds than are in Europe. There is a little beast seemingly of a species between a roe and a sheep, whose flesh is the most nourishing and delicious that can be tasted; these make a dish in all their feasts, and are chiefly reserved for that end. Their fowl, wild and tame, make the greatest part of their food, as to flesh-meat, of which they don't eat much, it being, as they think, too grofs a food. The rivers and lakes are stored with vast quantities of most exquisite fish, particularly a golden trout, whose belly is of a bright scarlet colour, as delectable to the palate as to the eye. They suppose fish to be more nourishing and easier of digestion than flesh, for which reason they eat much more of it; but having no rivers that run into the sea, they want all of that kind.

Their horses, as I observed before, are but small, but full of mettle and life, and extremely swift; they have a wild ass longer than the horse, of all the colours of the rainbow, very strong and profitable for burden and drudgery; but their great carriages are drawn by elks; the dromedaries are for travelling over the sands. The rivers, at least in the plain and low countries, are cut into canals, by which they carry most of their provision and effects all over the country.

country. This is only a small sketch of the nature of the country, because I know these matters don't fall under the cognisance of your Reverences, so much as the account of their religion, morals, customs, laws, and government. Yet I must say that for riches, plenty of all delicacies of life, manufactories, inventions of arts, and every thing that conduces to make this mortal state as happy as is possible, no country in the known world can parallel it; though there are some inconveniencies, as your Reverences will observe as I go on with my relation.

Before I come to the remaining occurrences of my own life, in which nothing very extraordinary happened till I came away, unless I reckon the extraordinary happiness I was placed in, as to all things of this life, in one of the most delicious regions of the universe, married to the regent's daughter, whose picture is there before you, and the deplorable loss of her, with my only remaining son, [Here he could not refrain from weeping for some time], as well as the present state to which I am reduced; though I must own I have received more favourable treatment than could well be expected: I shall give your Reverences a succinct account of their religion, laws, and customs, which are almost as far out of the common way of thinking

of

of the rest of the world, as their country.

Of their religion.

The religion of these people is really idolatry in the main; though as simple and natural as possible for Heathens. They indeed will not acknowledge themselves to be Heathens, in the sense we take the word; that is, worshippers of false gods *, for they have an abhorrence of idolatry in words as well as the Chinese, but are idolaters in effect, worshipping the material sun, and paying those superstitious rites to their deceased ancestors; of which part of their religion your Reverences have had a full account already. 'These people however acknowledge one supreme God, maker of all things, whom they call *El* †, or the most high of all. This they say natural reason

---

* This opinion was very ancient, and came originally from Egypt, where Pythagoras learned it: though perhaps not liking this way of employing it, he altered it quite from what these men held, which is the less irrational of the two. Though, with Signor Gaudentio's leave, I can never believe, these wise men really held that opinion, but only understood it allegorically; I must own, at the same time, some of the ancients did hold the other metempsychosis.

† The old Arabians by *Al*, or perhaps *El*, mean something very grand or high, as *Al-Cair*, for Grand Cair, *Alchymy* for the highest chymistry, &c. I wonder Signor Rhedi took no notice of this in his remarks.

teaches

teaches them from an argument, though good in itself, yet formed after a different way of arguing from other people: they say all their own wisdom, or that of all the wisest men in the world put together, could never form this glorious world in all its causes and effects, so justly adapted to its respective ends, as it is with respect to every individual species. Therefore the author of it must be a being infinitely wiser than all intellectual beings. As for the notion of any thing producing itself without a prior cause, they laugh at it, and ask why we don't see such effects produced without a cause? hence they hold one only independent cause, and that there must be one, or nothing could ever be produced. Though they make a god of the sun, they don't say he is independent as to his own being: but that he received it from this El. Some of the wiser sort, when I argued with them, seemed to acknowledge the sun to be a material being created by God; but others think him to be a sort of vicegerent, by whom the El performs every thing, as the chief instrumental cause of all productions. This is the reason that they address all their prayers to the sun, though they allow all power is to be referred originally to the El. The men look upon the moon to be a material being, dependent on the sun; but the women seem to make a goddess of her,

by

by reason of the influence she has over that sex; and foolishly think she brings forth every month when she is at the full, and that the stars are hers and the sun's children. They all of them, both men and women, rest satisfied in their belief, without any disputes or studied notions about a being so infinitely above them, thinking it much better to adore him in the inscrutability of his essence, in an humble silence, than to be disputing about what they cannot comprehend; all their search is employed in second causes, and the knowledge of nature as far as it may be useful to men.

[*Inquisitor*. I hope you don't deny but that some men may have wrong notions of the Deity, in which they ought to be set right by wiser and more learned men than themselves; by consequence all searches and disputes about the being and nature of God are not to be condemned.

Gaudentio. No, may it please your Reverences, for I presume you only understand me now as representing other people's opinions, not my own, which is entirely conformable to what the Catholic church teaches. I often told the Pophar, to whom I could speak my mind with all the freedom in the world, that as no mortal man could pretend to tell what belonged to the incomprehensibility

sibility of God's essence, yet our reason obliging us to believe his being; it was necessary, by the same reason, that we should be instructed by himself, or some lawgiver immediately commissioned by him, lest we should err in so material a point. This lawgiver we Christians believe he did send, by giving us his only Son, who was capable of instructing us in what belonged to the eternal Godhead; that he did not only give us the justest notions we could possibly have, but confirmed the truth of what he said, by such signs and wonders as none but one sent from God could perform.

Inquisitor. Go on.]

When I said, they address all their prayers, and most of the external actions of their worship to the sun, it is on account of their believing him to be the physical cause of the production of all things by his natural influence; which, though the wiser sort of them, when you came to reason more closely, will grant to be derived from the El, and some of them will own him to be a mere material being, moved by a prior cause, yet the generality of them don't reflect on this; but are really guilty of idolatry in worshipping a mere creature. Nevertheless, as to the moral effects of the universe, or the free actions of men
with

with respect to equity, justice, goodness, uprightness, and the like, which they allow to be properly the duty of rational creatures, and of much greater consequence than the physical part of the world: this, I say, they all refer to the supreme being, whose will it is they should be merciful, good, just, and equitable to all, agreeable to the just notions of the all-wise author of their existence, whose supreme reason being incapable of any irregular bias, ought to be the rule of his creatures that depend on him, and are in some measure partakers of his perfections. They confirm this notion by a very proper comparison; as for example, to act contrary to the laws of nature in physical productions, is to produce monstrous births, &c. so to act contrary to the ideas of the supreme reason in moral cases, must be a great deformity in his sight.

I own I was charmed with this natural way of reasoning, and asked them further, whether they believed the supreme being troubled himself about the moral part of the world, or the free actions of men? They seemed surprised at the question, and asked me, whether I thought it was possible he should leave the noblest part out of his care, when he took the pains (that was their expression) to create the least insect according to the most exact rules of art and knowledge, beyond all that the art of man can come up to ? I asked them again, what were the rules, which it was his will that free agents, such as man for instance, should follow in the direction of their lives ? They told me, reason, justice, and equity, in imitation of the supreme reason in him; for, said they, can you think the supreme being can approve of the enormous actions committed by men ; or that any vile practices can be according to the just ideas of his reason ; if not, they must be contrary to the best light of reason, not only in God, but man, and therefore liable to be punished by the just governor of all.

I submit these notions to your Reverences better judgment, but I thought them very extraordinary for persons who had nothing but the light of nature to direct them ; it is pity but they had been as right in their more remote inferences as they were in these principles. The sum therefore of the theoretical part of their religion, is,

First, that the El is the supreme intellectual, rational, and most noble of all beings ; that it is the duty of all intellectual beings to imitate the just laws of reason in him, otherwise they depart from the supreme rule of all their actions, since what is contrary to the most perfect reason in God, must be contrary to our own, and by
consequence

consequence of a deformity highly blameable in his sight; all their prayers, and whatever they ask of this supreme being, is, that they may be just and good as he is.

Secondly, that the sun is the chief, at least instrumental cause of their bodies, and all other physical effects. Your Reverences know better than I can inform you, that this is wrong: to him they address their prayers for the preservation of their lives, the fruits of the earth, &c.

Thirdly, that their parents are the more immediate instrumental cause of their natural being, which they derive partly from the El, and partly from the sun, and they reverence them the more on this account, as being the vicegerents of both, and believe them to be immortal, as to the spiritual or intellectual part, and consequently able and ready to assist them according to the respect they shew them by reverencing their tombs, and honouring their memories. Though, upon a nicer examination, I found that the superstitious worship they pay to their deceased ancestors, was as much a politic as a religious institution, because their government being patriarchal, this inviolable respect they shew to their parents makes them obey their elders or governors, not only with the most dutiful observance, but even with a filial love and alacrity.

There are some other points of less consequence, and reducible to these three heads, which your Reverences will observe in the course of my relation. As for the immortality of the soul, rewards and punishments in another life, they believe both, though they have an odd way of explaining them. They suppose, without any hesitation, that the soul is a being independent of matter, as to its essence, having faculties of thinking, willing, and chusing, which mere matter, let it be spun ever so fine, and actuated by the quickest and the most subtile motion, can ever be capable of; but their notion of their pre-existence with the El, before they were sent into bodies, is very confused. The rewards and punishments in the next life they believe will chiefly consist in this; that in proportion as their actions have been conformable to the just ideas of the supreme being in this life, partaking still more and more of his infinite wisdom, so their souls will approach still nearer to the beautiful intelligence of their divine model in the next. But if their actions in this life have been inconsistent with the supreme reason in God, they shall be permitted to go on for ever in that inconsistency and disagreement, till they become so monstrously wicked and enormous, as to become abominable even to themselves.

Of

Of their opinion concerning the tranfmigration of fouls, and the fcience of phyfiognomy.

I found the wifeft of them held the metempfychofis, or the tranfmigration of fouls *, not as a punifhment in the next life, as fome of the ancient Heathen philofophers did, but as a punifhment in this; the chief punifhment in the next was explained above. This tranfmigration of fouls is quite different from the received notion of the word. Inftead of believing, as the ancients did, that the fouls of wicked and voluptuous men, after their deaths, tranfmigrated into beafts according to the fimilitude of their vitious inclinations, till, paffing through one animal into another, they were permitted to commence men again; I fay, thefe people, inftead of believing this, hold a metempfychofis of quite a different nature; not that the fouls of men enter into brutes, but that the fouls of brutes enter into the bodies of men, even in this life. They fay, for example, that the bodies of men and women are fuch delicate habitations, that the fouls of brutes are perpetually envying them, and

---

* This notion of the tranfmigration of the fouls of brutes into men and women in this life, particularly into the latter, was not unknown to the ancients, though explained fomething after a different way: witnefs a remaining fragment of Simonides, a very ancient Greek poet, to that effect.

contriving

contriving to get into them; that, unless the divine light of reason be perpetually attended to, these brutal souls steal in upon them, and chain up the rational soul, so that it shall not be able to govern the body, unless it be to carry on the designs of the brutal soul, or at best only make some faint efforts to get out of its slavery. I took it at first, that this system was merely allegorical, to shew the similitude between the passions of men when not directed by reason, and those of brutes. But, upon examination, I found it was their opinion, that this transmigration did really happen; insomuch that in my last journey with the Pophar into Egypt, when he saw the Turks, or other strange nations, nay several Armenian and European Christians, he would say to me in his own language, There goes a hog, there goes a lion, a wolf, a fox, a dog, and the like; that is, they believe the body of a voluptuous man is possessed by the soul of a hog, of a lustful man by that of a goat, a treacherous man by that of a fox, a tyrannical man by that of a wolf, and so of the rest. This belief is instilled into them so early, and with so much care, that it is of very great benefit to keep them within the bounds of reason. If a young man finds himself inclined to any of these passions, he addresses himself immediately to some person whom he thinks of superior wisdom, who

who assures him that the soul of some certain brute is endeavouring to surprise and captivate his rational soul, and take possession of its place. This makes them always watchful, and upon their guard against their own passions, not to be surprised by such a merciless enemy. Their immediate remedy is, to look stedfastly at the divine light that shines within them, and compare it with its original, till by the force of its rays they drive away those brutal souls, which, as soon as fully discovered in their treacherous attacks, (for they come on, say they, by stealth, not daring to attack that divine light directly), are easily repulsed, before they have obtained possession, though it costs a great deal of pains to dislodge them, when once they are got in. The fear of being abandoned to the slavery of these brutal souls is so deeply imprinted in them from their infancy, that they look upon the temperance and regularity of their lives to be in a great measure owing to this doctrine. The same notions hold with their women; into whom their mothers and governesses instil them, as the wise men do to the men; only they believe the brutal souls that enter into women, are of a different species from those that enter into men. They say, for instance, that of a cameleon makes them false and inconstant; that of a peacock, coquettish and vain; that of a tygress, grefs, cruel and ill-natured ; and so of the rest. They add another difference between men and women, that when these brutal souls are entered into them, they are much harder to be driven out from them, than from the men; besides that these brutal souls will lurk undiscovered in women a great while, and are often scarce discernible, till the age of five and twenty or thirty ; whereas in most men they discover themselves presently after their entrance.

It was on account of this doctrine, as I found by repeated observations, that they were so addicted to the study of physiognomy, laying down rules to know by the countenance, the lines of the face, and unguarded looks of men, whether the brutal soul has got possession or not, in order to apply proper remedies. This science, however uncertain and doubtful among Christians, (who have greater assistance of grace and virtue to resist their passions, those treacherous invaders), is brought to greater perfection and certitude than one would imagine, among such of these people, who, having no such helps, take little care to cultivate and moderate their vitious inclinations, unless they are apprised and forewarned of the danger. Therefore their wise men, whenever they come in company of the younger sort, consider attentively with themselves all the lineaments of the countenance,

tenance, complexions, motions, habit of body, conſtitution, tone of the voice, make and turn of the face, noſe, ears, &c. but particularly they obſerve the ſtructure and glances of the eye, with innumerable ſigns proceeding from it, by which they pretend to diſcover thoſe paſſions. I ſay, they pretend to know by theſe what brutal ſoul lays ſiege to the rational ſoul, or whether it has already taken poſſeſſion of its poſt. If they are ſtrangers, they prudently take care to avoid their company, or at leaſt are on their guard not to have any dealings with them in matters obnoxious to the brutal ſoul they think them poſſeſſed by. But if the perſon attacked by theſe brutal ſouls be of their own nation, they immediately forewarn ſuch to be on his guard, by which, and the dread they have entertained from their youth of theſe brutal enemies, they are kept in ſuch order, that, as I ſaid, I never ſaw ſuch moral people in my life. The worſt is, they are extremely inclined to be proud, and have too great a value for themſelves, deſpiſing in their hearts all other nations as if they were nothing but brutes in human ſhape*.

* The Chineſe, whom I have proved to be deſcended from the firſt Egyptians, are ſubject to the like pride and contempt of other people; ſaying that all other nations have but one eye, whereas nature has given them two: ſignifying thereby, how much wiſer they think themſelves than other men.

However,

However, their wife men take as much care as possible to correct this fault, as far as the ignorance of the law of grace will allow; by putting them often in mind of the miseries and infirmities of human life, which being real evils, must be in punishment of some fault; that the most perfect are liable to death, which makes no distinction between them and the rest of the world. Besides, humility, and a commiseration for the defects of others, is one of the rays of the divine light that is to guide them. From such documents and instructions of the wiser sort, though they do not care to have any correspondence with other people, seeing them so possessed with those brutal souls, yet they are a most courteous and compassionate people in all their behaviour.

Of their laws and customs.

Over and above what has been said already of the nature and customs of these people, I shall here observe that their laws are very few in number; but then they are prodigious exact in the observance of them. I have often heard the Pophar, contrary to his custom, make very severe reflections on the lawyers of other countries, who make laws upon laws, and add precepts upon precepts, till the endless number of them makes the fundamental part to be forgotten; leaving

nothing

nothing but a confused heap of explanations; which may cause ignorant people to doubt, whether there is really any thing meant by the laws, or not. If I forbid my son, says he, to do any wrong to any one, what need is there of reckoning up all the particulars by which a person may be wronged? Shew but the fact on both sides, any man of sense and equity can tell, if there be any wrong done. For if you multiply an infinity of circumstances, it will be much more difficult to decide what is right, or what is wrong, than if you precisely and absolutely forbid all injury whatsoever. It is almost incredible, with what nicety and equity, and how soon, their judges determine the few disputes they have among them. To weigh the merits of the cause by the weight of the purse, would be counted by them one of the greatest enormities. There are no courts for disputes of this nature; all is done by laying the case before their public assemblies, or before any one or two prudent and just men; and the affair is finally decided at once. All the law for *meum* and *tuum* among them is, *Thou shalt do no wrong to any one*, without entering into any further niceties. Such explanatory suppositions, say they, oftener shew people how they may ingeniously contrive to do an injury, than how to avoid it.

Their laws therefore are nothing but

the first principles of natural justice, explained and applied by the elders, in the public hearing of all who have a mind to come in when the facts are brought into dispute.

The worship of the Deity, and that excessive and even superstitious reverence they pay to their parents, both alive and dead, is so carefully inculcated to them from their infancy, that there is no need of any written law to inforce it. They look on a man to be possessed with some brutal soul, who should pretend to call in question or neglect this duty.

There is a positive law among them, not to shed human blood voluntarily [*]. They carry this fundamental law of nature to

---

[*] These people descending from Misraim, who might know the patriarch Noah, and might have learned by tradition the punishment of Cain for the murder of his brother Abel, carried that opinion to an excess. Be these people who they will, or not be at all, I cannot but observe, how inexcusable the wickedness of men was from the beginning, without blaming God, as some libertines do, for leaving them in ignorance.

The wicked Ham, or Cham, was in the ark with Noah, and lived many years before the deluge, (the truth of which is attested by ancient history as well as by sacred scripture), and saw the dreadful punishment inflicted on the world for sin; could not he have learned godliness, and the reward for it, of his father Noah? Could not Ham have taught his own children, they theirs; and so on? But they corrupted their own ways, and thereby shewed the necessity of a revelation.

Such

such a height, that they never put any one to death, even for murder, which very rarely happens; that is, once in several ages. If it appears that a perſon has really murdered another, a thing they think almoſt impoſſible, the perſon convicted is ſhut up from all commerce of men, with proviſions to keep him alive as long as nature allows. After his death the fact is proclaimed, as it was when they ſhut him up, over all the Nomes. His name is blotted out of their genealogies; then his dead body is mangled juſt in the ſame manner as he killed the innocent, and afterwards burnt to aſhes, which are carried up to the higheſt part of the deſerts, and then toſſed up into the air, to be carried away by the winds blowing from their own country: nor is he ever more to be reckoned as one of their race, and there is a general mourning obſerved throughout the kingdom for nine days.

There is alſo an expreſs law againſt adultery and whoredom, which are likewiſe puniſhed after death. If perſons are caught in adultery, they are ſhut up apart till death; then they are expoſed naked as they were ſurpriſed, and the body of the woman treated after the moſt ignominious manner for three days. After which, they are burnt, and their aſhes diſperſed as before

fore *. Whoredom is only punished, in the man, by chaining him to a he-goat, and the woman to a salt bitch, and leading them thus round the Nome. All in the respective Nome, men and women, are to be present at the more signal punishments; and parents are obliged to explain to their children the wickedness and horror of the crime, for a warning for the future. I forgot to tell your Reverences, that if the woman brings forth by adultery, the child is preserved, till able to be carried with them when they go into Egypt, and there given to some stranger, with ample provision for its maintenance, but never to be heard of more †.

There is also one particular I should have mentioned, relating to injustice. If, for example, the elders find there has been any considerable injustice done, the criminal is obliged to restore nine times the value. If any one be convicted to have imposed upon the judges, he is to be sent out to the skirts of the country, to live by himself for a time

---

* See the learned Bishop of Meaux's universal history, concerning the Egyptians, par. 3. and of their punishments after death.

† With our author's leave, this is not such a just and compassionate part, to turn innocent children out among people whose customs they had such a horror of, only for their parents faults. For though the maxim be good, *Beware a breed;* yet the care they took of their youth, and the moral instruction they gave them, might make them abhor the crimes of their parents.

proportionable

proportionable to his guilt, with a mark on his forehead, for all persons to avoid him, lest he should instil his principles into others. All other matters are regulated rather by custom, than by laws, which will be seen, when I come to the form of their government, and other particular institutions.

Of their form of government.

Their form of government, as I had the honour to acquaint your Reverences before, is patriarchal, which they preserve inviolably, being the most tenacious people in the world of their primitive institutions. But the order of the succession is extremely particular, in order to keep up the equality of brotherhood and dignity as exact as they can. Your Reverences, I presume, remember that they all sprung from one family, (and lived as such when they were driven out of Egypt), the head of which was priest of the sun. This government they had observed ever since Misraim took possession of that land for his habitation. But when they were secured from all the world in the first vale, as was mentioned before, they established that form of government after a particular manner. The first Pophar settling in that vale with his five sons, and as many daughters with their husbands, governed

verned them during life, as father or patriarch of them all. Their prodigious veneration for their parents, and feparation from all other people, render this form infinitely more practicable than can well be imagined. As they were children of one man, the intereſt of the whole was the intereſt of every particular. All the nation of the firſt tranſmigration were children, grandchildren, or great-grandchildren of the good old man who conducted them thither. Having no wars, or voyages at fea, nor commerce with the diſtempers as well as vices of other nations, who generally differ in their way of living as well as their climate; having nothing of this, I fay, to deſtroy their people, they not only increaſed prodigiouſly, without plurality of wives, but by that and their almoſt primitive way of living, they preſerved their lives to a great old age, moſt of them living above a hundred years, and ſome above a hundred and fifty. The firſt Pophar (fay their memoirs) lived till an hundred and fifty-five, and his eldeſt ſon his fucceſſor, more robuſt ſtill, to a hundred and ſixty. Preſently after his eſtabliſhment in the firſt vale, he divided his ſmall dominions into five Nomes, or governments, under his five ſons, as was obſerved before. All were to be ſubordinate to the eldeſt; but it was only a patriarchal ſubordination, relating to the whole. The other governors,

and

and indeed all fathers of families, were entire ministers of the laws in their respective families; but these last were liable to the inspection of the more immediate superiors, and all to that of the Grand Pophar, assisted with such a number of counsellors as were established afterwards. To give your Reverences a more distinct idea of this wonderful government, it will come much to the same, whether we descend from the chief Pophar to every respective family, or from these upwards. The particularities of the succession I shall consider afterwards. However, it will be easier seen if we take them when their numbers were not so great, at the first beginning of their establishment.

The Pophar, then, having distinguished the bounds of every Nome, I mean in their first transmigration, each son took possession of it for himself and posterity. While each son's children were unmarried, they continued under the government of their father, who made use of as much land as was sufficient for the conveniencies and pleasures, as well as the necessaries of life. But as soon as any son was married, or at least when he could be called a father of a family, the father, with consent of the Pophar, allotted him likewise a sufficient quantity for the same end: so they spread and enlarged themselves as it were from the centre to to a farther extent, much in the same manner as they build their towns, till they had occupied the whole Nome. Here you will say, these people must in process of time increase *ad infinitum*, without lands sufficient to maintain them. This was really the case in the first plantation, which was so entirely occupied by them, that if the famous Pophar, who brought them into the vast continent they now enjoy, had not made that glorious discovery with the danger of his life, they must have returned into Egypt, or ate up one another; but where they are at present, they have room enough, notwithstanding their numbers, for several ages. However, I often represented to the Pophar, that it must come to that at last: the thought made him uneasy at first, and at length put him on a further discovery, as your Reverences will see in the sequel. But such vast numbers of them betaking themselves to arts and manufactures, and the country being so prodigiously fertile, there does not appear any great difficulty in that respect. Of all arts they look upon agriculture as the first in dignity next to the liberal sciences, since that nourishes all the rest; but it comes so easily, and the fruits and legumes are so rich and delicious, that they have little more trouble than to gather them: besides, having two summers, and two springs, each different

season

season produces its peculiar fruits. But to return to the idea of their government, each father of a family governs all his descendents, married or unmarried, as long as he lives. If his sons are fathers, they have a subordinate power under him; if he dies before he comes to such an age, the eldest son, or the eldest uncle, takes care of them, till they are sufficient to set up a family of themselves. The father, on extraordinary occasions, is liable to be inspected by five of the most prudent heads of that district; these by five of the five adjacent districts chosen by common consent; these last, by the heads of the five Nomes, and all the Nomes by the Grand Pophar, assisted with three hundred sixty-five elders, or senators, chosen out of every Nome. What is most particular in this government is, that they are all absolute in some manner, and independent, as looking on themselves as all equal in birth; yet in an entire dependency of natural subordination or eldership, which runs through the whole œconomy, as your Reverences will see when I come to the succession. They are in the same manner lords and proprietors of their own possessions, yet the Pophar and governors can allot and dispose of all for the public emolument, because they look on him to be as much the father of all, as the immediate natural father is of his proper children, and even in some

sense

sense their natural father by right of eldership, because they sprung originally from one man, whom the Grand Pophar represents. To this, that natural, or politic, or even superstitious respect they shew to their parents, contributes so much, that they never dispute, but, on the contrary, revere, the regulations made by their superiors; being satisfied that they are not only just and good, but that it is their own act, since it is done by virtue of a subordination to which they all belong.

The succession of eldership has something very particular, and even intricate in it. To express at the same time the superiority of the elder son, and the equality of independence, I shall endeavour to explain to your Reverences, as well as I can, the right thereof. The eldest son of the first Pophar is always Grand Pophar, when he is of age to govern, which, as I said, is at fifty at soonest; but if the direct line fails, not the uncle's son, nor any one in that Nome, but the right heir of the next Nome; and so of all the five Nomes. If they should fail in all the Nomes, the right heir of the second son of the first Nome, and so of all the rest. This, they say, has happened several times since their first establishment, which is not much to be wondered at, if they are so ancient as they pretend. Thus, though the grand popharship be confined to the eldest in some sense, in effect it belongs to them all; but if the next heir be a minor, as he is always judged to be till he is fifty years of age, the eldest of that age of the second son of the next Nome, is regent till the heir be out of his minority, and so on: insomuch that, in order to divide the superiority among them as equally as possible, he who has the next right to be Grand Pophar, is never to be regent. All other public officers, teachers of arts and sciences, overseers of all the public employments, &c. are constituted by the Grand Pophar, and sanhedrim, with associates of every Nome.

More particulars of their public œconomy.

Though, as I said, the Pophar is in some sense the proprietor of the whole country, as head of the government and chief patriarch; yet the paradox of this government consists in this, that they are joint lords, acknowledging no inequality, but merely eldership, and the respect due to dignitaries, which they esteem as their own, or redounding to themselves, because they all give their consent to their election for the public good. In a word, the whole country is only one great family governed by the laws of nature, with proper officers, constituted by the whole, for order

der and common preservation. Every individual looks on himself as a part of that great family. The Grand Pophar is the common father, esteeming all the rest as children and brothers, calling them universally by that name, as they all call one another brothers, bartering and exchanging their commodities as one brother would do with another; and not only so, but they all join in building their towns, public places, schools, &c. laying up all the stores and provisions, over and above the present consumption, in public places, for the use of the whole, with overseers and inspectors, constituted by common consent, who are to take care chiefly, that no disorder be committed. Thus every one contributes to all public expenses, feasts, and the like, which on some occasions are extremely magnificent; affecting external grandeur in all respects. Thus also every man, where-ever he goes, enters into what house he pleases, as if it were his own home; this they are doing perpetually throughout the whole country, rather visiting than merchandising; exchanging the rarities of each respective place with those of other parts, just like friends making presents to one another; so that all the roads are like streets of great towns, with people going backward and forward perpetually. They do this the more frequently to keep up a correspondence

respondence between the Nomes, lest distance of place should cause any forgetfulness of their being of one family. The plenty of the country affords them every thing that nature can call delightful, and that with such ease, that infinite numbers are employed in trades and arts, according to their genius, or inclinations; which, by their continual peace and plenty, their long establishment in one country, and under one form of government, the natural ingenuity of the people, the so early knowledge of arts, which they brought with them out of Egypt; by the improvements their wife men make in them from time to time; and from what they learn when they pay their visits to their deceased ancestors, they have brought to prodigious perfection. One may say of them, that they are all masters, and all servants; every one has his employment; generally speaking, the younger sort wait on the elders, changing their offices as is thought proper by their superiors, as in a well-regulated community. All their children universally are taught at the public expense, as children of the government, without any distinction but that of personal merit. As the persons deputed for that end, judge of their genius, or any particular inclination, they are disposed afterwards to those arts and callings for which they seem most proper; the most sublime sciences

sciences are the most in respect with them, and are chiefly the employment of their great men and governors, contrary to the custom of other countries; the reason of which is, because these being never chosen till they are fifty years of age, they have had more time to improve themselves, and generally are persons of more extensive capacities. They rightly suppose, that persons who excel others in the most rational sciences, are not only fittest to govern a rational people, but also most capable of making themselves masters of what they undertake; not but such men, knowing the governors are chosen out of that rank, have an eye in their studies to the rules and arts of governing, which are communicated at a distance by them, according to the talents they remark in the subjects. They do not do this out of any spirit of ambition, employments being rather an honorary trouble than an advantage, but for the real good of the whole. Agriculture, as I said, has the next place in honour after liberal arts; and next to that, those arts are most esteemed which are most necessary; the last of all are those which are of least use, though perhaps the most delightful.

Since every one is employed for the common good more than for themselves, perhaps persons may apprehend that this gives a check to industry, not having that spur
of

of private intereft, hoarding up riches, or aggrandizing their families, as is to be found in other nations. I was apprehenfive of this myfelf, when I came to underftand their government; but fo far from it, that poffibly there is not fuch an induftrious race of people in the univerfe. They place their great ambition in the grandeur of the country, looking on thofe as narrow and mercenary fpirits, who can prefer a part to the whole: they pride themfelves over other nations on that account; each man having a proportionable fhare in the public grandeur, the love of glory and praife feems to be their greateft paffion. Befides, their wife governors have fuch ways of ftirring up their emulation by public honours, harangues, and panegyrics in their affemblies, with a thoufand other ways of fhew and pageantry, and this for the moft minute arts, that were it not for that fraternal love ingrafted in them from their infancy, they would be in danger of raifing their emulation to too great a height. Thofe who give indications of greater wifdom and prudence in their conduct than others, are marked out for governors, and gradually raifed according to their merit. Whoever invents a new art has a ftatue erected according to the ufefulnefs of it, with his name and family inferted in public records. Whoever diftinguifhes himfelf by any particular excellency, has suitable marks of distinction paid him on public occasions, as garlands, crowns, acclamations, songs, or hymns in his praise, &c. It is incredible how such rewards as these encourage industry and arts in minds so affected with glory as these people are: on the other hand, their greatest punishments, except for capital crimes, which are punished as above, are by public disgraces.

But now I am speaking of their youth; as they look upon them as seeds of the commonwealth, which if corrupted in the bud will never bring forth fruit, so their particular care is laid out in their education, in which I believe they excel all nations. One cannot say there is one in the whole nation who may be called an idle person, though they indulge their youth very much in proper recreations, endeavouring to keep them as gay as they can, because they are naturally inclined to gravity. Besides daily recreations, they have set times and seasons for public exercises, as riding, vaulting, running, but particularly hunting wild beasts, and fishing for crocodiles and alligators, in their great lakes, which I shall describe to your Reverences on another occasion; yet they are never suffered to go alone, that is, a company of young men together without grave men and persons in authority along with them, who are a guard to them in all their actions: nay, they are

never

never suffered to sleep together, each lying in a single bed, though in a public room, with some grave person in the same room with them. Their women are kept much in the same manner, to prevent inconveniencies which I shall touch upon when I come to the education of their women: and this so universally, that as there are no idle companions to lead them into extravagancies, so there are no idle and loose women to be found to corrupt their minds. Their whole time, both for men and women, is taken up in employments, or public recreations, which, with the early care to instruct them in the fundamental principles of the morality of the country, prevents all those disorders of youth we see elsewhere. Hence too comes that strength of body and mind in their men, and modest blooming beauty in their women; so that among this people nature seems to have kept up to its primitive and original perfection. Besides, that universal likeness in them, proceeding from their conjugal fidelity and exclusion of all foreign mixture in their breed, (where all the lineaments of their ancestors, direct and collateral, meet at last in their offspring), gives the parents the comfort of seeing their own bloom and youth renewed in their children; though in my opinion this universal likeness is rather a defect; not but the treasures of nature are so inexhaustible, that

there

there are some distinguishing beauties in every face. Their young men and women meet frequently, but then it is in their public assemblies, with grave people mixed along with them. At all public exercises the women are placed in view to see and be seen, in order to inspire the young men with emulation in their performances. They are permitted to be decently familiar on those public occasions, and can chuse their lovers respectively, according to their liking, there being no such thing as doweries, or interest, but mere personal merit in the case; but more of this afterwards when I shall speak more particularly of the education of their women and marriages. This is a short sketch of the government and œconomy of a people, who are as much distinguished from the customs of others, as they are separated by their habitation and country.

Inquisitor. You seem, Sir, to have a very high idea of this patriarchal government, and look upon it according to the law of nature; I hope you don't deny but persons may be obliged by the law of nature to obey their forms of government, as well as a patriarchal one?

Gaudentio. No, Reverend Fathers, by no means, I don't enter into comparisons, but relate matter of fact. It is not to be doubted, but different forms of government may be proper for different nations;

nations; and where once a form of government is lawfully eſtabliſhed, perſons are obliged to obey, to avoid anarchy and confuſion; as for example, whoever ſhould endeavour to ſubvert a monarchical government once lawfully eſtabliſhed, muſt break in upon the laws of right and juſtice, which are obligations of the law of nature.

Inquiſitor. Read on.

Second *Inquiſitor.* Under favour, I muſt aſk him a queſtion or two firſt. I think, Signor Gaudentio, you make the Grand Pophar to be both prince and prieſt; that is, to be veſted both with temporal and ſpiritual power. Is it your opinion that the ſpiritual power is ſubject to the temporal?

Gaudentio. I ſpeak of Heathens, Reverend Fathers, and a Heatheniſh worſhip, where the Grand Pophar was both prince of the people, and chief prieſt of the ſun by his place. I acknowledge no head of the church but his Holineſs, as moſt agreeable to the primitive inſtitution of our religion.

Here he went on in his exalted notions of the ſovereign Pontiff, partly being a Roman Catholic, but chiefly, in all appearance, becauſe he was before the Inquiſition; for which reaſon the publiſher thought fit to leave it out.

Gaudentio.

Gaudentio. Is it your Reverences pleasure that I go on with my history?
Inquisitor. Ay, ay, read on.]

The education of their women, and marriages.

As for their women, the Pophar told me it was what gave them the most trouble of any thing in their whole government; that by their records their anceſtors had held frequent conſultations after what manner they were to be managed, there being great difficulties to be feared either from allowing them liberty, or keeping them under restraint. If you allow them liberty, you muſt depend on their honour, or rather caprice, for your own; if you keep them under confinement, they will be ſure to revenge themſelves the firſt opportunity; which they will find in ſpite of all you can do. The rules, ſaid he, by which men are governed, will not hold with women; ſolid reaſon, if you can make them ſenſible of it, will ſome time or other have an influence on moſt men; whereas humour is what predominates in women. Hit that, you have them; miſs it, you do nothing: and yet they are ſo far from being an indifferent thing in the commonwealth, that much more depends on the right management of them than people imagine. Licentiouſneſs of youth draws innumerable misfortunes on any government, and what greater incentives for
licentiouſneſs

licentiousness than lewd women, whether common prostitutes, wanton ladies, or adulteresses? For all loose women belong to one of these classes. Our women, continued he, are extremely beautiful, as you see; our men strong and vigorous; conjugal fidelity therefore and chastity must be the strongest bonds to keep them in their duty. As for our young men, we keep them in perpetual employment, and animate them to glory by every thing that can move generous minds; with our women, we endeavour the same by ways adapted to their genius. But our greatest care of all is, to make marriage esteemed by both parties the happiest state that can be wished for in this life. This we believe to depend on making the woman, rather than the man, happy and fixed in her choice; because, if the person be imposed upon her, contrary to her own inward inclination, dislike, or revenge, or perhaps a more shameful passion, will make her seek for relief elsewhere; and where women are not virtuous, men will be lewd. We therefore permit the woman to chuse entirely for herself, and the men to make their addresses where they please: but the woman is to distinguish her choice by some signal occasion or other, and that too not without great difficulties on both sides, which being surmounted, they esteem themselves arrived at the happy part of all their wishes.

wishes. The most ardent and tried love determines the choice: this endears the man to her on the one hand, and the difficulty of finding any woman who has not the same inducements to love her husband, leaves him no encouragement for his lawless desires among married women; and the single women are either so early engaged with their lovers, or so possessed with the notion that a married man cannot belong to her, that his suit would be entirely vain. In a word, we do not allow the least temporal interest to interfere in the choice, but rather wish our young people should be mutually attracted by esteem and affection. The whole business of courtship is to prove their constancy, and to make them so: when we are well assured of this, all obstacles are removed. We found this method to have the least inconveniencies of any, and the best means to preserve conjugal fidelity, on which the good of families so much depends.

When our nation, continued he, began to grow very populous, and the country full of riches and plenty; the promiscuous conversation of our young men and women, with some neglect on the part of the governors, was the occasion that the bounds of our innocent ancestors were not sufficient to keep them in their duty; strange disorders were crept in among our youth of both sexes;

sexes; our men grew enervated and effeminate, our women wanton and inflamed; unnatural abuses wasted their constitution; so that we lost thousands of our young men and women, without knowing what was the cause; even in the married state, the women began not to be contented with one man: on which account our ancestors had almost resolved to keep all our women from the sight of men till they were married, and then to deliver them up to their husbands, who should have a despotic right over them, as I am informed they have in other nations. They imagined this to be a certain means to ascertain the legitimacy of their children, and to prevent jealousy, the first cause, however dissembled, of the man's dislike to his wife. Others objected against this severe discipline, and said it was making the most beautiful part of the creation mere slaves, or at least mere properties; that it was to give a fatal check to the glory of a free people, to deprive the husband of the voluntary love of his moiety, and take away the most endearing part of conjugal happiness. To this the severer side answered, That the women were come to such a pass, that their abuses of liberty shewed they were scarce capable of making a proper use of it. However, a medium betwixt both carried it for that time. The injuries of the married state, and the corruption

ruption of youth, which was the occasion of it, were judged to be of such consequence to the commonwealth, that, resolved to put a stop to it at any rate, all the wise men and governors consulted together, and resolved unanimously to put the laws I mentioned against adultery and whoredom in execution, causing proclamations to be made for that intent throughout the whole empire. All corruptors of youth of both sexes were shut up immediately, with the regulations I related above, of having grave persons always in the company of young people, whether men or women. They married off all that were of age for it, as fast as they could; but quickly found the number of inhabitants did not increase as usual, their native vigour being exhausted or debilitated by their unnatural abuses. . . . .

[*Some paragraphs seem wanting in this part of Gaudentio's narrative which doubtless were very curious.*]

There is one peculiar method allowed by them, in which they differ from all other nations; for whereas these last endeavour to preserve their young people from love, lest they should throw themselves away, or make disadvantageous matches; the former, having no interested views in that respect, encourage a generous and honourable love, and make it their care to fix them in the

strictest

strictest bonds they can, as soon as they judge, by their age and constitution, of their inclinations: this they do sometimes by applauding their choice, but mostly by raising vast difficulties, contrived on purpose, both to try and enhance their constancy. They have histories and stories of heroic examples of fidelity and constancy in both sexes; but particularly for the young women, by which they are taught rather to suffer ten thousand deaths, than violate their plighted faith. One may say they are a nation of faithful lovers; the longer they live together, the more their friendship increases, and infidelity in either sex is looked upon as a capital crime. Add to this, that being all of the same rank and quality, except the regard paid to eldership, and public employments; nothing but personal merit, and a liking of each other, determines the choice; there must be signal proofs produced, that the woman prefers the man before all others, as his service must be distinguished in the same manner. Where this is approved of by the governors or elders, if the woman insists on her demands, it is an inviolable law that that man must be her husband. Their hands are first joined together in public, then they clasp each other in the closest embrace, in which posture the elder of the place, to shew that this union is never to be dissolved, takes a circle of the finest tem-

pered

pered steel, woven with flowers, and first lays it over their necks, as they are thus clasping each other, then round their waists, and last of all round their breasts, or hearts, to signify that the ardency of their love must terminate in an indissoluble friendship; which is followed by infinite acclamations and congratulations of the whole assembly. I believe the world cannot furnish such examples of conjugal chastity as are preserved between them by these means. Widowers and widows never marry single persons, and but rarely at all, except left young; when they are to gain each other as before. By such prudent precautions infinite disorders and misfortunes to the commonwealth are prevented, proceeding not only from disproportionate and forced marriages, but from the licentiousness of idle persons, who either marry for money, or live on the spoil of other people, till they can get an advantageous match. This is a short sketch of their government and customs, which I thought would not be unacceptable to your Reverences, though a great many other customs of less moment will occur in the sequel of my life, to which I now return.

The Pophar regent made choice of me for one of his attending companions, with the other young men who came home with us;

us; he had a great many other attendants and officers, deputed by common confent to wait his orders as regent; thefe were changed every five years, as were thofe attending the governors of the other Nomes, on account of improvement; for, being all of equal quality, they endeavour to give them as equal an education as is poffible, changing their employments, and waiting on one another in their turns, by the appointment of their refpective governors, except thofe whofe genius or choice determines them to arts and fciences, according to their œconomy defcribed before. I muft only add, that having fuch a high value for their race, no one thinks it a difgrace to perform the meaneft offices, being all to be attended in like manner themfelves when it comes to their turns, each looking on the honours done to every branch of their government, as their own. Hence all their public ranks and ceremonies are the moft magnificent that can be imagined; there is fcarce any thing done even in entertainments between the private tribes, but there are proper officers deputed for it, and all expenfes paid out of the common ftock, with deputies and overfeers for every thing. Their houfes are all open to one another with a long gallery, which runs from the end of one range of building to the other. The womens apartments join together;

with the men of each family joining to their own women, that is, their wives, sisters, and daughters. The women have their subaltern officers like the men. The first apartment of every break of a street belongs to the men, then the womens belonging to them, then the women of the next family joining to them, and their men beyond them, and so on, with large public halls at proper distances for public assemblies; so that every thing they do is a sort of paradox to us, for they are the freest and yet strictest people in the world, the whole nation, as I observed before, being more like one universal regular college, or community, than any thing else. The women are perpetually employed as well as the men; it is their business to work all the fine garments for themselves and the men, which being much the same except devices and flowers for their friends and lovers, are made with less difficulty; the chief difference is in the wearing them. But the chief distinction of sexes is in the ornaments of their necks, and hair. Crowns and fillets are worn by all, just after the model of the little picture your Reverences saw in the cabinet; all their tapestry, embroidery, and the like, with infinite other curiosities, are the works of their women, so that the chief qualification of their women or ladies, for they are all such, is to excel at the loom, needle, or distaff. Since

I

I came there, by the Pophar's defire, they have added that of painting, in which I believe, the vivacity of their genius will make them excel all the reft of the world. Not teaching for hire, I thought it no difgrace in me to inftruct fuch amiable fcholars in an art no man ought to be afhamed of. It is a thing unknown with thefe people for young ladies of any degree, or even young men, to have nothing elfe to mind or think of but vifits and drefs. When I gave them an account of the lives of our quality and gentry, they cried out, What barbarians! Can any thing become beauty more than knowledge and ingenuity? They feemed to have fuch a contempt, and even a horror for a life of that nature, that the young ladies afked me with great concern, if our ladies had any lovers? as if it were impoffible to love a woman who had nothing to recommend her, but what nature gave her. In fine, by the defcription I gave of the idle life of our ladies, they judged them to be no more than beautiful brutes. They afked me alfo, if I did not think myfelf fortunate by my captivity, where I met with ladies, who thought the ornaments of the mind more defirable than thofe of the body, and told me they imputed what they faw in me, to my good fortune of being born of their race by the mother's fide; nay, could fcarce believe but my father had a mixture of of their blood some way or other. I assured them, I esteemed myself very happy to be in the midst of so many charms of body and mind; and added, that though they had the inestimable happiness of being born all of one race, without any mixture of foreign vices, yet, in effect, all the world were originally brothers and sisters, as springing from one pair, since men and women did not rise out of the ground like mushrooms. This I said, to give them a little hint of natural and revealed religion, which are inseparably linked together. But to return to myself: The Pophar being my nearest relation, took me into his own family, as his constant companion and attendant, when he was not on the public concerns; where I likewise accompanied him sometimes, and received most distinguishing marks of his favour. He would often confer with me, and instruct me in their ways and customs, and the polity of their government, inquiring frequently into the particularities of our governments, both civil and religious. He never endeavoured to persuade me to conform to their religious ceremonies, and my own good sense told me it was prudence not to meddle with them.. I rather thought he seemed inclined to have more favourable sentiments of our religion, as such, than his own, though he was prodigiously bigotted to their civil customs.; saying,

saying, it was impossible ever to preserve a commonwealth, when they did not live up to their laws; which should be as few, and as simple as possible. For when once people come to break in upon fundamentals, all subsequent laws would not have half the strength as primary ones. To these he added many other reflections, that shewed him a man of consummate wisdom, and worthy the high post he bore. He had had two sons, both dead, and two daughters living; the one was about ten years old, when I arrived there, (it is she your Reverences saw in that picture), the other born the year before the Pophar set out for Grand Cairo. His lady, much younger than himself, shewed such fresh remains of beauty, as demonstrated that nothing but what sprung from herself, could equal her; both the Pophar and his consort looked on me as their own son, nor could I expect greater favour had I really been so. I took all the care imaginable not to render myself unworthy of it, and both revered and loved them beyond what I am able to express; though indeed, as I observed, the whole race of them was nothing but a kingdom of brothers and friends; no man having the least suspicion or fear of one another. They were so habituated to the observance of their laws, by their natural dispositions and the never-ceasing vigilancy of their governors, that they

they seemed to have a greater horror for the breach of their laws, than the punishments attending it; saying, that infinite disorders might be committed by the malicious inventions of men, if there was nothing but fear to keep them in their duty. Such force has education and the light of nature rightly cultivated; for myself I was left to follow what liberal employment I had a mind to. Philosophy, music, and painting had been the chief part of my study and diversion, till my unhappy captivity and the loss of my brother; but as I was fallen among a nation of philosophers, that noble science, the mistress of all others, made up the more serious part of my employment; though at some times, by the Pophar regent's earnest desire, I applied myself to the other two, particularly painting. They had a great many old-fashioned musical instruments, and an infinite number of performers in their way, who attended their feasts and public rejoicings; but their music, both vocal and instrumental, was not near so perfect as one might have expected of so polite a people, and did not come up to the elevated genius of our Italians. Their philosophy chiefly turned on the more useful part of it, that is, the mathematics and direction of nature: in the moral part of it they have a system, or rather notion, of which I forgot to acquaint your
                                    Reverences

Reverences before; it is a too high and exalted notion of providence, if that expreſſion may be allowed, by which they imagine all things to be ſo governed in this world, that whatever injury a man does to another, it will be returned upon him or his poſterity, even in this world, in the ſame manner, or even in a greater degree, than what he did to others.

[*Inquiſitor.* You will be pleaſed to explain your own ſentiments in this particular, ſince we hope you don't deny that fundamental law of nature and religion, *viz.* That the divine providence preſides over all things; and as for ſublunary things, we preſume you believe that providence does not only ſhew itſelf in the wonderful production and harmony conſpicuous in all natural cauſes and effects, beyond all the wit and art of men; but alſo over the moral part, that is, the free actions of men, by ſuitable rewards and puniſhments in this world or the next, to make an equal and juſt compenſation for all the good and evil of this life, as God is the juſt and equal father of all. So pray explain yourſelf, that we may know your real ſentiments on that head.

Gaudentio. I hope, Reverend Fathers, I ſhall convince you, my ſentiments are really orthodox in this point; no man has

has more reason to magnify Providence than myself; but Heathenish people may carry a just belief to superstition. That there is a providence over the physical part of the world, no man who has any just knowledge in nature can be ignorant, since he may be convinced by the least insect, every thing being adapted to its peculiar ends, with such art and knowledge in the author of it, that all the art and knowledge of men cannot do the like; and by consequence not being able to make itself, it must be produced by a cause infinitely knowing and foreseeing. Then, as to the moral part of the world, the same reason shews, that since the great creator descends so low as to take care of the least insect, it is incredible to think that the noblest part of the world, that is, the free actions of men, should be without his care. But as he has given them the glorious endowments of free will, the same providence knows how to adapt the direction of them by ways and means suitable to their beings; that is, by letting them know his will, and proposing suitable rewards and punishments for their good and bad actions; which rewards and punishments, it is evident, are not always seen in this life, since the wicked often prosper, and the good

good suffer, but by consequence must be reserved for another state.

But these people not having a just notion of the next life, though they believe a future state, carry matters so far, that they think every injury done to another, will be some way or other retaliated upon the aggressor, or his posterity, in this life; only they say, the punishment always falls the heavier the longer it is deferred. In this manner do they account for all the revolutions of the earth, that one wicked action is punished by another; that the descendents of the greatest monarchs have been lost in beggary for almost endless generations, and the persons that dispossessed them treated after the same manner by some of the descendents of the former; and so on: which notion, in my opinion, is not just, since a sincere repentance may wipe off the most grievous offences. But as persons, generally speaking, are more sensibly touched with the punishments of this life, it is not to be doubted but there are often most signal marks of avenging providence in this life, in order to deter the wicked.

Inquisitor. Go on.]

Finding the Pophar had a prodigious fancy for painting, by some indifferent pieces he had picked up, I applied myself, with

with extraordinary diligence, to that art, particularly since he would have me teach his daughter, whose unparallelled charms, though but in the bud, made me insensible to all others. By frequent drawing, I not only pleased him and others, but almost myself; every one there, men and women, were to follow some art or science; the Pophar desired me to impart my art to some of the young people of both sexes, saying there were very great encouragements for the inventors of any new arts, which I might justly claim a title to. I did so, and before I left the place, I had the pleasure to see some of them equal, or even excelling their master.

These were the chief employments of my leisure-hours; though I was forced to leave them for considerable intervals, to attend the Regent in the private visitations of his charge, which he did frequently from time to time, sometimes to one Nome, sometimes to another, having an eye over all, both officers and people. These visitations were rather preservatives against, than remedies for, any disorders. He used to say, that the commonwealth was like a great machine with different movements, which if frequently visited by the artist, the least flaw being taken notice of in time, was not only soon remedied, but was a means of preserving all the rest in a constant and regular

gular motion; but if neglected, would soon disorder the motions of the other parts, and either cost a great deal to repair, or bring the whole machine to destruction. Unless on public solemnities, which were always very magnificent, the Pophar (not to burden his people) went about without any great train, accompanied by only an assisting elder or two, the young Pophar, and myself. He had frequent conversations with the subalterns, and even with the meanest artisans, calling them his children; and they having recourse to him as their common father. For the first five years of his regency, the only difficulty we had of any moment to determine was an affair of the most delicate nature I ever heard: though it does not concern myself, I shall relate it to your Reverences for the peculiar circumstances of it, being a case entirely new, as well as unprovided for by the laws of their constitution.

The case was this: Two twin-brothers had fallen in love with the same woman, and she with them. The men and the woman lived in different parts of the same Nome, and met accidentally at one of their great solemnities; it was at the feast of the sun, which is kept twice a-year, because, as I informed your Reverences, their kingdom lies between the tropics, but more on this side the line than the other. This situation is the occasion that they have two springs and two summers. At the beginning of each spring, there are great feasts in every Nome, in honour of the sun; they are held in the open fields, in testimony of his being the immediate cause (in their opinion) of the production of all things. All the sacrifice they offer to him are five little pyramids of incense, according to the number of their Nomes, placed on the altar in plates of gold till they take fire of themselves. Five young men and as many women are deputed by the governors to perform the office of placing the pyramids of incense on the altar: they are clad in their spangled robes of the colour of the Nome, with crowns on their heads, marching up two by two, a man and a woman, between two rows of young men and women, placed theatre-wise one above another; and make the most beautiful show that eyes can behold. It happened that one of the twin-brothers was deputed, with the young lady I am speaking of, to make the first couple for the placing the incense on the altar. They marched up on different sides till they came to the altar: when they have placed the incense, they salute each other, and cross down, the men by the ranks of the women, and the women by the men, which they do with a wonderful grace becoming such an august assembly. The design of this

this is to encourage a decorum in the carriage of the young people, and to give them a fight of each other in their greatest luftre. When the five couple have performed their ceremony, the other ranks come two by two to the altar, faluting each other, and crofling as before; by which means the young people have an opportunity of feeing every man and woman of the whole company, though the placing of them is done by lot. If they have not any engagement before, they generally take the firft liking to one another at fuch interviews, and the woman's love and choice being what determines the marriage, without any view of intereft, being, as I faid, all equal in quality, the young gallants make it their bufinefs to gain the affection of the perfon they like by their future fervices. To prevent inconveniencies of rivalfhip at the beginning, if the man be the perfon the woman likes, he prefents her with a flower juft in the bud, which fhe takes and puts in her breaft. If fhe is engaged before, fhe fhews him one, to fignify her engagement; which if in the bud only, fhews the courtfhip is gone no further than the firft propofal and liking; if half blown, or the like, it is an emblem of further progrefs; if full blown, it fignifies that her choice is determined, from whence they can never recede; that is, fhe can change the man that prefents it, but he cannot

cannot challenge her till she has worn it publicly. If any dislike should happen after that, they are to be shut up, never to have any husband. If she has no engagement, but does not approve of the person, she makes him a low courtesy, with her eyes shut till he is gone away. The women, it is true, for all this, have some little coquettish arts, dissembling their affections now and then, but not often. If the man be engaged, he wears some favour or other to shew it; if he likes not the woman, he presents her with nothing; if the woman should make some extraordinary advances, without any of his side, she has liberty to live a maid, or to be disposed of among the widows, being looked upon as such, who, by the by, marry none but widowers. But to return to the twins. It happened that the brother who went with the lady to the altar, seeing she had no bud upon her breast, fell in love with her, and she with him; the awe of the ceremony hindered them from taking any further notice of one another at that time. As she went down the ranks, the other brother saw her, and fell in love with her likewise, and contrives to meet her with a bud in his hand, just as the ceremony ended; which she accepts of, taking him to be the person who had marched up with her to the altar; but being obliged to go off with the other young ladies, whether the

concern

concern she had been in, in performing the ceremony before such an illustrious assembly, or the heat of the weather, or the joy she conceived in finding her affection reciprocal, or all together, had such an effect, that she fell into a fainting-fit among her companions; who opening her bosom in haste, not minding the flower, it fell down, and was trod under foot. Just as she was recovered, the brother who performed the ceremony, came up and presented his bud; she thinking it had been that she had lost, received it with a look that shewed he had made a greater progress in her affections than what that flower expressed. The laws not permitting any further conversation at that juncture, they retired to their respective habitations. Some time after, the brother who had the luck to present the first flower, whom for distinction I shall call the younger brother, as he really was, found a way to make her a visit by stealth, at a grated window, which, as I observed, was publicly prohibited by the wise governors, but privately connived at to enhance their love. He came to her, and, after some amorous conversation, makes bold to present her the more advanced mark of his affection; which she accepted of, and gave him in return a scarf worked with hearts separated by little brambles, to shew there were some difficulties for him to overcome yet: however, they

they gave one another mutual assurances of love, and he was permitted to profess himself her lover, without declaring her name, for some private reasons she had. Not long after, the elder brother came, and procured an opportunity of meeting her at the same window. The night was very dark, so that he could not see the second flower which she had in her bosom; only she received him with greater signs of joy and freedom than he expected; but reflecting on the signs he had remarked in her countenance, and after her illness by a sort of natural vanity for his own merits, flattered himself that her passion was rather greater than his, excused himself for being so long without seeing her, and added, that if he were to be guided by the height of his flame, he would see her every night. She reflecting how lately she had seen him, thought his diligence was very extraordinary, but imputed it to the ardour of his passion; in fine, she gave him such assured signs of love, that he thought in himself he might pass the middle ceremony, and present her with the full-blown flower, to make sure of her. She took it; but told him she would not wear it for some time, till she had passed some forms, and had further proof of his constancy; but, for his confirmation of her affection, she put out her hand as far as the grate would permit,
which

which he kiffed with all the ardours of an inflamed lover, giving her a thoufand affurances of his fidelity, and fhe in return gave him a riband with two hearts interwoven with her own hair, feparated only with a little hedge of pomegranates almoft ripe, to fhew that the time of gathering the fruit was nigh at hand. Thus were the three lovers in the greateft degree of happinefs imaginable; the brothers wore her favours on all public occafions, congratulating each other for the fuccefs in their amours; but, as lovers affect a fecrecy in all they do, never telling one another who were the objects of their affection. The next great feaft drew on, when the younger brother thought it was time to prefent the laft mark of his affection in order to demand her in marriage, which was ufually performed in thofe public folemnities. He told her he hoped it was now time to reward his flame, by wearing the open flower, as a full fign of her confent, and gave her a full-blown artificial carnation, with gold flames and little hearts on the leaves, interwoven with wonderful art and ingenuity. She thinking it had been a repetition of the ardour of his affection, took it, and put it in her bofom with all the marks of tendernefs, by which the fair fex in all countries know how to reward all the pains of their lovers in a moment. Upon this he refolved to afk her of her parents;

rents; which was the only thing neceſſary on his ſide, the woman having right to demand any man's ſon in the kingdom, if he had but preſented her with the laſt mark of his affection. The elder brother having given in his ſome time before, thought the parents approbation was the only thing wanting on his ſide, and reſolves the ſame day on the ſame thing. They were ſtrangely ſurpriſed to meet one another; but ſeeing the different favours, they did not know what to make of it. When the father came, they declared the cauſe of their coming, in terms which fully expreſſed the agony of their minds: the father was in as great concern as they were, aſſuring them he had but one daughter, who, he was confident, would never give ſuch encouragement to two lovers at the ſame time, contrary to their laws; but ſeeing their extreme likeneſs, he gueſſed there muſt be ſome miſtake. Upon this the daughter was ſent for; who, being informed it was to declare her conſent in the choice of her lover, came down with four flowers in her boſom, not thinking but the two full blown had belonged to the ſame perſon, ſince ſhe had received two before ſhe had worn the fiſt. The deſcription the poets give of the goddeſs Venus riſing out of the ſea, could not be more beautiful than the bloom that appeared in her cheeks when ſhe came into

the

the room. I happened to be there prefent, being fent before by the Pophar, to let the father know of the regent's intended vifit; that being a confiderable officer, he might order his concerns accordingly. As foon as the young lady heard the caufe of their coming, and faw them indiftinguifhably like each other, with the public figns of her favours wrought with her own hand, which they brought along with them, fhe fcreamed out, " I am betrayed!" and immediately fell in a fwoon, flat on the floor, almoft between her two lovers. The father, in a condition very little better, fell down by his daughter, and bathing her with his tears, called to her to open her eyes, or he muft die along with her. The young men ftood like ftatues, with rage and defpair in their looks at the fame time. I being the only indifferent perfon in the room, though extremely furprifed at the event, called her mother and women to come to her affiftance; who carried her into another room, undreffed her, and, by proper remedies, brought her at laft to herfelf. The firft word fhe faid was, " Oh! Berilla, what have you done?" All the reft was nothing but fobs and fighs, enough to melt the hardeft heart. When fhe was in a condition to explain herfelf, fhe declared, fhe liked the perfon of the man who went up with her to the altar; that fome time after the fame perfon, as fhe thought,

thought, had presented her with the first marks of his affection, which she accepted of, and in fine had given her consent by wearing the full-blown flower; but which of the two brothers it belonged to, she could not tell; adding, that she was willing to submit to the decision of the elders, or to undergo what punishment they thought fit for her heedless indiscretion; but protested, that she never designed to entertain two persons at the same time, but took them to be the same person. The care of their marriages being one of the fundamentals of their government, and there being no provision in the law for this extraordinary case, the matter was referred to the Pophar regent, who was to be there in a few days: guards in the mean time were set over the brothers, for fear of mischief, till a full hearing. The affair was discussed before the Pophar regent, and the rest of the elders of the place. The three lovers appeared before them, each in such agony as cannot be expressed. The brothers were so alike, it was hard to distinguish one from the other. The regent asked them, which of the two went up to the altar with the young lady; the elder said it was he; which the younger did not deny. The lady being interrogated, owned she designed to entertain the person that went up with her to the altar, but went no further than the first liking.
Then

Then they asked which of the two brothers gave the first flower; the younger said, he presumed he did, since he fell in love with her as she went down the ranks, and contrived to give her the flower as soon as the ceremony was over, not knowing of his brother's affection, neither did she bear any mark of engagement, but accepted of his service; the lady likewise owning the receipt of such a flower, but that she lost it, fainting away in the croud; but when, as she thought, he restored it to her, she did not like him quite so well, as when she received it the first time, supposing them to be the same person. Being asked who gave her the second, third, and last mark of engagement, it appeared to be the younger brother, whose flower she wore publicly in her bosom; but then she received the full-blown flower from the elder brother also. The judges looked at one another for some time, not knowing well what to say to the matter. Then the regent asked her, when she gave her consent, if she did not understand the person to be him that went up with her to the altar? She owned she did; which was the elder: but in fact had placed her affections on the person who gave her the first flower, which was the younger. Then the two brothers were placed before her, and she was asked, that, supposing she were now at liberty, without any engagement,

ment, which of the two brothers she would chuse for her husband? she stopped, and blushed at the question, but at length said, the younger had been more assiduous in his courtship; and with that burst into tears, casting a look at the younger brother, which easily shewed the sentiments of her heart. Every one was in the last suspense how the regent would determine the case; and the young men expressed such a concern in their looks, as if the final sentence of life and death, happiness or misery, was to be pronounced to them. When the regent, with a countenance partly severe as well as grave, turning towards the young lady, Daughter, said he, your ill fortune, or indiscretion, has deprived you from having either of them: both you cannot have, and you have given both an equal right; if either of them will give up their right, you may marry the other, not else. What do you say, sons? says he, will you contribute to make one of you happy? They both persisted they would not give up their right till the last gasp. Then, says the regent, turning to the lady, who was almost dead with fear and confusion, since neither of them will give up their right, I pronounce sentence on you to be shut up from the commerce of men, till the death of one of your lovers; then it shall be left to your choice to marry the surviver. So giving orders to have her taken

away,

away, the court was going to break up, when the younger brother falling on his knees, cries out, I yield my right, rather than the adorable Berilla should be miserable on my account; let me be shut up from the commerce of men, for being the occasion of so divine a creature's misfortune. Brother, take her, and be happy; and you, divine Berilla, only pardon the confusion my innocent love has brought upon you; and then I shall leave the world in peace. Here the whole court rose up, and the young man was going out, when the regent stopped him; Hold, son, says he, there is a greater happiness preparing for you than you expect; Berilla is yours, you alone deserve her, you prefer her good to your own; and as I find her real love is for you, here join your hands, as I find your hearts are already. They were married immediately; the regent leaving behind him a vast idea, not only of his justice, but wisdom, in so intricate a case. I drew an historical piece of painting of this remarkable trial, expressing as nigh as I could the postures and agonies of the three lovers, and presented it to the divine Isyphena, the regent's daughter, telling her, that if she were to accept of flowers, as that young lady did, she would ruin all the youths of Mezorania. She received it blushing, and said she should never receive any but from one hand, nor even that, if she thought she should do him any harm; adding, that she thought her father had given a just judgment; then waved the discourse with such innocence, yet knowledge of what she said, that I was surprised to the last degree; not being able to guess whether I had offended her or not.

These visitations in the company of the Pophar, gave me an opportunity of seeing all the different parts and chief curiosities of the whole empire. Their great towns, especially the heads of every Nome, were built, as I said, much after the same form, differing chiefly in the situation, and are principally designed for the winter-residence, for their courts and colleges, but particularly for instructing and polishing their youth of both sexes; and such admirable care and œconomy, to avoid all dissoluteness and idleness, that, as I observed before, there is no such thing known, as for persons to have no other business on their hands but visits and dress; esteeming those no better than brutes and barbarians, who are not constantly employed in improving their natural talents in some art or science. Their villas, or places of pleasure, are scattered all over the country, with most beautiful variety : the villages and towns built for manufactures, trades, conveniency of agriculture, &c. are innumerable; their canals, and great lakes, some of them like
little

little seas, are very frequent, according as the nature of the country will allow; with pleasure-houses and pavilions, built at due distances round the borders, interspersed with islands and groves, some natural, some artificial, where at proper seasons you might see thousands of boats skimming backwards and forwards, both for pleasure and the profit of catching fish, of which there is an inexhaustible store. There are also vast forests of infinite variety and delight, distinguished here and there with theatrical spaces or lawns, either natural, or cut out by art, for the conveniency of pitching their tents in the hot seasons, with such romantic scenes of deep vales, hanging woods, and precipices, natural falls, and cascades, or rather cataracts of water over the rocks, that all the decorations of art are nothing but foils and shadows to those majestic beauties of nature; besides glorious prospects of different kinds over the edges of the mountains where we passed in our visitations, sometimes presenting us with a boundless view over the most delicious plains in the world; in other places, having our view terminated with other winding hills, exhaling their reviving perfumes from innumerable species of natural fruits and odoriferous shrubs. Travelling thus by easy journeys, staying or advancing in our progress as we thought fit, I had an opportunity of admiring with infinite delight the effects of induftry and liberty, in a country where nature and art feemed to vie with each other in their different productions, There was another extraordinary fatisfaction I received in thefe vifitations, which was the opportunity of feeing, and partaking of their grand matches, or rather companies, if I may ufe the expreffion, of hunting and fifhing. All the young people with their governors, or all who are able or willing to go, at particular feafons difperfe themfelves for thefe hunts all over the kingdom: the country being fo prodigious fertile, that it furnifhes them, almoft fpontaneoufly, with whatever is neceffary, or even delectable for life, the people living in fome meafure in common, and having no other intereft but that of a well-regulated community. They leave the towns at certain feafons, and go and live in tents for the conveniency of hunting and fifhing, according as the country and feafons are proper for each recreation; the flat part of the country (though it is generally more hilly than champaign) is ftocked with prodigious quantities of fowl and game, as pheafants, partridges of different kinds, much larger than our wild hens; turkeys, and peacocks, with other fpecies of game, which we have not in Italy; hares almoft innumerable, but no coneys that ever I faw; unlefs we call coneys a leffer fort of hare, which

which feed and run along the cliffs and rocks, but don't burrow as ours do. There is alſo a ſmall ſort of wild goat, much leſs than ours, not very fleet, of a very high taſte, and prodigious fat. They take vaſt quantities of all ſorts, but ſtill leave ſufficient ſtock to ſupply next ſeaſon, except hurtful beaſts, which they kill whenever they can. But their great hunts are in the mountains, and woodland parts of the country, where the foreſts are full of infinite quantities of maſt and fruits, and other food for wild beaſts of all kinds; but particularly ſtags of four or five different ſpecies; ſome of which, almoſt as big as a horſe, keep in the wildeſt parts, whoſe fleſh they dry and ſeaſon with ſpices, and is the richeſt food I ever taſted. Their wild ſwine are of two kinds, ſome vaſtly large, others very little, not much bigger than a lamb, but prodigious fierce. This laſt is moſt delicate meat, feeding on the maſts and wild fruits in the thickeſt part of the groves; and multiplying exceedingly, where they are not diſturbed, one ſow bringing ſixteen or eighteen pigs; ſo that I have ſeen thouſands of them caught at one hunting-match, and ſent in preſents to the other parts of the kingdom, where they have none; which is their way in all their recreations, having perſons appointed to carry the rarities of the country to one another, and to the governors,

nors, parents, and friends left behind. When they go out to their grand hunt, they chuse some open vale, or vast lawn, as far in the wild forests as they can; where they pitch their tents, and make their rendezvous: then they send out their most courageous young men, in small bodies, of ten in a company, well-armed, each with his spear and his fusil flung on his back, which last of late years they find more serviceable against the wild beasts than spears, having got samples of them from Persia. These go quietly through the wildest parts of the forest at proper distances, so as to meet at such a place, which is to view the ground, and find a place proper to make their stand, and pitch their toils. They are often several days out about this; but are to make no noise, nor kill any wild beast, unless attacked, or they come upon him in his couch, at unawares, that they may not disturb the rest. When they have made their report, several thousands of them surround a considerable part of the forest, standing close together for their mutual assistance, making as great a noise as they can, with dogs, drums, and rattles, and other noisy instruments, to frighten the game towards the centre, that none may escape the circle. When this is done, all advance in a breast, encouraging their dogs, sounding their horns, beating their drums and rattles,

tles, that the most courageous beasts are all roused, and run before them towards the centre, till by this means they have driven together several hundreds of wild beasts, lions, tygers, elks, wild boars, stags, foxes, hares, and in fine all sorts of beasts that were within that circle. It is most terrible to see such a heap of cruel beasts gathered together, grinning and roaring at one another, in a most frightful manner: but the wild boar is the master of all. Whoever comes near him in that rage, even the largest lion, he strikes at him with his tusks, and makes him keep his distance. When they are brought within a proper compass, they pitch their toils round them, and inclose them in, every man joining close to his neighbour, holding out their spears to keep them off. If any beast should endeavour to make his escape, which some will do now and then (particularly the wild boars), they run against the points of the spears, and make very martial sport. I was told, that a prodigious wild sow once broke through three files of spears, overturned the men, and made a gap, that set all the rest a running almost in a body that way, so that the people were forced to let them take their career, and lost all their labour. But now they have men ready with their fusils to drop any beast that should offer to turn ahead. When they are inclosed,

there

there is moſt terrible work, the greateſt beaſts fighting and goring one another, for rage and ſpite, and the more fearful running into the toils for ſhelter. Then our men with their fuſils drop the largeſt as faſt as they can. When they intend to ſhoot the wild boars, three or four aim at him at a time, to be ſure to drop him or diſable him, otherwiſe he runs full at the laſt that wounded him, with ſuch fury, that ſometimes he will break through the ſtrongeſt toils ; but his companions all join their ſpears to keep him off. When they have dropped all that are dangerous, and as many as they have a mind, they open their toils, and diſpatch all that are gaſping. I have known above five hundred head of beaſts of all ſorts killed in one day. When all is over, they carry off their ſpoil to the rendezvous, feaſting and rejoicing, and ſending preſents as before.

There is oftentimes very great danger, when they go through the woods to make diſcovery of their haunts ; becauſe, if, in ſmall companies, ſome ſtubborn beaſt or other will attack them directly ; every man, therefore, as I ſaid, has a fuſil flung at his back, and his ſpear in his hand for his defence. Being once in one of their parties, we came upon a prodigious wild boar, as he was lying in his haunt ; ſome of us were for paſſing by him, but I thought ſuch a

noble

noble prey was not to be let go; fo we furrounded him, and drew up to him, with more courage and curiofity, than prudence; one of my companions, who was my intimate friend, being one of thofe who conducted me over the deferts, went up nigher to him than the reft, with his fpear in his hands, ftretched out ready to receive him, in cafe he fhould come at him; at which the beaft ftarted up of a fudden, with a noife that would have terrified the ftouteft hero, and made at him with fuch a fury, that we gave him for loft. He ftood his ground with fo much courage, and held his fpear fo firm and exact, that he run it directly up the mouth of the beaft, quite into the inner part of his throat; the boar roared, and fhook his head in a terrible manner, endeavouring to get the fpear out, which if he had done, all the world could not have faved the young man. I, feeing the danger, ran in with the fame precipitancy, and clapping the muzzle of my gun almoft clofe to his fide, a little behind his forefhoulder, fhot him quite through the body; fo he dropped down dead before us. Juft as we thought the danger was over, the fow, hearing his cry, came rufhing on us, and that fo fuddenly, that before I could turn myfelf with my fpear, fhe ftruck at me behind with her fnout, and pufhing on, knocked me down with her impetuofity;

and

and the place being a little fhelving, fhe came tumbling quite over me, which was the occafion of faving my life. Afhamed of the foil, but very well apprifed of the danger, I was fcarce got up on my feet, and on my guard, when, making at me alone, though my companions came in to my affiftance, fhe pufhed at me a fecond time with equal fury. I held my fpear with all my might, thinking to take her in the mouth; but miffing my aim, I took her juft in the throat, where the head and neck join, and thruft my fpear with fuch force, her own career meeting me, that I ftruck quite through her windpipe, the fpear fticking fo faft in her neck-bone, that when fhe dropt, we could fcarce get it out again. She toffed and reeled her head a good while before fhe fell; but her windpipe being cut, and bleeding inwardly, fhe was choaked. My companions had hit her with their fpears on the fides and back; but her hide and briftles were fo thick and hard, they did her very little damage. They all applauded my courage and victory, as if I had killed both the fwine. But I, as juftice required, gave the greateft part of the glory, for the death of the boar, to the courageous dexterity of the young man, who had expofed himfelf fo generoufly, and hit him fo exact in the throat. We left the carcafes there, not being able to take them with us; but

but marking the place, we came afterwards with some others to carry them off. I had the honour to carry the boar's head on the point of my spear; which I would have given to the young man, but he refused it, saying, that I had not only killed it, but saved his life into the bargain. The honour being judged to me by every one, I sent it as a present to the divine Hyphena; a thing allowed by their customs, though as yet I never durst make any declarations of love : she accepted of it, but added, she hoped I would make no more such presents; and explained herself no further.

These people having no wars, nor single combats with one another, which last are not allowed for fear of destroying their own species, have no other way of shewing their courage, but against wild beasts; where, without waiting for any express order of their superiors, they will expose themselves to a great degree, and sometimes perform exploits worthy the greatest heroes.

Their fishing is of two kinds; one for recreation and profit; the other to destroy the crocodiles and alligators, which are only found in the great lakes, and the rivers that run into them, and that in the hotter and champaign parts of the country. In some of the lakes, even the largest, they cannot live; in others they breed prodigiously. As they fish for them only to destroy them,

them, they chufe the propereft time for this purpofe, that is, when the eggs are hatching; which is done in the hot fands, by the fides of the rivers and lakes. The old ones are not only very ravenous at that time, but lie lurking in the water near their eggs, and are fo prodigious fierce, that there is no taking their eggs, unlefs you firft contrive to kill the old ones. Their way to fifh for them is this: They beat at a diftance, by the fides of the rivers and lakes, where they breed, which makes the old ones hide themfelves in the water. Then twenty or thirty of the young men row quietly backward and forward on the water where they fuppofe the creatures are; having a great many ftrong lines with hooks, made after the manner of fifh-hooks, well armed as far as the throat of the amimal reaches. Thefe hooks they faften under the wings of ducks and water-fowls, kept for the purpofe, which they let drop out of the boat, and fwim about the lake. Whenever the ducks come over the places where the creatures are, thefe laft ftrike at them, and fwallow the poor ducks immediately, and fo hook themfelves, with the violence and check of the boat. As foon as one is hooked, they tow him, floundering and beating the water, at a ftrange rate, till they have brought him into the middle of the water at a diftance from the reft of his companions,

who

who all lie nigh the banks; then the other boats surround him, and dart their harping-spears at him, till they kill him. These harping-spears are pointed with the finest tempered steel, extremely sharp, with beards to hinder them from coming out of his body; there is a line fastened to the spear, to draw it back, and the creature along with it; as also to hinder the spear from flying too far, if they miss their aim. Some of them are prodigious dexterous at this; but there is no piercing the creature but in his belly, which they must hit as he flounces and rolls himself in the water.—If a spear hits the scales of his back, it will fly off as from a rock, not without some danger to those who are very nigh, though they generally know the length of the string. I was really apprehensive of those strange fierce creatures at first, and it was a considerable time before I could dart with any dexterity; but the desire of glory, and the applauses given to those that excel, who have the skins carried like trophies before their mistresses, these, and the charms of the regent's daughter, so inspired me, that I frequently carried the prize.

It is one of the finest recreations in the world; you might see several hundred boats at a time, either employed, or as spectators, with shouts and cries, when the creature is hit in the right place, that make the very banks tremble. When they have killed all the old ones, they send their people on the shore, to rake for the eggs, which they burn and deftroy on the fpot; not but fome will be hatched before the reft, and creep into the water, to ferve for fport the next year. They deftroy thefe animals, not only for their own fecurity in the ufe of the lakes, but alfo to preferve the wild fowl and fifh, which are devoured and deftroyed by the crocodiles.

But the fifhing on the great lake Gilgol, or lake of lakes, is without any danger; there being no alligators in that water; and is only for recreation, and the profit of the fifh. The lake is above a hundred Italian miles in circumference. At proper feafons, the whole lake is covered with boats; great numbers of them full of ladies to fee the fport, befide what are on the iflands and fhores, with trumpets, hautboys, and other mufical inftruments, playing all the while. It is impoffible to defcribe the different kinds of fifh the lake abounds with; many of them we know nothing of in Europe; though they have fome like ours, but much larger, as pikes, or a fifh like a pike, two or three yards long; a fifh like a bream, a yard and a half over; carps forty or fifty pound weight; they catch incredible numbers of them; fome kinds in one part of the lake, fome in another. They fifh in this

this manner, and afterwards feast on what they catch, for a fortnight or three weeks, if the season proves kind, retiring at night to their tents, either on the islands, or shore, where there are persons employed in drying and curing what are proper for use; sending presents of them into other parts of the country, in exchange for venison, fowl, and the like. Though there are noble lakes and ponds, even in the forests, made by the inclosures of the hills and woods, that are stored with excellent fish; yet they are entirely destitute of the best sort; that is, sea-fish, which we have in such quantities in Europe. When this fishing is over, they retire to the towns, because of the rainy seasons, which begin presently after.

I am now going to enter on a part of my life, which I am in some doubt, whether it is proper to lay before your Reverences, or not: I mean the hopes and fears, the joys and anxieties of a young man in love; but in an honourable way, with no less a person than the daughter of the regent of this vast empire. I shall not however enter into the detail of the many various circumstances attending such a passion; but shall just touch on some particular passages, which were very extraordinary, even in a passion which generally of itself runs into extremes. Your Reverences will remember, that there is no real distinction of quality in these people,

nor

nor any regard either to intereſt or dignity, but merely to perſonal merit; their chief view being to render that ſtate happy which makes up the better part of human life. I had nothing therefore to do in this affair, but to fix my choice, and endeavour to pleaſe and be pleaſed. My choice was ſoon determined; the firſt time I ſaw the incomparable Iſyphena, the regent's daughter, though ſhe was then but ten years old, ten thouſand budding beauties appeared in her, with ſuch unutterable charms, that though I as good as deſpaired of arriving at my wiſhed-for happineſs, I was reſolved to fix there, or no where.

I obſerved, when I was firſt introduced into her company by the regent her father, that ſhe had her eye fixed on me, as a ſtranger, as I ſuppoſed, but yet with more than a girliſh curioſity. I was informed afterwards, that ſhe told her playfellows, that that ſtranger ſhould be her huſband, or no one. The wife Pophar her father had obſerved it, and whether it was from his knowledge of the ſex, and their unaccountable fondneſs for ſtrangers, or whether he diſapproved of the thought, I cannot tell, but he was reſolved to try both our conſtancies to the utmoſt. I was obliged by the Pophar to teach her and ſome other young ladies, as well as ſome young men, to paint; but it was always in the father or mother's company. Not to detain

tain your Reverences with matters quite foreign to, and perhaps unworthy your cognifance, it was five years before I durſt let her ſee the leaſt glimmering of my affection. She was now fifteen, which was the height of her bloom. Her father ſeeing ſhe carried no mark of any engagement, aſked her in a familiar way, if her eyes had made no conqueſts: ſhe bluſhed, and ſaid, ſhe hoped not. He told me alſo as a friend, that I was older than their cuſtoms cared to allow young men to live ſingle; and with a ſmile aſked me, if the charms of the Baſſa's daughter of Grand Cairo had extinguiſhed in me all thoughts of love. I told him there were objects enough in Mezorania, to make one forget any thing one had ſeen before, but that being a ſtranger I was willing to be thoroughly acquainted with the genius of the people, leſt I ſhould make any one unhappy. I was juſt come back from one of our viſitations, when I was ſtruck with the moſt lively ſenſe of grief I ever felt in my life. I had always obſerved before, that Iſyphena never wore any ſign of engagement, but then I found ſhe carried a bud in her boſom. I fell ill immediately upon it; which ſhe perceiving, came to ſee me without any bud, as ſhe uſed to go before, keeping her eyes upon me to ſee what effect it would have. Seeing her continue without any marks of engagement, I recovered, and made bold to tell her one day,

day, that I could not but pity the miferable perfon, whoever he was, who had loft the place in her bofom he had before; fhe faid unconcernedly, that both the wearing and taking away the flower from her bofom, was done out of kindnefs to the perfon. I was then fo taken up with contrary thoughts, that I did not perceive fhe meant to try whether fhe was the object of my thoughts or not. However, finding fhe carried no more marks of engagement, I was refolved to try my fortune for life or death; when an opportunity offered beyond my wifh. Her mother brought her to perfect a piece of painting fhe was drawing: I obferved a melancholy and trouble in her countenance I had never feen before; that moment the mother was fent for to the regent, and I made ufe of it to afk her, what it was that affected her in fo fenfible a manner? I pronounced thefe words with fuch emotion and concern on my own part, that fhe might eafily fee I was in fome very great agony. She expreffed a great deal of confufion at the queftion, infomuch, that, without anfwering a word, fhe got up, and went out of the room, leaving me leaning againft the wall almoft without life or motion. Other company coming in, I was roufed out of my lethargy, and flunk away to my own apartment, but agitated with fuch numberlefs fears, as left me almoft deftitute of reafon. However, I was refolved to make a

moft

moſt juſt diſcovery, and to be fully determined in my happineſs or miſery. There was a grated window on the back-ſide of the palace, where I had ſeen Iſiphena walk ſometimes, but never dared to approach; I went thither in the evening, and ſeeing her by-herſelf, I ventured to it, and falling on my knees, aſked her for heaven's ſake what was the matter, or if I had offended her? She immediately burſt into tears, and juſt ſaid, " Aſk no more," and withdrew; though I cannot ſay with any ſigns of indignation. Some time after, I was ſent for to inſtruct her in the finiſhing of her piece. I muſt tell your Reverences, that I had privately drawn that picture of her which you ſaw, and put the little boy in afterwards. In a hurry I had left it behind me in my cloſet, and the Pophar finding it by accident, had taken it away without my knowledge; and ſhewn it to the mother; and making as if he did not mind Iſyphena, who ſtood by, and ſaw it (as ſhe thought, undiſcerned), ſeemed to talk in a threatening tone to the mother about it. When I came in, I had juſt courage enough to caſt one glance at Iſyphena, when, methought, I ſaw her eyes meet mine, and ſhew a mixture of comfort and trouble at the ſame time. As this ſubject cannot be very proper for your Reverences ears, I ſhall compriſe in half an hour what coſt me whole years of ſighs and ſollicitude; though happily

pily crowned at laſt with unſpeakable joys.
This trouble in Iſyphena was, that having
made herſelf miſtreſs of the pencil, ſhe had
privately drawn my picture in miniature,
which ſhe kept ſecretly in her boſom, and it
having been diſcovered by the mother, as
that which I had drawn was by the father, to try her conſtancy he had expreſſed the utmoſt indignation at it: but Iſyphena's greateſt trouble was, leſt I ſhould know
and take it for a diſcovery of her love, before I had made any overtures of mine. In
proceſs of time we came to an eclairciſſe-
ment; ſhe received my two firſt flowers;
but becauſe I was half a ſtranger to their
race, we were to give ſome more ſignal
proof of our love and conſtancy than ordinary: we had frequently common occaſions
offered us, ſuch as might be looked upon
as the greateſt trials. She was the paragon
not only of the kingdom, but poſſibly of
the univerſe, for all perfections that could
be found in the ſex. Her ſtature was about
the middle ſize, the juſt proportion of her
ſhape made her really taller than ſhe ſeemed
to be; her hair was black * indeed, but of a
much finer gloſs than the reſt of the ſex, nor
quite ſo much curled, hanging down in eaſy
treſſes over her ſhoulders, and ſhading ſome

---

* The author being an Italian, did not think black hair
ſo beautiful.

part

part of her beautiful cheeks. Her eyes, though not so large as our Europeans, darted such lustre, with a mixture of sweetness and vivacity, that it was impossible not to be charmed with their rays; her features were not only the most exact, but inimitable and peculiar to herself. In fine, her nose, mouth, teeth, turn of the face, all concurring together to form the most exquisite symmetry, and adorned with a bloom beyond all the blushes of the new-born aurora, rendered her the most charming, and the most dangerous object in nature. The noblest and gayest youths of all the land paid their homages to her adorable perfections, but all in vain: she avoided doing hurt where she could do no good; she did not so much scorn, as shut her eyes to all their offers, though such a treasure gave me ten thousand anxieties before I knew what share I had in it; but when once she received my addresses, the security her constant virtue gave me was proportionable to the immense value of her person. For my part, I had some trials on my side. I was surrounded with beauties, who found a great many ways to shew me they had no dislike to me. Whether being a stranger, of different features and make from their youth, gave them a more pleasing curiosity, or the tallness of my stature, something exceeding any of theirs, or the gaiety of my temper, which
gave

gave me a freer air than is usual with them, being, as I observed, naturally too grave, (be that as it will), Isyphena's bright sense easily saw I made some sacrifices to her. But we had greater trials than these to undergo, which I shall briefly relate to your Reverences, for the particularity of them. When I thought I was almost arrived at the height of my happiness, being assured of the heart of the divine Isyphena, the Pophar came to me one day with the most seeming concern in his countenance I ever remarked in him, even beyond that of the affair with the great Bassa's daughter: after a little pause, he told me, he had observed the love between his daughter and myself; that, out of kindness to my person, he had consulted their wise men about it, who all concluded, that, on account of my being a stranger, and not of their race by the father's side, I could never marry his daughter; so that I must either solemnly renounce all pretensions to her; or be shut up for ever without any commerce with his people, till death. But, says he, to shew that we do justice to your merit, you are to have a public statue erected in your honour, because you have taught us the art of painting; which is to be crowned with a garland of flowers by the most beautiful young woman in the kingdom; thus you will live to glory, though you are dead to the world. But if you

you will renounce all pretenfions to my daughter, we will furnifh you with riches, fufficient, with the handfomenefs of your perfon, to gain the greateft princefs in the world, provided you will give a folemn oath never to difcover the way to this place. I fell down on my knees before him, and cried out, " Here take me, fhut me up, " kill me, cut me in a thoufand pieces, I " will never renounce Ifyphena."—He faid no more, but that their laws muft be obeyed. I obferved tears in his eyes, as he went out, which made me fee he was in earneft. I had fcarce time to reflect on my miferable ftate, or rather was incapable of any reflection at all, when four perfons came in with a difmal heavinefs in their looks, and bade me come along with them; they were to conduct me to the place of my confinement. In the mean time, the Pophar goes to his daughter, and tells her the fame thing; only adding, that I was to be fent back to my own country, loaded with fuch immenfe riches as might procure me the love of any woman in the world: for, fays he, thofe barbarians (meaning the Europeans) will marry their daughters to any one who has but riches enough to buy them; the men will do the fame with refpect to the women; let the woman be whofe daughter fhe will, if fhe had but money enough to purchafe a kingdom, a king would marry her. Before

fore he had pronounced all this, Isyphena had not strength to hear it out, but fell down in a swoon at his feet: when she was come to herself, he endeavoured to comfort her, and added, that she was to have the young Pophar's son, a youth about her age; for though he was not old enough to govern, he was old enough to have children. He went on and told her, I was to have a statue erected in honour of me, to be crowned by the fairest woman in all Mezorania, which, says he, is judged to be yourself; and, if you refuse it, Amnophilla is to be the person. This was the most beautiful woman next Isyphena, and by some thought equal to her, whose signs of approbation and liking to my person, I had taken no notice of, for the sake of Isyphena. She answered with a resolution that was surprising, even to her father, That she would die before she would be wanting to her duty, but that their laws allowed her to chuse whom she pleased for her husband, without being undutiful; that as for the crowning of the statue, she accepted of it, not for the reason he gave, but to pay her last respects to my memory, who, she was sure, would never marry any one else. As for the young Pophar, she would give her answer when this ceremony was over. When all things were ready for it, there was public proclamation made in all parts of the Nome, that whereas

I

I had brought into the kingdom, and freely communicated to them the noble art of painting, I was to have a public statue erected in my honour, to be crowned with a crown of flowers by the hand of the fairest woman in all Mezorania. Accordingly, a statue of full proportion, of the finest polished marble, was erected in one of their spacious squares, with my name ingraven on the pedestal in golden characters, setting forth the service I had done the commonwealth, &c. The statue had the picture of Isyphena in one hand, and the emblems of the art in the other. The last kindness I was to receive, was to be permitted to see the ceremony with a perspective glass, from the top of a high tower belonging to the place of my confinement, from whence I could discern every minute circumstance that passed. Immediately the croud opened to make way for Isyphena, who came in the regent's triumphant chariot, drawn by eight white horses, all caparisoned with gold and precious stones, herself more resplendent than the sun they adored. There was a scaffold with a throne upon it just close to the statue, with gilt steps for her to go up to put the crown on the head of it. As soon as she appeared, a shout of joy ran through the whole croud, applauding the choice of her beauty, and the work she was going to perform; then proclamation was made again for the same intent, setting forth the rea-

sons of the ceremony. When all was silent, she steps from the throne to the degrees with the crown in her hand, holding it up to be seen by all, supported by Amnophilla and Menifa, two of the most beautiful virgins after herself. There appeared a serenity in the looks of Isyphena beyond what could be expected, expressing a fixed resolution at the same time. As soon as she had put the crown on the head of the statue, which was applauded with repeated shouts and acclamations, she stood still for some time, with an air that shewed she was determined for some great action; then turning to the officers, ordered them to make proclamation, that every one should remark what she was going to do. A profound silence ensuing through the whole assembly, she went up the steps again, and taking out the most conspicuous flower in the whole crown, first put it in the right hand of the statue, and then clapped it into her bosom, with the other two she had received from me before, as a sign of her consent for marriage, which could not be violated. This occasioned a shout ten times louder than any before, applauding such an heroic act of constancy, as had never been seen in Mezorania. The regent ran up to her, and embracing her with tears of joy trickling down his cheeks, said, she should have her choice, since she had fulfilled the law, and supplied all defects by that extraordinary act of fidelity: and
immediately

immediately gave orders to have that heroic action regiſtered in the public records, for an example and encouragement of conſtancy to poſterity. But the people cried out, Where is the man! where is the man! let their conſtancy be rewarded immediately...

Here the reader, as well as the publiſher, will lament the irreparable loſs of the ſheets, which were miſlaid at his coming over. He does not pretend to charge his memory with what they contained; juſt having had time to run them over in the Italian, when Signor Rhedi got them copied out for him. As far as the publiſher remembers, the loſt ſheets contained ſeveral diſcourſes between the Pophar and Gaudentio, concerning religion, philoſophy, politics, and the like; with the account of the loſs of his wife and children, and ſome other accidents that befel him during his ſtay in the country, which, as we ſhall ſee, induced him to leave the place, with ſeveral curious remarks of Signor Rhedi: all which would doubtleſs have given a great deal of ſatisfaction to the reader. But no one can be ſo much concerned for the loſs as the publiſher, ſince they cannot now be repaired, by reaſon of the death of the ſame Signor Rhedi, never to be ſufficiently regretted by the learned world.]

Theſe diſcourſes * made very great impreſſions on the mind of a perſon of ſo

---

* Probably about the Chriſtian religion.

much penetration as the regent was, insomuch that he seemed resolved, when his regency was out, which wanted now but a year, to go along with me into Europe, during the stay he was to make at Grand Cairo, that he might have an opportunity of examining matters at the fountain-head; wisely judging a consideration of such consequence, as that of religion, to be no indifferent thing. For my own part, notwithstanding the beauty and riches of the country, I could find no satisfaction in a place where I had lost all that was dear to me, though I had the comfort to have my dear Isyphena, and her three children, all baptized by my own hand before they died: neither could length of time allay my grief; but, on the contrary, every thing I saw revived the memory of my irreparable loss. I considered the instability of the fleeting joys of this world, where I thought I had built my happiness, for a man of my fortune, on the most solid foundation. But alas! all was gone as if it had been but a dream, and the adorable Isyphena was no more. The good old Pophar was in a very little better condition, having lost his dearest daughter, and his little grandchildren, particularly the eldest boy, who is in that picture with his mother. This reflection on the vanity of human felicity, made him more disposed to hear the truths of our divine religion, so that he was resolved to go and search further

ther into the reasons for it. There was another yet more forcible reason induced me to solicit the Pophar for my return to my native country, which was the care of my future state. I had lived so many years without the exercise of those duties our church obliges us to perform, and, though I had not been guilty of any great crimes, I was not willing to die out of her bosom: however, to do all the good I could to a country where I had once enjoyed so much happiness, this being the last year we were to stay, I at length persuaded the regent, that there might be some danger of an invasion of his country, from the opposite side towards the southern tropic; at least, I did not know, but there might be some habitable climate not so far over the sands, as towards Libya and Egypt. I had often signified my thoughts to him in that respect. I told him, that though his kingdom was safe, and inaccessible to all but ourselves on that side, it was possible, it might be nigher the great ocean on the opposite one, or that the sands might not be of such extent; or, in fine, there might be ridges of mountains, and from them rivers running into the ocean, by which, in process of time, some barbarous people might ascend, and disturb their long uninterrupted rest, without any fence to guard against such an emergency. This last

last thought alarmed him; so we were resolved to make a new trial, without communicating the design to any but the chief council of five, where we were sure of inviolable secrecy. What confirmed me in my notion was, that, when we were on the utmost point of our mountains southward, looking over the deserts, I could perceive something like clouds, or fogs, hanging always towards one part. I imagined them to be fogs covering the tops of some great mountains, which must have habitable vales. Being resolved to make a trial, we provided all things accordingly, and set out from the furthest part of the kingdom southwards, taking only five persons in our company, steering our course directly towards that point of the horizon, where I observed the thick air always hanging towards one place. We took provisions and water but for ten days, leaving word that they should not trouble themselves about us, unless we made a considerable stay, because in case we found mountains, we should always find springs and fruits to subsist on, by making a further search into the country: otherwise, if we saw no hopes at the five days end, we would return the other five, and take fresh measures. The third day of our voyage, we found the deserts nothing so barren as we expected, the ground grew pretty hard; and the fourth day

day we difcovered fome tufts of mofs and fhrubs, by which we conjectured we fhould foon come to firm land; the evening of that day we difcovered the tops of hills, but further off than we thought; fo that though we travelled at a great rate all that night and moſt of the next day, we could only arrive at the foot of them the fifth day at night. After fome little fearch we came to a fine fpring, and, to our comfort, no figns of inhabitants; if there had, we fhould have returned immediately to take further advice. The next morning we got up to the top of the higheft hill to difcover the country; but found it to be only the point of a vaft mountainous country, like the worft part of our Alps, though there were fome fertile vales and woods, but no footfteps of its ever having been inhabited, as we believed, fince the creation. Finding we could make good provifion for our return, we were in no great pain about time; but wandered from place to place, viewing and obferving every way. After proceeding along thofe craggy hills and precipices in this manner for five days, they began to leffen towards our right, but feemed rather to increafe the other way: at length, in the moft difmal and horrid part of the hill-brow, one of our young men thought he fpied fomething like the figure of a man, fitting by a little fpring under a craggy rock

juſt

just below us ; we sent three of our people round another way to keep him from running into the wood, while the Pophar and myself stole quietly over the rock where he was. As soon as he saw us, he whips up a broken chink in the rock, and disappeared immediately : we were sure he could not get from us; so we closed and searched, till we found a little cave in the windings of the rock, where was his retiring place. His bed was made of moss and leaves, with little heaps of dried fruits, of different sorts, for his sustenance. When he saw us, he was surprised, and rushed at us like a lion, thinking to make his way through us, but being all five at the mouth of the cave, he stood ready to defend himself against our attempts. Viewing him a little nigher, we saw he had some remains of an old tattered coat, and part of a pair of breeches, with a ragged sash, or girdle, round his waist, by which, to our great surprise, we found he was a European. The Pophar spoke to him in Lingua Franca, and asked him who, or what he was ; he shook his head as if he did not understand us. I spoke to him in French, Italian, and Latin, but he was a stranger to those languages ; at length he cried out *Inglis, Inglis*. I had learned something of that language, when I was a student at Paris : for knowing my father had a mind I should learn as many languages

ges as I could, I had made an acquaintance with several English and Scotch students in that university, particularly with one F. Johnson, an English Benedictine; and could speak it pretty well for a foreigner, but had almost forgot it for want of use. I bid him take courage, and fear nothing, for we would do him no harm. As soon as ever he heard me speak English, he fell down on his knees, and begged us to take pity on him, and carry him to some habitable country, where he might possibly get an opportunity of returning home again, or, at least, of living like a human creature. Upon this he came out to us, but looked more like a wild beast, than a man; his hair, beard, and nails were grown to a great length, and his mien was as haggard, as if he had been a great while in that wild place; though he was a stout well built man, and shewed something above the common rank. We went down to the fountain together, where he made us to understand, that his father was an East-India merchant, and his mother a Dutch woman of Batavia; that he had great part of his education in London; but being very extravagant, his father, whose natural son he was, had turnned him off, and sent him to Batavia, to his mother's friends; that, by his courage and industry, he was in a way of making his fortune, being advanced to be a lieutenant in the Dutch guards at Batavia; but was

unhappily

unhappily caſt away on the coaſt of Africa, where they had been on a particular adventure: That he and his companions, four in number, wandering up in the country to ſeek proviſions, were taken by ſome ſtrange barbarians, who carried them a vaſt unknown way into the continent, deſigning to eat them, or ſacrifice them to their inhuman gods, as they had done by his companions. But being hale and fat at the time of his taking, they reſerved him for ſome particular feaſt: That, as they were carrying him through the woods, another party of barbarians, enemies to the former, met them, and fell a-fighting for their booty: which he perceiving, knowing he was to be eaten if he ſtaid, ſlunk away in the ſcuffle into the thickeſt woods, hiding himſelf by day, and marching all night he did not know where, but, as he conjectured, ſtill higher into the country. Thus he wandered from hill to hill, and wood to wood, till he came to a deſert of ſands, which he was reſolved to try to paſs over, not daring to return back, for fear of falling into the hands of thoſe merciless devourers. He paſſed two days and two nights without water, living on the fruits he carried with him, as many as he could, till he came to this mountainous part of the country, which he found uninhabited; taking up his abode in that rock, where he never had any

hopes

hopes of seeing a human creature again: neither did he know himself where he was, or which way to go back. In fine, he told us he had lived in that miserable place, now upwards of five years. After we had comforted him, as well as we could, I asked him, which way the main sea lay, as near as he could guess, and how far he thought it was to it? He pointed with his hand towards the south, a little turning towards the east, and said, he believed it might be thirty or forty days journey; but advised us never to go that way, for we should certainly be devoured by the barbarians. I asked him whether the country was habitable from that place down to the sea; he told me yes, except that desert we had passed; but whether it was broader in other places, he could not tell.

All the time he was speaking, the Pophar eyed him from top to toe; and calling me aside, What monster, says he, have we got here? There is a whole legion of wild beasts in that man. I see the lion, the goat, the wolf, and the fox, in that one person. I could not forbear smiling at the Pophar's skill in physiognomy, and told him we should take care he should do no harm. Then I turned to the man, and asked him, whether he would conform himself to the laws and rites of the country, if we carried him among men again, where he should
want

want for nothing. He embraced my knees, and laid, he would conform to any laws or any religion, if I would but let him fee a habitable country again. I ftared at the man, and began to think there was fome truth in the Pophar's fcience. However, I told him, if he would but behave like a rational creature, he fhould go along with us: but he muft fuffer himfelf to be blindfolded, till he came to the place. He ftartled a little, and feemed to be prodigious fufpicious, left we fhould deceive him. But on my affuring him on the faith of a man, that he fhould come to no harm, he confented.

After we had refrefhed ourfelves, being both glad and concerned for the information we had received of the nature of the country, which was the intent of our journey, in order to guard againft all inconveniencies, we covered his eyes very clofe, and carried him back with us, fometimes on foot, fometimes on one of the fpare dromedaries, till we arrived fafe from where we fet out. Then we let him fee where he was, and what a glorious country he was come into. We clothed him like ourfelves, that is, in our travelling-drefs, to fhew he was not an entire ftranger to our race. He feemed loft in admiration of what he faw, and embraced me with all the figns of gratitude imaginable. He readily conformed to all our cuftoms, and made no
fcruple

scruple of assisting at all their idolatrous ceremonies, as if he had been as good a Heathen as the best of them. Which I seeing, without declaring myself to be a Christian, told him I had been informed, the people of the country where he was educated, were Christians; and wondered to see him join in adoring the sun. Pugh! says he, some bigotted people make a scruple, but most of our men of sense think one religion is as good as another. By this I perceived our savage was of a new set of people, which I had heard of before I left Italy, called *Politici* *, who are a sort of Atheists in masquerade. The Pophar, out of his great skill in physiognomy, would have no conversation with him, and commanded me to have a strict eye over him. However, the information he had given us of the possibility of invading the kingdom the way he came, answered the intent of our voyage, and my former conjectures; about which there was a grand council held, and orders given to secure the foot of our outermost mountain southwards, which ran a great way into the desert; so that it was sufficient to guard against any of those barbarous invaders of the continent. But to return to our European savage; for he may be just-

---

* These *Politici* were forerunners of our modern freethinkers, whose principles tend to the destruction of all human society, as our author shews incomparably well by and by.

ly called so, being more dangerous in a commonwealth, than the very Hyckloes themselves; though he was a person who had had a tolerably civilized education, bating the want of all sense of religion, which was owing to his perpetual conversation with libertines: He had a smattering of most kinds of polite learning, but without a bottom in any respect. After he had been with us some time, his principles began to shew themselves in his practice. First, he began to be rude with our women; married or single, it was all alike to him; and, by an unaccountable spirit of novely or contradiction, our women seemed to be inclined to be very fond of him; so that we were at our wits ends about him. Then he began to find fault with our government, despising and condemning all our ceremonies and regulations: but his great aim was, to pervert our youth, enticing them into all manner of liberties, and endeavouring to make them believe, that there was no such thing as moral evil in nature; that there was no harm in the greatest crimes, if they could but evade the laws and punishments attending them. As I had endeavoured to create a confidence in him, he came to me one day, and said, that since I was an European as well as himself, we might make ourselves men for ever, if I would join with him: You see, says he, these men cannot fight;

fight; nay, will rather be killed themselves, than kill any one else: can't you shew me the way out of this country, where we will get a troop of stout fellows well armed, and come and plunder all the country? we shall get immense riches, and make ourselves lords and masters of all. I heard him with a great deal of attention, and answered him, that I thought the project might easily take, only for the horrid wickedness of the fact; especially for us two, who had received such favours from the Pophar and his people; he, in his being delivered from the greatest misery; and myself, in having been freed from slavery, and made one of the chief men of the kingdom: that the action would deserve to be branded with eternal infamy, and the blackest ingratitude: beside the infinite villanies, injustices, crimes, and deaths of innocent persons, who must perish in the attempt; which would always stare us in the face, and torment us with never-ceasing stings of conscience till our death. Conscience! says he, that is a jest; a mere engine of priest-craft: all right is founded in power: let us once get that, and who will dispute our right? As for the injustice of it, that is a mere notion; distinction of crimes, mere bigotry, and the effect of education, ushered in under the cloak of religion. Let us be but successful, and I will answer for all your scruples. I told him, it was a matter not to be refolved on on a fudden; and that I would confider on it. But I bid him be fure to keep his matters to himfelf. I went immediately to the Pophar, and gave an account of what had paffed. He was ftruck with horror at the recital; not fo much for the confequences, as that human nature could be brought to fuch a monftrous deformity. If, fays he, your Europeans are men of fuch principles, who would not fly to the furtheft corner of the earth, to avoid their fociety? Or rather, who can be fure of his life among fuch people? Whoever thinks it no greater crime in itfelf, to kill me, than to kill a fly, will certainly do it, if I ftand in his way. If it were lawful, continued he, by our conftitutions to kill this man, he deferves a thoufand deaths, who makes it lawful to deftroy all the world befides. I anfwered, that all the Europeans were not men of his principles, nor even thofe of his nation, who were generally the moft compaffionate and beft-natured men in the world. But that he was of a new fet of wretched people, who called themfelves *Deifts*, and interiorly laughed at all religion and morality, looking upon them as mere engines of policy and prieftcraft. Interiorly! fays he; yes, and would cut any man's throat exteriorly and actually, if it were not for fear of the gallows. Shut him up, cried he, from all commerce of men, left his breath fhould infect the whole world; or rather, let us send him back to his cave, to live like a wild beast; where if he is devoured by the savages, they do him no injury, on his own principles. I represented to him, that we were, just on our journey back to Grand Cairo, where we might carry him blindfold, that he should not know our way over the sands, and there give him his liberty; but that we would shut him up till then. This being agreed on, I took a sufficient number of men, to seize him; and to do it without any mischief, for he was as stout as a lion, we contrived to come upon him in his bed, where we caught him with one of our young women. Three of our men fell upon him at once, and kept him down, while the rest tied his hands and legs, and carried him into a strong-hold, whence it was impossible for him to escape. The woman was shut up apart, according to our laws. When he found himself taken, he called me by the most cruel names he could think on, as the most wicked and treacherous villain that ever was, thus to betray him, and the trust he had put in me. Yes, says I, it is a crime to discover your secrets, and no crime in you to subvert the government, and set all mankind a-cutting one another's throats, by your monstrous principles: so I left him for the present. Some time after, I went to him, and told him, our council had decreed he should be carried back from whence he came, and be delivered over to the savages, either to be devoured by them, or to defend himself by his principles, as well as he could. He cried out, Sure we would not be guilty of such horrid barbarity! Barbarity! said L; that is a mere jest: they will do you no injury; if your flesh is a rarity to them, when they have you in their power, they have full right to make use of it. He begged by all that was dear, we would not send him to the savages; but rather kill him on the spot. Why, says I, you are worse than the greatest cannibals; because they spare their friends, and only eat their enemies; whereas your principles spare no body, and acknowledge no tye in nature. At length he owned himself in a mistake, and seemed to renounce his errors; when I told him, if he would engage his most solemn promise, to suffer himself to be blindfolded, and behave peaceably, we would carry him to a place where he might find an opportunity to return to his own country. But, says I, what signify promises and engagements in a man who laughs at all obligations, and thinks it as just and lawful to break them, as to make them? No, he cursed himself with the most dreadful imprecations, if he were not tractable in all things we should command him. But, says he again, won't you deliver me back to the savages? I answered in the same tone, Should we do you any wrong, if we did? At length,

to

to appeafe him, I promifed him faithfully we would put him in a way to return into his own country : but bid him confider, if there were no fuch thing as right and wrong, what would become of the world, or what fecurity could there be in human life ?

In a few weeks, the time drew on for our great journey to Grand Cairo, where I was in hopes of feeing my native country once more. All things were now as good as ready; the Pophar and myfelf had other defigns than ufual, and were in fome pain to think of leaving that once fo happy country. Though, as I faid, all things that could make me happy, were buried with my dear Ifyphena. The Pophar had fome ferious thoughts of turning Chriftian; the evidences of our religion were foon perceived by a perfon of his deep penetration; though perfons of little learning, and great vices, pretend they don't fee them. But, like a wife man, he was refolved to examine into it, in the places where it was exercifed in the greateft fplendour. We provided a good quantity of jewels, and as much gold as we could well carry, for our prefent expenfes at Grand Cairo, and elfewhere, in future exigencies. I went to my Deift in his grotto, and threw him in as much gold and jewels as were fufficient to glut his avarice, and make him happy in his brutal way of thinking. But I would not truft myfelf with

with him alone, for all his promises, as he, on his side, expressed still a diffidence of trusting any body; I suppose from the consciousness of his own vile principles. Then I threw him a blinding-cap, which we had made for him, that he should not see our way over the deserts. This cap was made like a head-piece, with breathing places for his mouth and nose, as well as to take in nourishment, opening at the back part, and clasping with a spring behind, that being once locked, he could not open it himself. He put it on his head, two or three times, before he durst venture to close it. At length he clasped it, and he was as blind as a beetle. We went to him and tied his hands, which he let us do quietly enough; but still begged us, that we would not betray him to the savages. I bid him think once more, that now his own interior sense told him, that to betray him would be a crime; by consequence there was such a thing as evil.

All things being in readiness, we mounted our dromedaries. The Pophar and all the rest kissed the ground as usual; I did the same, out of respect to the place which contained the remains of my never too much lamented Isyphena, the ashes of whose heart are in the hollow of the stone, whereon is her picture. Not to mention the ceremonies of our taking leave, we were conducted

in

in a mournful manner over the bridge, and lanched once more into the ocean of fands and deferts, which were before us. Our favage was on a dromedary which would follow the reft, but led by a cord faftened to one of them, for fecurity. It ftumbled with him twice or thrice, and threw him off once, but without any great hurt. But the fear of breaking his neck put him into a great agony; and though he was as bold as a lion on other occafions, he was prodigioufly ftartled at the thoughts of death. We arrived at Grand Cairo at the ufual period of time, without any particular difafter. As foon as we were fettled, the Pophar ordered me to fend the Deift packing as foon as we could. This brutal race, fays he, next to the cannibals, are the fitteft company for him. I unlocked the blinding-helmet, and told him, we had now fulfilled our promife; that he was at Grand Cairo, where he might find fome way or other to return into Europe; and, to convince him, carried him to fome European merchants who affured him of the fame. Delivering to him his gold and jewels, I begged him to reflect on his obligations to us, and the grateful acknowledgments due to our memory on that account: we had taken him from a miferable folitude, where he lived more like a wild beaft than a man; and where he was in danger of being found and

and devoured by the cannibals: we had brought him into one of the happiest countries in the world, if he would but have conformed to its laws; and now had given him his liberty to go where he pleased, with riches sufficient to make him easy, and benefits to make him grateful all his life: I then took my leave of him. But to our sorrow we had not done with him yet. As soon as the Pophar and the rest had performed the ceremony of visiting the tombs of their ancestors, or rather the places where the tombs had been, the good old man and myself began to think of measures for our journey into Italy. He ordered his people to stay at Grand Cairo till the next annual caravan; and in case he did not return by that time, they were to go home, and he would take the opportunity of the then next following caravan, because he was upon business that nearly concerned him. We had agreed with a master of a ship to carry us to Venice, which, as I had the honour to acquaint your Reverences before, was a French ship, commanded by Monsieur Godart. We had fixed the day to go abroad, when, behold! our savage, at the head of a band of Turks, came and seized every one of us, in the name of the great Bassa. By great good fortune, while I staid at Grand Cairo, I had the grateful curiosity to inform myself what was become of the former Bassa's fa's daughter, we left there five and twenty years ago. The people told me, the daughter was married to the Grand Sultan, and was now Sultanefs, mother to the prefent Sultan, and regent of the empire; adding that her brother was their prefent great Baffa. This lucky information faved all our lives and liberties. We were carried prifoners before the great Baffa, the faithlefs favage accufing us of crimes againft the ftate; that we were immenfely rich, (a crime of itfelf fufficient to condemn us), and could make a difcovery of a country of vaft advantage to the Grand Signior. To be fhort, we had all been put to the torture, had not I begged leave to fpeak a word or two in private to the great Baffa. There I told him who I was; that I was the perfon who had faved his fifter's, the now Emprefs, life; and, to convince him, told him all the circumftances except that of her love, though he had heard fomething of that too: I fhewed him the ring fhe had given me for a remembrance, (which he alfo remembered), adding, that we were innocent men, who lived honeftly according to our own laws, coming there to traffic, like other merchants, and had been traduced by one of the greateft villains upon earth. In a word, this not only got us off, and procured us an ample paffport from the great Baffa for our further voyage; but he alfo ordered the

informing

informing wretch to be feized, and fent to the galleys for life. He offered to turn Turk, if they would fpare him. But being apprifed of his principles, they faid he would be a difgrace to their religion ; and ordered him away immediately. Upon which, feeing there was no mercy, being grown mad with rage and defpair, before they could feize his hands, he drew out a piftol, and fhot himfelf through the head; not being able to find a worfe hand than his own. The Pophar, good man! bore thefe misfortunes with wonderful patience, though he affured me his greateft grief was, to fee human nature fo far corrupted, as it was in that impious wretch, who could think the moft horrid crimes were not worth the notice of the fupreme governor of the univerfe. But we fee, fays he, that providence can make the wicked themfelves the inftruments of its juft vengeance : for can any thing be fo great a blot upon human nature, as to be its own deftroyer, when the very brutes will ftruggle for life till the laft gafp? However, he was uneafy till he had left that hateful place. Befides, there were fome figns of the plague breaking out ; fo we went down to Alexandria as faft as we could. And to encourage Monfieur Godart, he made him a prefent beforehand of a diamond of a confiderable value. We fet fail for Candy, where Monfieur
Godart

Godart was to touch, the 16th day of August, *anno* 1712. But, alas! whether thefe troubles, or not being ufed to the fea, or fome infection of the plague he had caught at Grand Cairo, or all together, is uncertain; but that great good man fell fo dangeroufly ill, that we thought we fhould fcarce get him to Candy. He affured me, by the knowledge he had of himfelf and nature, that his time was come. We put in at the firft creek, where the land-air a little refrefhed him; but it was a fallacious crifis; for, in a few days, all of us perceived his end draw near. Then he told me he was refolved to be baptized, and die in the Chriftian faith. I got him inftructed by a Reverend prieft belonging to Monfieur Godart; his name was Monfieur Le Grelle, whom I had formerly known when he was a ftudent in the college for foreign miflions; and, what was the only comfort I had now left, I faw him baptized, and yield up the ghoft with a courage becoming the greateft hero, and the beft of men. This was the greateft affliction I ever had in my whole life, after the death of his daughter. He left me all his effects, which were fufficient to make me happy in this life, if riches could procure happinefs.

We had fome days to ftay, before Monfieur Godart could make an end of his bufinefs.

finess. I was walking in a melancholy posture along the sea-shore, and reflecting on the adventures of my past life, occasioned by those very waters whereon I was looking, when I came, or rather my feet carried me, to a hanging rock, on the side of the island, just on the edge of the sea, and where there was scarce room enough for two or three persons to stand privately under covert, very difficult to be discerned; where going to sit down, and indulge my melancholy thoughts, I espied a Turk and two women, as if concealed under the rock. My own troubles not allowing me the curiosity to pry into other people's concerns, made me turn short back again: but the elder of the two women, who was mistress of the other, seeing by my dress, that I was a stranger and a Christian, (being now in that habit), came running to me, and falling on her knees, laid hold of mine, and begged me to take pity on a distressed woman, who expected every moment to be butchered by one of the most inhuman villains living, from whose violence they had fled and hid themselves in that place, in expectation of finding a boat to convey them off. I lifted her up, and thought I saw something in her face I had seen before, though much altered by years and troubles. She did the same by me, and at length cried out, O heavens! it cannot be the man I hope! I remembered
confusedly

confusedly something of the voice, as well as the face; and, after a deal of astonishment, found it was the Curdish lady, who had saved my life from the pirate Hamet. Oh! says she, I have just time enough to tell ye, that we expect to be pursued by that inhuman wretch, unless you can find a boat to carry us off before he finds us, otherwise we must fall a sacrifice to his cruelty. I never staid to consider consequences, but answered precipitately, that I would do my best; so ran back to the ship as fast I could, and with the help of the first man brought the boat to the rock. I was just getting out to take hold of her hand, when we heard some men coming rushing in behind us, and one of them cried, Hold, villain, that wicked woman shan't escape so; and fires a pistol, which missing the lady, shot the man attending her, into the belly, so that he fell down presently, though not quite dead. I had provided myself with a Turkish scymitar, and a case of pistols, under my sash, for my defence on shipboard; I saw there was no time to deliberate, so I fired directly at them, for they were three, and had the good luck to drop one of them. But Hamet, as I found afterwards, minding nothing but his revenge on the woman, fired again, and missing the lady a second time, shot her maid through the arm, and was drawing his scymitar to cleave her down, when I stept in before the lady; but shooting with too much precipitancy, the bullets passed under his arm, and lodged in the body of his second; he started back at the fire so near him, which gave me time to draw my scymitar. Being now upon equal terms, he retired two or three paces, and cried, Who art thou that venturest thy life so boldly for this wicked woman? I knew his voice perfectly well, neither was he so much altered as the lady. I am the man, said I, whose life thou wouldst have taken, but this lady saved it, whose cause I shall now revenge as well as my own, and my dear brother's. We made no more words, but fell to it with our scymitars, with all our might; he was a brave stout man, and let me see I should have work enough to hew him down. After several attacks, he gave me a considerable wound on my arm, and I cut him across the cheek a pretty large gash, but not to endanger his life; at length the justice of my cause would have it, that striking off his turban at once stroke, and with another falling on his bare head, I cut him quite into the brains, that some of them spurted on my scymitar. He fell down, as I thought, quite dead, but after some time he gave a groan, and muttered these words, Mahomet, thou art just, I killed this woman's husband, and she has been the occasion of my death; with these words

words he gave up the ghoſt. By this time the lady's attendant was dead; ſo I took the lady and her woman without ſtaying, for fear of further difficulties, and putting them in the boat, conducted them to the ſhip. Monſieur Godart was extremely troubled at the accident, ſaying we ſhould have all the iſland upon us, and made great difficulty to receive the lady; but upon a juſt repreſentation of the caſe, and an abundant recompenſe for his effects left behind, we got him to take her in, and hoiſt ſail for Venice as faſt as we could. The lady had now time to thank me for her delivery, and I to congratulate my happy fortune in being able to make a return for her ſaving my life. During our paſſage, I begged her to give us the hiſtory of her fortunes ſince I left her, which I prognoſticated then could not be very happy, conſidering the hands ſhe was fallen into. Says ſhe, You remember I made a promiſe to Hamet, that I would marry him on condition he would ſave your life. Yes, Madam, ſaid I, and am ready to venture my own once more in return for ſo great a benefit. You have done enough, ſays ſhe; and with that acquainted us, that when I was ſold off to the ſtrange merchants, Hamet carried her to Algiers, and claimed her promiſe. I was entirely ignorant, ſays ſhe, of his having a hand in the death of my dear lord; but, on the contrary,

the villain had contrived his wickedness so cunningly, that I thought he had generously ventured his own life to save his, and being, as you know, a very handsome man, of no very inferior rank, and expressing the most ardent love for my person, and I having no hopes of returning into my own country, fulfilled my promise made on your account, and married him. We lived contentedly enough together for some years, bating that we had no children, till his constant companion, who was the man attending me at the rock, and was killed by that villain, fell out about a fair slave, which Omar, so he was called, had bought, or taken prisoner in some of their piracies. Hamet, as well as he, fell in love with her, and would have taken her for his concubine, but the other concealed her from him: they had like to have fought about it; Hamet vowed revenge. The other, who was the honester man of the two, was advised to be upon his guard, and to deliver the woman to him; which he never would consent to, but was resolved to run all risks, rather than the young lady should suffer any dishonour. In the mean time, her friends, who were rich people of Circassia, hearing where she was, made interest to have her ransomed, and taken from both of them, by the authority of the Dey of Algiers, who was otherwise no friend to Hamet. This last had
been

been informed, that Omar, becaufe he could not enjoy her himfelf, contrived to have her ranfomed from his rival, and I myfelf had a hand in the affair, for which he threatened revenge on both of us; and being alfo difgufted with the Dey, he gave orders to have his fhips ready to remove, and follow his trade of piracy. Then Omar informed me how Hamet had murdered my firft hufband, by hiring the Arabians to do it, while he pretended to defend him to avoid my fufpicions, with fuch circumftances of the fact, that I faw the truth was too clear. The horror and deteftation I was in, is not to be expreffed, both againft Hamet, and againft myfelf, for marrying fuch a monfter. Omar added, that he was certainly informed, that as foon as he had us out at fea, he would make away with us both; and told me, if I would truft myfelf with him, he would undertake to carry me off in a boat, and conduct me into my own country. I was refolved to fly to the fartheft end of the earth to avoid his loathed fight; fo refolved to pack up our moft precious things, and go along with him. He procured a boat to meet us, at a little creek of the ifland, by a perfon he thought he could confide in, but who betrayed the whole affair to Hamet. Of which alfo we had timely notice, and removing from the ftation where we expected the boat, and

and fled along the coast as privately as we could, and hid ourselves under the rock where you found us, expecting either to find some favourable occasion to be carried off, or to die by the hand of Hamet, which we certainly had done, had not he met with his just death by yours. The lady had scarce given us this short account of her misfortunes, and we were not only congratulating her for her deliverance, but admiring the justice of providence, which reached this villain, both to bring him to condign punishment for the murder of the innocent Curd, and make him die by my hand, five and twenty years after he had robbed and killed my brother with all his crew, sold me for a slave, and attempted to kill me also, had not the strange lady saved my life : I say, we were making such like reflections on this strange accident, when they told us from above, two vessels seemed to come full sail upon us, as if they were pursuing us with all their might. We made all the sail we could, but our ship being pretty heavily loaded, we saw we must be overtaken. Some of us were resolved to fight it out to the last, in case they were enemies. But Monsieur Godart would not consent to it, saying the Bassa's passport would secure us, or by yielding peaceably, we might be ransomed. They came up to us in a short time, and saluted us with a volley of shot, to shew what we were to trust truft to. We ftruck our fails, and let them board us without any refiftance. Monfieur Godart, with too mean a fpirit, as I thought, told them with cap in hand, that he would give them any fatisfaction, and affured them he would not willingly fall out with the fubjects of the Grand Signior. They feized every man of us, and fpying the lady and me, There they are, faid they; the adulterefs and her lover, with the fpoils of her murdered hufband. Which words, fhewing they were Turks in purfuit of us from Candy, quite confounded Monfieur Godart at once, and made me imagine, I fhould have much ado to find any quarter. They haled us upon deck, making fhew, as if they were going to cut off my head. I never thought myfelf fo nigh death before; but had the prefence of mind to cry out in the hearing of the whole crew, that we were fervants of the Grand Sultanefs; and produced the paffport of the great Baffa her brother, charging them on their peril not to touch us. This ftopt their fury a little; fome cried out, Hold, have a care what you do; others cried, Kill them all for robbers and murderers, the Sultanefs will never protect fuch villains as thefe. When the hurlyburly was fomething appeafed, Monfieur Godart reafoned the cafe with them, and told them, if they murdered us, they could never conceal it; fince all the crew

crew of the three ships heard our appeal to the Sultanefs mother, the paffport fetting forth among other things, that I had faved the life of the Grand Sultanefs. This brought them to a demur. The chief of them began to confult among themfelves what was beft to be done. When I, begging leave to fpeak, told them, if they would carry us to Conftantinople, we would willingly fubmit our lives, and all that belonged to us, in cafe the Sultanefs did not own the fact, and take us into her protection: that, in cafe they put us to death, fome one or other, in fuch a number, would certainly inform againft them, the confequences of which they knew very well. I touched alfo but tenderly on the death of Hamet, and our innocence. The firft part of my fpeech made them pafs over the other. They demurred again, and at length refolved to carry us to Conftantinople, and proceed againft us by way of juftice, not doubting to make good prize of us, on account of our being Chriftians. Thus was our journey to Venice interrupted for fome time by this accident. When we came to the port, Monfieur Godart got leave to fend our cafe to Monfieur Savigni, the French refident; who found means to reprefent to the Sultanefs mother, that there was a ftranger in chains, who pretended to be the perfon who had faved her life, when fhe was at Grand Cairo, and would give her proofs of it, if he could be admitted to her

Highnefs's

Highness's presence. I would not send the ring she gave me, for fear of accidents. The Sultaness gave orders immediately, I should be brought to her presence; saying, she could easily know the person, for all it was so long before. I put on the same kind of dress I was in when she first saw me, which, if your Reverences remember, was the travelling dress of the Mezoranians. When I was brought into her presence, I scarce knew her, being advanced to a middle age, and in the attire of the Grand Sultaness. She looked at me with a great deal of emotion, and bid me approach nigher. I immediately fell on my knees, and holding the ring in my hand which she gave me at parting, as if I were making a present of it, Madam, said I, behold a slave, who had the honour to save your Highness's life, and now begs his own, and that of his companions; and most humbly requests your Highness to accept of this jewel, as a token of our last distress. Instead of answering me, which put me in great pain, as doubting whether I was right or not, she turned to her nighest attendants, and said in a pretty soft voice, It is he, I know him by his voice, as well as dress: and rising off her seat, came and took the ring. Then looking attentively at it, Yes, Sir, said she, I own the ring and bearer; and acknowledge you to be the person who saved

my

my life. For which reason, I give you yours, and all that belongs to you, forbidding all under pain of death, to give you the least trouble; and withal ordered a very rich Turkish robe to be thrown over my shoulders, as a sign of her favour. Immediate orders were sent to the port to set Monsieur Godart and all his crew at liberty, and to feast us as particular friends of the Grand Sultaness. The company being dismissed, she made a sign for me to stay, having further business with me. When all were gone, but two of her chief favourite women, she came to me without any ceremony, and taking me in her arms, as if I had been her brother, embraced me with a great deal of tenderness; her joy to see me, making her lay aside her grandeur, and yield to the transports of undisguised nature. She led me by the hand into a most magnificent apartment; saying, Come, Signior Gaudentio, for so I think you are called; after you have refreshed yourself, you shall tell me your adventures. She made no scruple to sit down with me, being now not only mistress of herself, but of the whole Ottoman empire, as well as sure of her attendants. We had a refreshment of all the rarities of the East, with the richest wines for me, though she drank none herself. I long to hear your adventures, continued she, of so many years absence. So I told her

her in fhort, how I was carried by that ftrange merchant into an unknown country; without telling her the way we went thither; where I had married the regent's daughter. She blufhed a little at that part, and fhewed the remains of all her former beauty. But it put me in mind of my own indifcretion, to touch on fuch a nice point. She paffed it off with a great deal of goodnefs; and, recovering myfelf, I continued to acquaint her of the reafons of my return, as well as how I was taken by Hamet the firft time, which fhe had not been acquainted with before; and laftly, how I met with the fame Hamet again, killed him, and by that means came into that misfortune. I called it then a misfortune, faid I, but look upon it now to be one of my greateft happineffes; fince, by that occafion, I have the honour of feeing your Highnefs in that dignity of whch you are the moft worthy of any one in all the Ottoman empire. She feemed to be in admiration at the courfe of my life; and added, I think, Signor, you faid you were married; is your fpoufe with you? No, Madam, faid I: alas! fhe is dead, and all my children, and I am going to retire, and lead a private life in my native country. With thefe and other difcourfes we paffed the greateft part of the day, when fhe bid me go back to the fhip in public, attended with all the marks of her

high

high favours; but she said she would send for me privately in the evening; for, added she, I have a thousand other things to ask you. Accordingly I was introduced privately into the seraglio; which she, being Sultaness-regent, could easily do. There she entirely laid aside her grandeur. We talked all former passages over again, with the freedom of friends and old acquaintances. In our conversation, I found she was a woman of prodigious depth of judgment, as indeed her wading through so many difficulties, attending the inconstancy of the Ottoman court, particularly the regency, evidently shewed. I made bold to ask her, how she arrived at that dignity, though she was the only person in the world that deserved it; and took the liberty to say in a familiar way, that I believed her Highness was now sensible of the service I did her, in refusing to comply with her former demands, since the fates had reserved her to be the greatest empress of the world, not the consort of a wandering slave. Had I not been entirely assured of her goodness, I should not have dared to have touched on that head. She blushed with a little confusion at first, but putting it off with a grave air, Grandeur, says she, does not always make people happy. Ten thousand cares attend a crown; but the indifference I have for all things, make mine sit easier than it might

might have done otherwife. It is true, continued fhe, that young people very feldom fee their own good, and oftentimes run into fuch errors, by the violence of their paffions, as not only deprive them of greater bleffings, but render their misfortunes irretrievable. Some time after you were gone, my father the Grand Baffa was accufed by fome underhand enemies, of maleadminiftration, a thing too frequent in our court, and privately condemned to be ftrangled. But having fome trufty friends at the Porte, he had notice of it, before the orders came : he immedeately departed from Grand Cairo, and took a round-about way towards Conftantinople, to prevent, as the way is, the execution of them. He fent me before to prepare matters, and to intercede with the young Sultan, my late deceafed Lord, for his life, leaving word where I might let him know of the fuccefs of my interceffion. I prefented myfelf before the Sultan with that modeft affurance, which my innocence, my youth, and grief for my father's danger, gave me. I fell down on my knees, and, with a flood of tears, begged my father's life. The Sultan looked at me with fome amazement, and, whatever it was he faw in my face, not only granted my requeft, and confirmed my father in his former poft ; but made a profeffion of love to my perfon.; and even continued it with more constancy, than I thought a Grand Sultan capable of, having so many exquisite beauties to divert him, as they generally have. I consented, to save my father's life; and whether the indifferency I had for all men, made him more eager, I cannot tell; but I found I was the chief in his favour. He had some other mistresses now and then, of whom he was very fond. But never teasing him, nor fretting myself about it, I easily found I continued to have the solid part of his friendship; and bringing him the first male child, the present emperor, I became the chief Sultaness; and by his death, and the minority of my son, am now regent; by which I am capable of rendering you all the service the Ottoman empire can perform: which I esteem one of the happiest events of my life. I returned her the most profound bow, and humble thanks a heart full of the most lively sense of gratitude could profess. She offered me the first post of the Ottoman empire, if I would but become a mussulman, or only so in appearance. Or if, said she, you had rather be nigh me, you shall be the chief officer of my houshold. I have had assurance enough, added she, that neither your inclinations nor principles can be forced; neither will I endeavour to do it, but leave you as much at your liberty, as your generous master did, when he bought you

of

of Hamet. I expreſſed all the grateful acknowledgments poſſible, for ſo generous an offer; but aſſured her with an air that even expreſſed ſorrow for the refuſal, that I lay under religious obligations, which bound me indiſpenſably to return into my own country. She was become now as much miſtreſs of her inclinations, as ſhe had acquired prudence and experience by the long command ſhe had over her huſband's heart, and the whole Ottoman empire. So after a month's ſtay ſhe let me go, with all the marks of honour her dignity would ſuffer her to expreſs. She would have puniſhed the perſons that took us, but I interceded for them. Monſieur Godart, who was well rewarded for the loſs of his time and confinement, can teſtify the truth of this hiſtory. The laſt words ſhe ſaid to me, were, to bid me remember, that a Turk and a woman were capable of generous gratitude and honour, as well as Chriſtians. So we ſet ſail for Venice.

[*Secretary.* Here one of the inquiſitors came in with a gold medal in his hand, and turning to the examinant, ſaid, Signor Gaudentio, I believe you have found a relation in Italy, as well as in Africa, and one of the ſame nation with your mother. It is the Perſian lady you brought along with you, whom we ſecured the ſame time we did you; but would not let you know it, till we could procure intelligence from Venice, and a person who could speak the Persian language. We own we find her in the same story with you, and nothing material against you from Venice. Upon the examining her effects, we found this medal of the same make with yours by which you knew who your mother was. She says it was about her neck, when she was sold to the Persian merchant. But since we shall give you both your liberties in a short time, she shall be brought unto you, and we give you leave to say what you will to her, with the interpreter by. Upon this the lady was introduced, with her maid and the interpreter. As soon as she saw our examinant in good health, and seemingly at liberty, a joyful serenity spread itself over her countenance, such as we had not seen before. Our examinant asked her, to be pleased to give an account of her life, as far as she thought proper, and how she came by that medal.

Lady. All I know of myself, said she, is, that the noble Curd, who bought me of a Persian merchant for a companion for his only daughter, about my own age, whom he thought I resembled very much, often declared to me, that the merchant bought me of a Turkish woman,

man, who left that medal about my neck, suppofing it to be fome charm or prefervative againft diftempers, or becaufe a fifter of mine had the fame faftened about her neck, with a gold chain, which could not be taken off without breaking; but who, or where the fifter was, I never knew. The noble Curdifh Lord, who bought me, grew prodigious fond of me, and bred me up as another daughter; and not only fo, but having an only fon, fomething older than myfelf, he connived at a growing love he perceived between his fon and myfelf; which, after fome difficulties on both fides, at length came to a marriage; though it coft my generous benefactor and father-in-law his life. For another young Lord of Curdiftan, falling in love with me, often challenged Prince Cali (that was my dear hufband's name) to decide their pretenfions by the fword, which I had always forbid him to do; faying, that man fhould never be my hufband who expofed my reputation by a duel; fince the world would never believe, that any man would expofe his life for a woman, unlefs there had been fome encouragement given on both fides: whereas I never gave the leaft to any but Prince Cali. However, the other met him one day, and attacked him so furiously, that Prince Cali was forced to kill him in his own defence, making a thousand protestations, that he had almost suffered himself to be killed, rather than to disobey my orders. But the father of the prince who was slain, with a company of assassins, laid an ambuscade for Prince Cali and his father, in which this latter was killed, and most of his train. But by the valour of his son, and two of his companions, the chief assassins were laid dead on the spot, and the rest put to flight. But Prince Cali, after the death of his father, fearing further treachery of that nature, presently after we were married, removed to another part of the kingdom; from whence being sent on a commission by his king, he was inhumanly murdered by the barbarous Hamet. This is the sum of my unfortunate life, till I had the good fortune to save yours.

Secretary. We permitted the nephew and the aunt (for so they were found to be by the medal) to embrace one another; Signor Gaudentio assuring her, that by all appearance he was the son of her sister and the mother's sister that was lost, and both of them preserved to save each other's life. The lady then declared, she would turn Christian, since her misfortunes were come to that period; and that

that she was resolved to leave the world, and retire into some of our monasteries. We put her among the nuns of our order, where she promises to be a signal example of virtue and piety. The inquisitors ordered the examinant to give them the remaining part of his life, which, in all appearance, if they found his story to agree with their informations, might purchase him his liberty. Upon which Gaudentio proceeded as follows.]

I was telling your Reverences, that at length we set sail from the Porte, and steered our course directly for Venice, where we happily arrived without any considerable accident, the 10th of December 1712. I do not question but your Reverences are already informed, that such persons did arrive at Venice about that time. Monsieur Godart is well known to several merchants, and some of the senators of that famous city, whom he informed of what he saw with his own eyes. But there were some particular passages, unknown to your Reverences, wherein I had like to have made shipwreck of my life, after so many dangers; as I did here of my liberty; though I do not complain, but only represent my hard fortune to your Reverences consideration. It happened to be the carnival time during our stay at Venice. Curiosity led me, as well as a great many other strangers of the first rank, to see the nature of it. I put on my Mezoranian habit, spangled with suns of gold, and the fillet-crown on my head, adorned with several jewels of very great value, which I believe was the most remarkable and magnificent dress of any there. I went unmasked, being assured my face and person were unknown to all the world. Every one's eyes were upon me. Several of the masqueraders came up to me, and talked to me, particularly the ladies. They spoke to me in several languages, as Latin, French, Italian, Spanish, High Dutch, &c. I answered them all in the Mezoranian language, which seemed as strange to them, as my dress. Some of them spoke to me in the Turkish and Persian language, in Lingua Franca, and some in an Indian language I really did not understand. I answered them still in the Mezoranian, of which no body knew one word. Two ladies particularly, very richly dressed, followed me where-ever I went. The one, as it proved afterwards, was Favilla, the celebrated courtesan, in the richest dress of all the company; the other was the lady who was with me when I was taken up, and who was the occasion of my settling at Bologna; I mean the true occasion, for I will conceal nothing from your Reverences. Notwithstanding their diligence, I got away unknown at that time.

time. The next time I came, I appeared in the same dress, but with richer jewels; I had more eyes upon me now than before. The courtesan pursued me again in a different, but richer dress than the former. At length she got me by myself, and pulling off her mask, shewed me a wonderful pretty face, only there was too fierce an assurance in it. She cried in Italian, O Signor, you are not so ignorant of our language, as you would seem to be! you can speak Italian and French too: though we don't know who you are, we have learned you are a man of honour. If you would not understand our words, you may understand a face, which very great personages have been glad to look at; and with that put on one of the most ensnaring airs I ever saw. I don't doubt but your Reverences have heard of that famous courtesan, and how the greatest man in Venice was once her slave. I was just going to answer her, when the other lady came up, and pulling off her mask also, said almost the same things, but with a modesty more graceful than her beauty, which was most exquisite, and the likest the incomparable Isyphena I ever saw. I made them both a most respectful bow, and told them, that it had been much safer for me, if I had kept myself still unknown, and never seen such dangerous charms. I pronounced these words with an air, that

shewed,

shewed, that I was more pleased with the modesty of the last lady, than the commanding assurance of the first. The courtesan, though a little nettled at the preference she thought I gave the other, put on a more serious air, and said, she had been informed, there was something very extraordinary in my character, and should be glad to hear more of it by herself; that her name was Favilla, and that she lived in such a street, where I should find her house remarkable enough. The Bolognian lady, whom your Reverences knew very well, and who was then at Venice, on account of the death of her uncle, one of the senators, who had left her all his effects, said modestly, If where I favour her with a visit, as she had been informed that I was a learned man and a virtuoso, being inclined that way herself, she should be glad of an hour's conversation with me on that subject, telling me her name, and where she lived; adding, if I would inform myself of her character, I need not be ashamed of her acquaintance; nor, I hope, of mine, Madam, says the other, thinking she had been reflected on by that word. It was Monsieur Godart, who, with a levity peculiar to his nation, had made the discovery who I was, though he knew nothing of me but what passed since I came from Grand Cairo. I was going to reply to the ladies, when company came up, up, and broke off the difcourfe. I was refolved to fee neither of them, and would go no more to the affembly, though almoft unavoidably I faw both afterwards. I inquired into Favilla's character, though I fcarce doubted of it by what I faw and heard, and was informed that fhe was an imperious courtefan, who had enflaved feveral perfons of the firft rank, of different nations, and enriched herfelf by their fpoils: this determined me not to fee her. But, as Monfieur Godart and myfelf were walking to fee the town, he brought me either induftrioufly, or accidentally, by her door; fhe was fitting at the window of one of the moft magnificent palaces in Venice, (fuch fpoils had fhe reaped from her bewitched lovers.) As foon as fhe efpied me, fhe fent a fervant to tell me, that that lady would fpeak with me; I made fome difficulty, but Monfieur Godart told me, a man of honour could not refufe fuch a favour as that; fo I went in, and Monfieur Godart with me. The lady received me with a moft charming agreeable air, much different from her former affurance, and conducted me into a moft magnificent apartment, leaving Monfieur Godart entertaining a very pretty lady, her companion. Not to detain your Reverences too long, when I would not underftand what fhe meant, fhe offered me marriage, with the inheritance of all her effects;

I was put to the last nonplus. I assured her with a most profound bow, that though I was not worthy of such a happiness, I had an indispensable obligation never to marry. All the blood immediately came into her face: I did not know what she was going to do, but finding her in that disorder, I made another bow, saying, I would consider further on her proposal; and walked directly out of the house, designing to leave Venice as soon as my affairs would give me leave. Some time after Monsieur Godart came to me, and told me, he was forced to do as I did; that the lady was in such an outrageous fury he did not know what might be the consequence. Three nights after, as Monsieur Godart and a young kinsman of his, and myself, were going towards the Rialto, in the dusk of the evening, four ruffians attacked us unawares; two of them set upon me, the other two attacked Monsieur Godart and his kinsman; the poor young gentleman was run through the body the first push; I made shift to disable one of my adversaries, but in doing it, the other run me through the ribs, but the sword took only part of my body, and missing my entrails, the point went out on the side of my back. Monsieur Godart, who, to give him his due, behaved with a great deal of courage and bravery, had killed one of his men, and wounded the other; and the ruffians,

fians, seeing us now two to two, though fit to march off as well as they could. I was forced to be led to my lodging, not doubting but the wound was mortal, though it proved otherwise. The affair made a great noise about town: we very rationally supposed it was Favilla who had set the assassins on; but we knew her to be so powerful with the senators, that there was no hopes of justice. While I was recovering, I was told there was a lady, with two waiting women, desired to see me on very earnest business, if it would not be incommodious to me. (Monsieur Godart would not stir from my bedside, for fear of accidents). Who should this be but Favilla, who came all in mourning for my misfortune. I pretended to be a dying man, and took the liberty of telling her of her way of living, to what a dismal pass her passions had brought her; in fine, I said so much, and begged her, by all that was dear to her, to consider her state, that, bursting into a flood of tears, she promised me, if I died, she would become a penitent nun. I effected so much by letters afterwards, that, though I recovered, she performed her promise.

The Bolognian lady had heard of my misfortune, and, by a goodness peculiar to the tender sex, particularly with regard to strangers, she sent often to know how I did, with prefents of the richeft cordials that could be got in Venice. Finding my illnefs continued longer than was expected, fhe fent me word, that, though it was not fo decent for her to make the firft vifit, fhe had heard fo much of my adventures, as very much raifed her curiofity to hear them from my own mouth, when I was capable of converfation without doing me any prejudice. I had informed myfelf of her character from very good hands; fo that I was very curious to converfe with a perfon of thofe incomparable talents I heard fhe was miftrefs of. She was the only woman, next to Ifyphena, and the great Baffa's daughter, I ever much liked in my life. To fum up all in fhort, fhe came feveral times to fee me, infomuch that we contracted the moft virtuous friendfhip, by our mutual inclination to learning and the fympathy of our tempers, that ever fubfifted between two perfons of different fexes. It was on her account I refolved to fettle at Bologna; and having fome knowledge in nature and phyfic, I took on me that character, to be the oftener in her company without fcandal. We were neither of us inclined to marry. As fhe is one of the moft virtuous women living, and I am pretty much advanced in years, being both entirely mafters of ourfelves, we thought our innocent friendfhip could be offenfive to no one. What has paffed fince I came to this

town,

town, I don't doubt but your Reverences are apprifed of.

This is a true and full account of my life hitherto; whatever is blameable in it I hope your Reverences will pardon, as I fubmit it entirely to your judgments.

Secretary. As I had the honour to inform you before, we inquired into all thofe facts which he faid happened to him in the company of Monfieur Godart; which finding to be true, we judged the reft might be fo. We afked him, if he would conduct fome of our miffionaries to that ftrange country he mentioned; he told us he would: but not willing to truft him entirely, as not knowing what he might do with them, when he had them in unknown countries, we thought fit to give him his liberty firft to go where he would, even out of Italy, with affurances, if he came back of his own accord, we would fend miffionaries along with him. He went to Venice and Genoa about his concerns, and is now come back, and with us; fo that we believe the man to be really what he profeffes himfelf to be.]

FINIS.

www.ingramcontent.com/pod-product-compliance
Lightning Source LLC
Chambersburg PA
CBHW021208230426
43667CB00006B/614